THE KLEIN - LACAN DIALOGUES

edited by
BERNARD BURGOYNE
& MARY SULLIVAN

REBUS PRESS

Rebus Press
76 Haverstock Hill
LONDON
NW3 2BE

ISBN 1 900877 06 6

CONTENTS

Phantasy

Sexuality

Counter-transference

The Unconscious

Klein and Lacan in the 1990's

FOREWORD

It is with particular pleasure that I write the Foreword to this collection of THERIP's *Psychoanalytic Seminars: The Klein - Lacan Dialogues* .

The Higher Education Network for Research and Information in Psychoanalysis - THERIP - was founded in 1988. It is an essential part of THERIP's function to provide a platform for the exchange of ideas and information in psychoanalysis, not only in the UK but abroad as well. Equally it is an essential part of THERIP's function to broaden debate within and about psychoanalysis.

THERIP also produces a Register giving information on members' research in the field. This enables researchers to establish contact with each others' work. The *Psychoanalysis Newsletter* publishes a wide variety of articles and an extensive Events Diary.

THERIP organizes a series of lectures each year. Topics are addressed by speakers from different schools of psychoanalysis. In keeping with THERIP's role as a forum for discussion, the organization is not affiliated to any particular school. Much of THERIP's unique contribution to psychoanalytic debate lies in this very impartiality.

This is the second collection in a series of lectures published to reach a wider audience. It covers the academic year 1994 to 1995. As the title, *The Klein - Lacan Dialogues* suggests, the lectures take the form of panel discussions. These were very well received by the audience who were present at the time.

On behalf of THERIP may I thank all our contributors: Robin Anderson, Bice Benvenuto, Catalina Bronstein, Bernard Burgoyne, Filip Geerardyn, Robert Hinshelwood, Darian Leader, Dany Nobus, Vicente Palomera, Margaret Rustin, Jane Temperley and Robert Young.

It is also my pleasant duty to thank Bernard Burgoyne and Mary Sullivan for editing this collection. My thanks are also due to Oliver Rathbone of Rebus Press and to Kirsty Hall for her editorial work on behalf of Rebus Press, our publishers. Guy Hall has kindly provided us with an introduction.

I should like to express appreciation of many organisations for their cooperation with THERIP. These include: The Association for Group and Individual Psychotherapy, The British Association of Psychotherapists, The British Psycho-Analytical Society, The Centre for Freudian Analysis and Research, The Guild of Psychotherapists, The Institute of Group Analysis, The London Centre for Psychotherapy, The Philadelphia Association, Regent's

College, The Society for Analytical Psychology, The Tavistock Clinic, TheFreud Museum (London), The Freud Museum (Vienna). I should also like to acknowledge the contribution of UAPS (The Universities Association for Psychoanalytic Studies) and of the Directors and students of courses in psychoanalysis in the Universities.   These include, Brunel, Dublin (LSB College and University College), East London, Ghent, Goldsmith's, Kent, Leeds Metropolitan, Manchester and Middlesex Universities.

Finally, I should like to pay tribute to Bernard Burgoyne and Audrey Cantlie of the Management Committee for the tireless work they do for THERIP.   I should also like to acknowledge Martin Stanton's advice and support.

The broad spectrum of acknowledgements clearly reflects THERIP's position within the field of psychoanalysis. We hope that readers will welcome the discussion in its topicality and that everyone will find something of interest and enjoyment in this collection of the *Klein - Lacan Dialogues.*

Dr. Liz Reid
Chair THERIP

INTRODUCTION

Guy Hall

In 1994-5, a series of discussions took place between Kleinian and Lacanian psychoanalysts. The aim of the presentations and the debates that followed was to allow for dialogue, as well as controversy to take place. The difference is important and the process with its successes and failures, is both revealed and recorded on the following pages. Both camps came with their supporters, but many others attended, intrigued and curious as to what might happen. The purpose was not to systematically teach, but to get a clearer idea of what it was that each school shared, and in what ways they differed. Respecting the convictions of the other and allowing their expression in their own terms became a prerequisite (and sometimes a problem) in the dialogue. Learning to understand such terms was a duty which befell all who attended, one that was only successful in part. The meetings provided an opportunity for reflection upon the implications for respective positions and an appreciation of the sensitivities of both schools. The aim of such a dialogue was not conversion, but to encourage an awareness of what changes could be brought about in the understanding of their theoretical perspectives, as a result of such an encounter. This was not to remove the right to disagree with an expressed opinion, but it came with a responsibility for not misrepresenting, or disparaging another's point of view.

It became clear during the course of the meetings, that ignorance and misconceptions about the theory and practice of each school was held by the other. Thus the meetings had to cope with the anxiety of unresolved opposites, and not give in to a total denial of the validity of the other. Nor could the contradictions be ignored, in order to pretend that all theories were compatible, acceptable and of equal value.

These debates were not about reconciliation. At times, there was an aggressive if not crusading nature to the encounters. It would be disingenuous to pretend that for some this was not an attraction for attending, in order to see just how bruising the meetings would be. At times the quoting of proof-texts was essayed, as if to give a knock-out blow against an opposing case; perhaps such use reveals a desire for the assurance of an authority, rather than an aid which can clarify an argument. A statement attributed to Klein or Lacan cannot be used as the last word on the matter: it may be the starting point for a discussion but it does not necessarily end it. The process

of acquiring psychoanalytic understanding can be seen as the result
of a cumulative process which should include contemporary
thinkers.

The formal training required to be a psychotherapist takes many
years and some considerable commitment to complete. The investment required is enormous and the result is often that you become
a member of an esoteric, closed and self-perpetuating system. It is
an all or nothing situation. One result of such a training can be a
lack of self-criticism from within the schools. It is not unknown for
those who have rejected a part of a systematic theory to be disciplined, or even expelled. Criticism can result in the calling into
question of the efficacy of a training analysis. Attacking an individual, rather then dealing with the issues raised, is a well-tried tac-
tic which avoids engaging in a fresh examination of the case under
debate. The infighting within some therapeutic organisations, however appalling such confrontations can be, is an indication of the
importance (and at other times impotence) of theory. The courage to
engage in a public discourse, by the representatives of both schools
who took part, is to be applauded, not only for being prepared to
take the necessary risks, but in the setting out of positions, and for
the exchanges that followed.

It is in the nature of such theoretical debates that extracts from
actual cases, give the impression of a scientist dispassionately
observing "clinical material". Some analysts might support such a
view, but others would stress the importance of a personal therapeutic relationship. It is easy to loose sight of the importance of the
personality of the therapist and qualities such as empathy. If psychoanalysis was strictly a science it could easily be taught from
books, and no doubt, the technique from a single volume. If the
human qualities of therapy disappeared at times in the formal presentations, they were rediscovered in the discussions that followed.

The belief of adherents of each school is that ultimately the deepest insights of psychoanalysis in reality belong to them. A genuine
dialogue has to recognize this, along with a hidden (and sometimes
not so hidden,) deep desire for the other to 'come over', and accept
a different version about the basis of psychoanalysis. The paradox
is that there can be no dialogue until the magnitude of the differences that exist are recognised and that only from this can common
ground be sought. It is significant that what is shared is the realization that mutual understanding can come about through the
acceptance of a particular set of convictions, which by definition
exclude the other's set of convictions, and that such contradictions
cannot with any sense of integrity easily be accommodated. There

is a great temptation not to resist the deception of levelling down differences, or making inauthentic harmonies. Instead a reformulation of one's irreducible constructs is required. Exposing one's thinking to another's questioning is to be in a vulnerable position, but a reformulation need not mean the loss of an original idea, for it can lead to its growth and development. Such action calls for both great boldness and humility. It may not be a commitment that both partners can enter into at the start of a dialogue. Indeed the dialogue may be called into question if one partner feels that the other is not fully involved. The answer comes with the realization that we are always aware of the sacrifices that we bring to a dialogue situation. It is much harder to truly appreciate the sacrifices that the other has had to make.

If the nature of the dialogue does not go beyond scoring points, then there is little purpose in meeting. Real dialogue begins when doubts, uncertainties and failures can be shared between the two camps, rather then defending the whole canon of a particular theory. The willingness to acknowledge to another when there are parts in the other's system which can be appreciated and valued, is an important step in dialogue. It helps move the debate away from triumphalism. If one party feels that it has the Truth, then there can be no place in an absolutist system for others. Neither can there be any space for evolution. The result is a kind of psychoanalytic fundamentalism. There is a second paradox - simply winning all the intellectual arguments is in itself no guarantee that others will be convinced. In the process of dialogue, honesty is more important then cleverness. Appearing to have all the answers may ultimately be both self-defeating and self-deluding. In these meetings the process of dialogue was not completed, but it was an original first step, which required great tenacity. All those involved are to be thanked and congratulated and it is to be hoped that this book will encourage the process to be continued.

CHILD PSYCHOTHERAPY WITHIN THE KLEINIAN TRADITION

Margaret Rustin

In this contribution to dialogue I intend to concentrate on current practice and points of interest but it seems appropriate to begin with a brief review of Melanie Klein's contributions to child analysis.

Rather than starting with theory, I shall offer quite a simple description of her technique, so that we can try to imagine the experience of a child who went to see her for a psychoanalytic session. The child would be offered a small collection of toys for his personal use during the sessions, including drawing and modelling materials, small dolls representing both adults and children, toy animals, a selection of both wild and domestic species, small model cars, small wooden bricks and so on. The toys and all the child's own creations during the sessions would be kept in a safe place and gradually become an aspect of the shared narrative of the analysis. The child was invited to do as he wished during analysis, to talk or play, and Mrs Klein conveyed that the toys could be useful, because she wanted to get to know and understand the child's thoughts, feelings and worries, and that playing was a good way for her to learn to understand what was important from the child's point of view. Her belief was that children's playing was serious work since she found, through careful observation of her child patients, that the sequence of play activities could be seen as the child's equivalent of the free associations of adult analysis.

She began to describe to the child the story of the play and to link this systematically with her understanding of the child's internal world. Her interpretations explored this inner world and the evolving relationship to herself. The child's play activities, verbal communications and overall behaviour in the consulting room provided the evidence of the nature and evolution of the transference. Recent Kleinian preoccupation with something usually referred to as the 'transference to the total situation' is very much rooted in child analysis, where the necessity to bear in mind the total situation is paramount. So much of the relevant evidence is in the child's relationship to the room and the impact he has on the analyst.

Klein's theory developed in parallel with her clinical approach. She believed that babies experience anxiety from birth onwards, and that they turn towards those caring for them, their primary objects, not only for physical care - the relief of hunger and bodily discomfort - but also for containment of their distress and over-whelming early anxiety. Much of what was implicit in her theory of mother-infant relations is of course elaborated in Bion's writings, and the importance of his concept of containment has been immense in subsequent theory and practice, particularly in making it possible to work with a wider population of child-patients, including children who have not yet developed a capacity for symbolic play.

Klein believed that the baby brings to his post natal existence some constitutional factors, including his mental and physical endowment which influence his expectations of the world. We can now draw on a greater understanding of the foetus' experience of life in the uterus to amplify Klein's picture. The nature of the experience of birth, the first encounter with the world outside mother's body, is an important backcloth in considering an infant's exploration of his mother from outside. This is a mother whose interior he already knows, but who must seem very different when perceived across space through his as yet inexperienced organs of perception; eyes, ears, nose, mouth, skin. Klein described the internal world as formed on the bedrock of unconscious phantasy. This concept of the internal world, peopled by internal objects, is fundamental to her thinking. Variations of it appear in other modern theories of infant development. For example, Bowlby's 'internal working models' seem to me to be a theoretical construct which tends to emphasize the element of experience of the external world and to reduce the contribution of unconscious phantasy to the structuring of the mind. Unconscious phantasy in Kleinian theory is both the continuous process of unconscious mental activity, which elaborates the relationship between self and objects, suffused with a whole range of passionate emotion, and also the outcome of this mental activity, that is the body of unconscious phantasies that influence our perceptions of the world. It is not a static entity but one evolving throughout life, embodying the impact on us of our relationships with our internal and external objects.

The psychoanalysis of children is thus an exploration through the technique of undirected play and careful observation of the child's overall behaviour of the nature of the child's internal world. To a very considerable degree, the setting in which Klein worked with her child patients is the basis for a current Kleinian child psychotherapist's professional framework. There has been some modification of the kind of toys found useful for work with particular children. For example, some therapists use non-miniature dolls with children who have experienced abuse, and for very immature or very ill patients such as autistic children, who have developed little capacity for symbolic play, toys more characteristic of a toddler's domestic world are being introduced. Nonetheless, classical practice is still largely based on the idea of a personal set of small toys very much modelled on Mrs Klein's toys, because these can be used with great flexibility according to the child's phantasies, since their defining characteristics are minimal and they do not therefore prescribe play. Klein's own intuitive grasp of infantile emotional states enabled her to think about them on the basis of her personal and clinical experience but the average psychoanalytic practitioner has to work without her genius. One of the most fruitful tools in helping us towards understanding infantile states has proved to be the observation of infants and their mothers and the study of our own reactions. It is not possible to talk about pioneering work with children today without some attention to the central role of infant observation in training. What does this experience offer? Although researchers approach it with the belief that they will learn much about infant development, and indeed they do, they learn more deeply and often in a disturbing way about the feelings of the infant and the feelings of the parent in trying to care for the infant. The degree of disturbance felt by the observer is related to the relative inactivity of the observer's role and consequent openness to profound identification with the members of the family observed. The observer is drawn into the struggle to give meaning to the baby's body language as well as his vocalisations, that is to learn the pre-verbal language of the infant. Observers also face becoming aware of the carer's emotional state and the impact this has on the baby. They are thus potentially in touch with the multi-generational unconscious force field which is the infant's inheritance. Here is an example, to demonstrate what I have in mind.

The observer I am thinking of is visiting a ten month old baby girl, Angela, and her mother Carole. This is the first baby in a comfortable middle class family. The observer had learnt recently that the maternal grandmother had been a twin, whose twin had died at birth, and this information has thrown some light on the predominantly manic atmosphere of Carole's style in relation to her baby. The observer felt that anxieties about silence, stillness, unresponsiveness were playing a part in Carole's intense dependence on Angela's providing immediate positive feedback. There had been two areas of difficulty in the care of the baby. A good early breast-feeding relationship had been replaced by a very distressing conflict over feeding and there were also recurrent serious sleeping difficulties. On the occasion of this visit, Carole is complaining about

Angela's temper, clinginess, miserableness, and sleep disturbance and implicitly about her own immense exhaustion, which has led to a decision to get a part-time nanny in order to have some time to herself. The surface presentation by the mother is of an irritatingly superficial and narcissistic woman, but the defensive quality of this seems very evident to the observer, who felt agonised by the mutual frustration of mother and baby. The seminar group discussing the observation was also struck by the critical stance the observer was adopting towards the mother.

Here is an extract from the observational notes:

> Angela reached for two glossy magazines that Carole had removed from her, but had placed behind herself on the floor. She handed first one then the other to her mother, who again put them out of reach. Angela grizzled and reached once more. The top one was a copy of Elle with a large picture of a woman's face on the cover. This the baby again tried to hand to her mother, but tore the magazine in doing so, and the magazine fell to the ground. "That's terrific, that one hadn't even been opened" said Carole in a jokey, irritated tone, removing the torn cover. Angela gave her mother the other magazine and then reached out to pick up the torn one. Carole moved both out of reach. Angela burst into deep sobs and her body collapsed in a slump. Perplexed, Carole said "This is just temper. What do you want?" She then picked up one of the magazines, opening her arms to Angela who stared at the picture intently while Carole continued her jokey comments. She turned the page. "Do you like this one or this one? Oh look at this". She seemed unable to follow Angela's gaze or pause on one page, but flicked through at speed. Angela quickly became frazzled and began to cry again. She struggled down to the floor out of mother's arms and crawled away. Carole removed the magazines totally and Angela stopped in the middle of the floor and cried bitterly and desperately. This went on for a long time, Angela sitting alone while Carole mocked her, to the great discomfort of the observer who felt she was in complicity against the baby.

Now I think there is much in this fragment of observation to suggest Angela's preoccupation with the weaning process that is underway. She seems to me to be trying to communicate with her mother about the possession of the shiny, beautiful mummy. She shows us her attempt to hand something back to mother, to return to mother symbolically the breast which the baby has had temporary possession of in the breastfeeding months. Angela is not ready for them to disappear totally out of reach. Indeed, at the end of this particular observation, after an appallingly frustrating effort to feed her solid food, Carole offered Angela the breast, which she instantly accepted. This led mother and baby to a peaceful contact for the first time in the whole hour. Angela is also very easily tantalised by the feeling that the objects of desire are so near and yet so far, just out of reach. The seminar puzzled about the observer's experience of being trapped, which was evident in her tone of voice in the presentation. She seemed stuck in a hostile and critical stance towards the mother, who she also felt to be in agony in her failure to please the child. It seemed clear that Carole felt doubtful about having anything good to offer the baby, and that this anxiety underlies her hasty move from thing to thing. So little does she believe that there could be a satisfying moment between them, that she does not even scan her baby's face to discover what might attract her: she is sure she will be rejected, and that whatever Angela wants it is not her.

To understand this, and the observer's pained awareness of her hypercritical stance, some of the mother's history may be relevant. Her mother, the one who had lost a twin at birth, was unable to care for Carole, who had been more or less brought up by her grandmother. One might surmise that the shadow of the dead baby had laid heavily over the living child, who could, we may imagine, not be seen with joy by her mother because of the pain associated with the lost baby. Perhaps we see an echo of this in Carole's great difficulty in responding to Angela's developing capacities at the beginning of the observational extract. She complained about Angela having worked out how to open drawers, which she saw only as a source of persecution; she could not see her baby's lively curiousity about the world, or her increasing dexterity, as delightful achievements, but rather as rejections of herself, indications that she is not wanted except as a victim. There seems to be an inner critical voice within mother bitterly attacking the value of her maternal care. Often she seems to attribute this to Angela, but also at times to the observer, whose eyes are felt not to watch with sympathy, but with hostility and mockery.

These interchanges provide some vivid examples, I think, of the processes of projective identification, the crucial psychological mechanism first described by Melanie Klein and now so valuable a theory in clinical practice. The observer who unwillingly mocks the mother in her tone of voice during her presentation to the seminar has been overtaken by an identification with a hostile internal object in the mother's internal world, temporarily lodged in the observer through projection. The baby who slumps in despair and sobs may be carrying not only her own despair but also her mother's, for one senses that just below the brittle surface maintained by mother lies great unhappiness.

The child analyst is peculiarly exposed to projective pressures since a relationship must be maintained not only with the child patient but also with the child's parents if an analytic setting is to be sustained. The experience of infant observation, in which emotions are pulled this way and that, in contradictory identifications, is an enormously helpful preparation since it opens up awareness of projections in both directions - child into parent and parent into child. I think the understanding of the impact of adult projections into the immature mind of the child is one of the growth points of clinical practice, an area where significant shifts are taking place.

Now let me describe the task of the child analyst. Firstly comes the provision and maintenance of the setting. This can at times be such a huge thing that it may be the only thing that can be attended to. Sessions must be at regular and reliable times, and for younger children this means the analyst is dependent upon the support of the family. There needs to be a structure for term times and holiday breaks, and the structure of the analytic year needs to become gradually transparent to the child - not just equated with school or with family arrangements for holidays, so that there can be meaningful contrast between the analyst's absence and presence. And enough reliable ordering of sessions for the frustrations of absence to be tolerable. It is not possible to treat a child who is brought very often late or irregularly for sessions, since the exploration of the child's response to frustration cannot be satisfactorily gathered into the transference relationship with the analyst. There also has to be a suitable room available, tough enough to withstand some misuse, safe enough in terms of potential damage to objects or persons to provide the analyst with some support in dealing with an aggressive child, and there has to be a commitment to an open ended and reasonably lengthy period of therapy. Once these fundamentals are in place the analytic work can begin. This initial work is what Meltzer helpfully describes as the "gathering of the transference", the focusing on responses of the child to the analyst and the analytic situation as they begin to unfold.

A case example may be most helpful in conveying what these

ideas mean. I have chosen some material from the last few months of my work with an adopted boy aged twelve at the time of the session I will describe.

Tim was referred by his adoptive parents who felt they had been unable to get close to him. They were worried by his lack of warmth, his aggressiveness, his sexualised play with other children, his lying and stealing. He proved to be a very difficult child to treat, as underneath the thin veneer of charm was a boy who believed that the only way not to be a victim was to manoeuvre himself into a position to inflict on others the hurt and humiliation that he dreaded. His cruelty, contempt and violence could take my breath away at times. As a small child, he had been both physically and sexually abused and received into care temporarily many times before social services ultimately removed him permanently aged two and a half. In therapy, I was, unsurprisingly, on the receiving end of a great deal of mistreatment.

There were sessions in which he would create chaos in my room, upturning all the chairs and using most of the furniture to barricade himself in a camp from behind whose walls he would pelt me with missiles from every angle. I recall the mockery with which he greeted most of what I said. One day he told me I was a tramp, I stank, I lived in a cardboard box on the Embankment, I needed a bath etc. In the course of this session I felt clearly as I looked around my room that I had indeed become homeless. There was nowhere I could sit down because he had all the furniture. I was totally exhausted by the struggle of preventing either of us getting hurt in any major way. I was hot, sweaty and weary, and indeed I wanted a bath badly, since one of Tim's weapons was spitting at me. I felt an object of total derision. Thus concretely did Tim teach me of what he had made of his experience of living in twelve different places in the course of his first year of life, and of being the child of a prostitute, who was at times quite unable to look after him.

At a later period I learnt what it is like to be exposed to loveless and brutal sexuality. Tim spent time enacting ugly sexual scenes, lying on top of a cupboard in my room where he was very close to the ceiling. I had to watch him while he was up there because I had to make sure that he was safe, and not about to fall off, as the cupboard offered only a narrow ledge on which he could lie and it was quite high up. I also had to monitor his efforts to poke holes in the ceiling tiles! But what I had to watch was pretty unbearable, as in word and gesture perverse sexual intercourse went on relentlessly. I felt sickened, assaulted and degraded. Any attempt to bring it to an end by getting him to come down from the cupboard was interpreted by Tim as my attempt to join in as he claimed I was so excited by his display. I felt I got to know what it must have been like to be a baby continuously exposed to the horror of his mother's way of life as a prostitute.

Tim soon realised he could make my life even more excruciating if he ran out of sessions to create mayhem in the corridor outside my room. His pleasure in my humiliating attempts to prevent him misusing the goods lift or climbing up to dangerous windows at the end of the corridor was enormous. He could calibrate his provocativeness very finely: if someone else appeared he would seem not to be out of control, and yet he could create an atmosphere of my being helplessly and foolishly inept, waiting around while he played at being Lord of the clinic. The fury evoked in me by being rendered helpless on my own territory was sometimes very difficult to process, but it certainly made me understand what he might have been enduring.

Here is a brief account of a recent session. This therapy is a once-weekly treatment.

The week before, he had not felt well and had slept for much of the session, tucked up on the couch. Today he arrived with his mother ten minutes late, which is extremely unusual, and he looked tense. He began by making a paper aeroplane which did not satisfy him despite his considerable efforts. He then threw it out of the window ignoring my requests to the contrary. He then folded a piece of paper to make a bomb-like object, and exploded it with a great pleasure. I talked of his feeling explosive today. He ran out of the room down towards the goods lift, playing with the call buttons. I waited at the door of my room from where I could see him. He tried to interest me in his malicious excitement and get me to collude against those who might possibly be inconvenienced by his hogging of the lift. He read out a milk order which was chalked up on a board inside the lift, apparently uncomprehending. He seemed possibly to become a bit anxious - I thought probably because he was aware of someone trying to call the lift. He ran off to the loo. While he was there the cafe manager came along to investigate what was going on with his lift and scowled suspiciously at me. When Tim returned, the lift had gone and he then came into my room, extremely angry. He threw various things at me and the atmosphere became threatening, as he began to use his ruler as a catapult. I talked about the fact that we have a problem in how to deal with his explosive feelings. I linked this to how frustrated he was now the lift was unavailable and also because he'd missed ten minutes of his session today. I also talked about how hard he found it not to be in complete control. He then looked in his drawer, where his toys are kept, for a red pen and climbed up on the cupboard I have mentioned near the ceiling, on which he can lie full length, and he began to write with the red pen on the cupboard, the wall and the light fitting. First his name, and then a list of his friends' names, then my name and a range of choice expletives.

This activity went on for a long period and it was clear that he had found a very satisfying way of expressing himself. I said that he wanted to reassert today that Tim was boss: his name was at the top of the list. I said that this might feel urgent today as he was feeling that he wasn't as much in control as he wanted to be. After a while I talked about his fear of being forgotten, that he felt he could force me to remember him by writing his name up on my wall, and I spoke of the feelings of the little Tim, feelings about being forgotten by his long ago first mother. Now that we were thinking together about ending his therapy he felt too that I was an unreliable mummy, that I could just toss him out of my mind. I linked this to his throwing things at me, his wish to leave a hurt, a mark, so that I wouldn't be able to forget him. The pain he caused was to be a reminder of him. Later I spoke of his writing up the names of his friends because he might be thinking how important they are. He wants them to be there for him after his therapy ends. As the writing continued, I talked about how he might feel jealous about people coming to see me and want to force them to be aware of Tim's place here by leaving marks in the room. This is a well rehearsed theme, and his ingenuity in asserting his right to my room is truly amazing. In response to this, he wrote Fuck and Shit in huge letters. I responded by talking about his worry that I would be glad when he leaves. The Tim who behaves badly when he's here must sometimes feel that I hate him and long to be rid of him. Towards the end of the session I spoke about how upset he's been since we made the decision to end his sessions. I described how much he had wanted myself and his parents to agree that therapy should come to an end, because he had really wanted us to say how much better he was coping and express some confidence in him, and he had also wanted me to see that he could make efforts to stick to our agreed rules in the therapy. But I pointed out that since the decision had actually been made, to his great surprise he'd been feeling differently, feeling suspicious of me, worried that I don't like or care about him. He said "I won't come back in September". This was a session in June and it was as if he felt I was putting up a case for needing to continue. He then climbed down from his perch, got a cloth, asked me for detergent and thoroughly cleaned the wall, the cupboard and the light, including drying everything - and the walls were absolutely dripping with red water! So it was quite a major job and took quite some time. At the end of the session as he got ready to leave he asked for a drink of water, drank a huge quantity, and then told me he's going ice skating on Saturday.

I think this material gives rather a vivid picture of the relationship between a haunting past, a current state of mind and thoughts also of the future. It shows us a boy who has discovered, at least from time to time, that terrible past times are actually past. They do not need to be continually relived in the present. There is the possibility of memories, as distinct from being in the grip of feelings in which past and present are not distinguished. In the present, it is possible to do something different. His decision to clear up himself is an example of this, and took me by total surprise. His twelve year old capacities help him not to be stuck in the position of the much less well-equipped two year old, faced with abandonment as he had repeatedly been.

The orientation towards the future represented by his reference to going skating is also striking. At that moment he seems to be able to clear away the details of the past; he has a chance to take off and find his own way. In my talk with him, I referred to the way in which infantile worries about loss are being evoked by the present circumstances, and I also described his characteristic omnipotent defence of becoming the boss when confronted with anxiety, trying to control people and force them to take care of him as he does not trust that they will wish to do so; but I balanced this attention to the past with comments on his current anxiety, his jealousy towards rivals here in the clinic for example, and his current defences, his wish to have a group of friends by whom he could feel supported. Tim took up my reference to the future with his remark about September, and interestingly spent time in subsequent sessions making complicated calenders to show the whole structure of the term in relation to his sessions, with the last session's date coloured in with a distinctive colour and a complex code to permit interpretation of this calender. He used to see endings as dead endings, and had a near breakdown when a boy he knew was killed when he tried to leap over a railway line during Tim's summer holiday from therapy. Tim told me that the boy called out to his mother to hold him when he fell, recreating the tragedy in the therapy room in a very life-like way, and allowing us to understand the terrifying meaning for him of the summer holiday from therapy, a gap in which he could fall to his death.

This clinical example provides a glimpse of how reconstruction can play a part in the psychotherapy of children who have been traumatised. It also shows how close reconstruction and here-and-now interpretation of the transference can be to the past, so that it seems sometimes to be happening all over again. With a very traumatised child like Tim there may be very little disguise or imaginative accretion once the really serious issues of the analysis are broached. The therapist's problem is less to know and understand what is happening, to decode complex transformations, more to find a way to contain the projected pain until the child is ready to be put in touch with it. This containment does not mean the passive enduring of whatever is inflicted. Unless the scrutiny of the counter-transference and the self analytic efforts of the therapist are powerfully mobilised, the indigestible overwhelming painfulness cannot be modified in a way that can lead to useful interpretation. A container has not only to receive projections, but also to hold on to them, to feel and explore their quality and ponder them before the transformation from the unthinkable to the communicable can be achieved. I think these are the distinctive elements in therapeutic practice which have grown out of Klein's discoveries and the developments made possible by subsequent theoretical and technical advances based on her ideas. I believe that the gradually widening appreciation of her contribution to psychoanalysis is because in clinical experience her conceptualizations are so helpful in unlocking meaning.

ONCE UPON A TIME: THE INFANT IN LACANIAN THEORY[1]

Bice Benvenuto

Childhood seems to contain in itself the mystery of our origin. It is the foundation for any further development. That the quest for the mystery of origins holds strong in psychoanalysis can be seen in the way it traces man's relation to the world further and further back into the mists of an original state, as if to catch it at its birth. Like storytellers, psychoanalysts would also like to start the story with a 'Once upon a time'.

As in biology there is the cell and in physics the atom, so does psychoanalysis look for the irreducible unit of the psychic world. Object relations theory, in spite of all its variations of emphasis, postulates the irreducible relation to a primary object - namely the breast - which will determine to a greater or lesser extent the internal world of the infant and thus, eventually, the adult. As for the nature of this object, there are different emphases according to different schools: there is the question of whether it is an external or an internal object, and the way in which phantasy and external reality interact in the constitution of the psychic object.

Generally, the advocates of this original unit, which is specifically the mother-child one, reproach Freud for not having gone further with the reconstruction of childhood in analysis, implying that if he had done so he would inevitably have realised the importance of earlier and earlier stages of development. But such a reproach does not take into account that the one they hold responsible for such a 'lacuna' is the very discoverer of psychic infantile development, and that his developmental pre-Oedipal stages , with their fundamental importance in our sexual choice, are still the unchallenged milestones on which all later work on infancy is based.

There is an air of denial, or else of naivety, in the belief that Freud accidentally overlooked the importance of what he was discovering and trying to systematise and communicate. Freud never takes his discoveries for the truth of his patients, but states what they unequivocally are for him: speculations. Freud too works within a unit, but he conceives of it as the triangular one of father, mother and child, rather than a dual one. The third term of the triangle, which tends to be misrecognised by the dual relation theorists, both determines and breaks the desired idyllic union of the child with the mother. The one-to-one relation does not account for what makes this union fail most of the time. Father, as representing what makes man's relation to the world problematical, is a function which is only too easily repressed by the analysts themselves, even though they are dealing with it at a clinical level, albeit with a greater or lesser awareness.

Although Melanie Klein stressed the importance of the relation to the mother, and saw the father's object, namely his penis, as a subsidiary one inside the wide insides of the mother's phantasised body, she still regarded the father function as the determining factor in the conflictual aspect of the relation to the maternal object.

The Psychoanalytical Object

What, then, is the psychoanalytical object for Lacan? It is neither the real object as seen by science, nor the one perceived by the ego or our consciousness.

The analytical object can only be accounted for by the subject of the Unconscious, which is the proper interlocutor of the psychoanalyst.

Birth entails a trauma, a real separation from the body of the mother. But how can the baby know that it has separated from another? There is a non-differentiation between 'me' and the 'other', and it is from this state of unity that birth inaugurates the principle of separation. However, it is not from another that the baby has separated, but from itself. It has not as yet lost the mother or the breast (neither of which it has ever met before), but a part of itself. For Lacan, it is in this way that the very first encounter is neither with the breast nor any other object or person, but with the lack of object; this amounts to saying a lack of oneself, as oneself and the other have not yet started their process of mental separation for the infant.

The lack of object does not imply this or that object, as the baby does not know what it is lacking as part of its world. Birth breaks the world and oneself into pieces. This seems to be the origin of Bion's catastrophes, Winnicott's unbearable anxiety at not being held, and Klein's phantasies of fragmentation and persecution in early infancy. The baby would never be able to indicate this loss if not for the fact that it has crying as a means of expression. If we do not know what it wants, at least we know that it wants something because of this crying. The baby cries and a breast comes in the way of its want, offering itself as an external object in the place of the enveloping object. We could use a metaphor and compare the breast to the womb turned inside out. By losing its envelope and source of life so far it has lost a part of itself, and it is demanding this missing part to make itself whole again; but what it is faced with is an external object other than itself. Wholeness is lost for man from that point on, and he will desire it and strive to regain it for ever. This corresponds to what Lacan calls desire as the pure desire for something unattainable. desire leaks between and beyond the need for nourishment and the demand for satisfaction (pleasure).

In most analytical theories the newborn baby is seen as dependent, fragmented, without a sense of Self and dominated by external objects. Nevertheless, the Kleinian approach maintains that the baby has an internal world; a phantasy world which, even if fragmented and partial, is operative from the start together with the external one. Now the problem for the various Object relations schools is to determine how and to what extent phantasy and external reality interlink, where phantasy is seen by them as an internal reality. I wonder why the distinction between phantasy and reality is never defined: how much of the internal world is inborn and how much of it is determined by the external one?

For Freud, the analytical object is the one cathected by the libido. As in the example of the amoeba, the object is included within the auto-erotic net of the infant. It is an object which becomes attached to one's own pleasure, and pleasure is the core of any sense or concept of a Self. Oneself and the world are not yet distinguished, so if there is a subject at all in the little newborn, it will reside *in nuce* in this pleasure (libido) which strives for an object. But the problem for the little auto-erotic being is that because this object is other than him, it resists a unification with the auto-erotic subject. The object is something which ultimately always escapes our grasp. Even the breast and the maternal body do not belong to the baby, but are gifts of the mother's love, and are given and taken away at the mother's discretion.

The mother is the only carrier of the desired object and, because the baby will never own it, he is totally at her mercy. However generous or good enough the mother is, she will never make her breast her baby's; and her efforts to do so will only deceive the baby as to such a possibility.

I will now take a case from one of my infant observations. Right from the first encounter with the pregnant mother, I could see all the elements of her anxiety about her own role, both in relation to the baby as her own responsibility, and in relation to the 'other mother': to her husband's ex-wife and to myself. What unfolded during the first few weeks of observation was the conflict between her own mother's precepts and her own leanings and judgement.

With her pain and her visits to the hospital, mother was still in the foreground in the first observation, while baby Ivana appeared merely as somebody to be changed, fed, and talked about. To mother's surprise, Ivana did not even draw attention to herself to protest during the changing of nappies. She left mother as the main character of the scene to worry about everything: shortage of nappies, equipment and of the warm blankets that her own mother reproached her for not supplying. Mother seemed to think that she did not have enough of what she was supposed to be giving baby, and frequently compensated for the shortage with a supply of her milk. On the other hand, baby was not distressed by any shortage, and seemed uninterested in the supply of her mother's milk. Her obvious enjoyment at the breast seemed to irritate mother: as the milk supplier, she did not think her breast was supposed to be a plaything! Once she was offered the other breast, Ivana went to sleep. Baby and mother did not actually come into an overt conflict, but they nevertheless acted on each other sideways. Neither was doing what they should have been doing; on the one hand baby was not being hungry or crying when expected , and on the other hand mother was not covering her up and enveloping her with nappies and blankets. Although nothing was quite right, it did not seem to matter too much to either of them; only to the father who was troubled by the naughty girl!

Crying became the main issue in the third week. For mother the immediate connection with the cry was baby's hunger - but why so much of it? And to the point of making herself sick? 'Baby thinks she is hungry, but she is not,' says mother, and to distract baby from her breast she starts to talk to her: replacing her breast with her voice as a substitute object, as it were, which baby partially accepts, (for Lacan the voice is one of the primary objects). Although baby calms down she still looks distressed, her cry no longer being a cry of hunger but of pain. The object which cannot fill up her irreducible hole pains her with its excessive presence, and in wanting to cork the hole, the object becomes a 'colic'. Kleinians would say it turns into a bad object. But the bad object is nothing other than the object which is expected to fill up the hole, and can only do this at the cost of pain. One of the Lacanian maxims is 'the lack cannot lack', (unless at the cost of psychosis). For mother, Ivana's cry is both a cry of hunger and a cry of colic pain. For the Kleinians, unfortunately, the good and the bad object are one and the same!

Let's try to look at the baby's relation to the object in some other way, one amongst many. After all, there is never just one way to observe, one always observes one's own understanding of things rather than understanding what is observed in itself.

Dependence

The baby is dependent on an object which is not itself or part of itself, but is another's and part of the other. This state of helplessness matches well with the biological theory of man's 'specific prematurity of birth', which makes man dependent in his childhood so much longer than any other animal. Biology has always aided psychoanalysis in its theoretical speculations as there is a contiguity between the two fields which, however, tends also to mislead as to their difference. 'Biology is destiny', said Freud when discussing the biological difference of the sexes in relation to man's originary-bisexuality. Even though the biological and the psychical work elbow to elbow with common givens, such as sexuality, the senses, capacities, the body, etc., the two levels are, unfortunately, not in harmony with each other. On the contrary, Freud realised that psychic pain and pleasure do not respond to the laws of necessity and need, but to a surplus of energy (libido) which exceeds any biological satisfaction. Think of homosexuality, drug addiction, perversion - the existence of mental pain is evidence that the two do not coincide but only relate to each other; and this is often characterized by great conflict.

Need and Pleasure

Instinct aims at the satisfaction of a need, for example, hunger. So, libido cannot be an instinct as its aim is the satisfaction of a pleasure, whether or not this pleasure was originally drawn from the satisfaction of a need. In her sensitivity to this overlapping of need and pleasure, Ivana's mother articulates the confusion for the baby: 'You think it is hunger, but it isn't'. Freud did not need endless observations of babies and nannies to deduce from his work with adult patients that their regressions did not point to oral or anal needs, but to oral or anal erotism - that is, pleasure. Ivana's greed points to such an erotic energy which exceeds any purely biological satisfaction. Eroticism is something essentially scandalous because it only rarely respects our wise needs. In spite of a satisfying feed, Ivana enjoys sucking beyond the milk that the breast offers; she plays with it, sucks her own thumb or mine, and goes so far as to make herself sick from too much sucking. Nevertheless, we had to wait for Freud before such a simple observation could be made. It seems easier to interpret babies' greed and pleasure as hunger for milk, even if the simplest nanny could tell us that most of the time the baby's cry is only a demand for pleasure and love. It is demanding a recognition of the erotic nature of its demand from the other. It is demanding Eros and mother gives it a sign of this; her breast is a sign of love. As can be seen in my observation, the confusion between need and pleasure resides not with the mother or the baby, but with the analysts themselves, including those who have translated Freud's 'Trieb' by instinct. The theoretical confusion starts here: if instinct serves need which looks for satisfaction, it is the drive which serves the libido which looks for erotic pleasure.

The Cry

As the abundant range of perversions and addictions to useless and harmful objects shows us, pleasure in the adult distances itself more and more from need. In the baby, pleasure seems to find its satisfaction in the breast as the only object offered to it, and as this is the object of feeding, it is offered to him for the satisfaction of his hunger. We could say that the baby has no other choice but to enjoy the breast. Therefore even the most satisfied baby wails; it would be worrying if it did not. Unlike all other animals, babies are born crying, and this is the sign that they are alive and well. Human beings seem to be born into this fundamental crying state, into an inarticulable want. Their cry bears witness to a split between need and pleasure; something is being demanded by the baby that is beyond satiation. Its total dependence on the care of another places it in a state of demand. But demand for what? Is it the breast that is being demanded by the baby as soon as it is pushed out of the maternal womb? The baby - 'the king' - cries, and mother offers it her breast, her milk; that is, she responds to the demand of the baby with the satisfaction of a need. But does the baby know what it is demanding? What is going to make it stop crying? It will know when mother puts her nipple into its mouth and shuts it up with her food. Mother has interpreted what it wants, but what the baby wanted before it met the breast, nobody knows. A mother's offering of her breast is a gift. A gift is not a needed object but a loving object; the gift always represents love. No one today, or at any other time, believes that maternity is a cow's function. Bottle feeding is as much a part of our customs of upbringing today, as wet nurses were the past. A woman choosing to breast feed her baby is doing so as a mere gift of love, and not as a necessity. Mothers know that what their breasts offer to the baby is a gift of love rather than the wanted object. However much a mother loves her child, she will never fulfil his demand to be One with her. In Ivana's mother we see an example of how a mother's anxiety consists of not being able to give the baby what it wants. Ivana's demanding helplessness seems to be interpreted by her mother as an absolute demand on her: baby wants more than her milk. What is this 'more' about? Is it the demand for the total consumption of the object and of herself (her colic)? Who is going to put a stop to this 'more and more'? The people like her mother or the observer who says that she should not give in? This mother does not yet know the 'rules' of her own mothering , and she clings to the empty rules of others without being able to apply them. I abstain from giving her other meaningless rules, and it is only as a response to this that she turns her gaze from me to her watch to make a choice and state it: 'I will not allow baby to cry more than ten minutes'! She gets her first rule not from me but from the scansion of time. A mother's anxiety arises from her recognition that she does not have what the baby wants (and this coincides with her recognition that the baby is not all she wants). The most loving mother cannot give back to her baby this mythological, originary unity. All she can give is some comforting gifts which are not 'it', but which represent 'it'. Love comes in the place of unity, but it is not unity. Most analysts agree, and most mothers know, that to satiate hunger is not all baby wants from the breast. It is quite common not to consider milk as everything the baby wants from life, but rather as a comfort that pacifies the desperately demanding infant.

The next session is characterised by a break, or a 'fast break', in the form of a breakfast. This time it was mother who ate, and she asked me to wait and let her enjoy her break from baby. She was 'nearly' sure now about what made baby cry, but she did not need to be completely certain, because what she is sure about is that it is not herself that baby cries for: it is because of the colic. She calmly tells me about baby playing and not sucking. I can relate to Ivana for the first time without mother. The action is slow and confident, with no hurry and no panic. Feeding can be interrupted and resumed later. Mother has decided to adopt her own rules and rhythms, knowing how much to give and how much not. As she says herself, she is indeed falling in love with her baby. From the anxiety of not feeling maternal - that is, short of love but full of anxiety - this mother very plainly describes to me how she is falling in love by breaking off the reciprocal devouring and sticky vicious circle of the previous two weeks. It is not the unmeetable need that preoccupies mother in the second and third week, but the dimension of play where the object is offered for pleasure by another as a sign of love. Love comes in the place of the needy relation, thus allowing for the breast or mother to be withdrawn.

The Partial Object

The Other, who knows and has what baby wants, responds to the baby's intransitive demand by offering an object in the place of the unknowable lost one. The breast has probably assumed such importance in psychoanalytical theory because feeding is the first response from the other to the inarticulable demand of the infant; it represents the object of desire, but only as an approximation. By offering her supply of milk, mother creates a demand for it. Some psychoanalysts think that because the baby gets satisfaction from its food and shows frustration when a limit is set, then all's well that ends well. Melanie Klein did not think so: the oral stage is populated by devouring and terrifying fantasies in relation to the breast. Such a relation is not a matter of fact, it entails a process of adaptation to the breast as an external object that never satisfies; in other words, that is partial. Lacan applied this concept of 'partial' to an object that only partially acquits its function of satisfaction. The object is partial by definition, because for the baby, nothing is whole. The most classical Object relations theories conceive of a world split up into parts. Psychoanalysis, of whatever persuasion, always has to deal with splits and divisions, and the Lacanian one is no exception . On the contrary, it makes the split the centre of its theory and attempts to look at it rather than trying to neutralise or deny it. The lack is not pathological, it is the core of the human mind; as an analyst one deals with it rather than trying to fill it or sew it up. Even mother has to frustrate the baby. We all know that bringing up a child is not simply a question of providing food and sweets. Frustration is part of growing up. But the child does not seem to take it very well, and even the most peaceful child can throw a tantrum for what seems to the parents to be a very minor frustration. Frustration cannot explain the excesses and the naughtiness of children who want more and more, and who push to the limit what can be given by parents; these are demands for absolute love - that is, perfect wholeness. Frustration concerns the baby's absolute demand where the complete object is lacking, rather than the satisfaction of a need or a pleasure. But it is only through the satisfaction of needs and pleasure that the baby can demand anything at all. Thanks to the presence of mother and her 'objects' the baby can demand something of somebody else; and it is thanks to these objects that mother and child can have their first conversation, as it were. Their physical contact functions as a means of communication. The divided newborn is not alone. The principle that there is an Other (with a big O, that is, not an object but rather closer to a

Deus ex machina who regulates our being in the world) is introduced by the presence and function of mother. Her object , the breast for instance, is a response from the Other to the absolute demand of the baby and, as such, acquires a psychic relevance. The breast offers itself to the inarticulate cry as a possibility of articulation. After the encounter with the breast the baby can ask for and from another; in this way it is introduced into the essence of the human world, that is, a shared world with meaning through common points of reference. The 'primal scream' finds its channels of communication with the other. The baby is alienated from its absolute demand by the intervention of the meaningful objects of the mother. In Lacanian terms, we could say that the 'holding mother' or 'good enough mother' is the one who is supplies meanings or the means of communication through which the baby can articulate its otherwise inexpressible, absolute demand.

But this alienation of demand to the maternal objects does not proceed as a matter of fact, it has its consequences. As the absolute demand is never met by mother's efforts, the latter stimulates it rather than satisfies it. This explains much about Melanie Klein's concern for greed, which she saw as an inborn affect. Others see it as an effect of either 'spoiling' or deprivation. Rousseau would have thought of Ivana's mother's earlier approach in his *Emile ou de l'Education*: 'the long cries of an infant who is neither tied up nor ill, and who is cared for completely, are only the cries of habit and obstinacy. They are not the work of nature, but of its nurse, who, incapable of bearing the importunity, multiplies it, while not imagining that by shutting up the infant today she is inciting it to cry more tomorrow'. The other who is in charge of the baby presents him/herself as whatever has been lost; as the big absolute Other, he/she embodies the role of what is desperately wanted. The omnipotence is on the side of mother, said Lacan, not of the infant. And it knows, or soon learns, that its desire is in the hands of the arbitrary desire of the other; its very life depends on it. The other, who is so present to the infant and yet so discordant in relation to it, is in total charge of the lost and desired object. Mother too is subjected to the law of absolute demand, she also demands that the baby be satisfied with what she has to offer. Mother demands that the baby's wants will be satisfied by her breast, her love, her care and so on. In this way the maternal objects are assimilated into the object of the original demand. And the world would stop here, in this illusory self-sufficiency of the mother-child relation, in this circularity of demand where nothing would be left to be desired. The world could stop at the circularity of the mother's breast which fills and the holding embrace. But it does not. The circularity of baby's and mother's demand has always given rise to an idealisation of the mother-child couple on the one hand, and on the other, to the conviction that all that goes wrong with a subject is originally the mother's fault. However reassuring and meaningful the mother-child couple might appear when taken in isolation, it is doomed to an impasse. This is also evident in Klein's postulation of Oedipal conflicts taking place earlier than the one postulated by Freud at around four years. By working with very young children and by exploring the infantile world, she realised that the relation to mother introduced a relation to the larger world. The body of the mother contains external elements in the child's fantasies: her body contains the father's penis, other babies, weapons and a whole series of conflicting and intruding objects. With Klein one has the impression that the baby relates to the world through and in spite of mother rather than communicating to her. The baby in the Kleinian fantasy world lives inside the empire of mother's body.

Mother's Gaze

In this stage, commonly called symbiotic, when the baby tries to find its completeness in the offerings and in the body of mother, Winnicott introduces the idea that among the mother's objects that link the baby to her there is also a special one, mother's gaze. This 'object' is very important for Winnicott because it functions as a mirror for the baby, in that he sees himself in mother's face; it is also important for Lacan because it triggers off the scopic drive, which involves taking in through the eyes rather than the mouth or fingers, as we have observed in Ivana. The world of images and the image of the world, which is still oneself, have set in. The image of oneself in the mother's eyes (in Latin the word pupil has the meaning of 'little girl', which is the little image of oneself that one sees in the pupil of the person who is looking at one) introduces both a separation of the image from oneself and an identification; the baby is in the face of the mother.

Mirror Stage

But for Lacan the importance of the mirror goes beyond the gaze of the mother. The mirror in which the baby can see its own reflection determines an overturning of the baby's perception of the world. According to Lacan this event takes place around the sixth month of life which is, interestingly enough, the same age that

Klein's depressive position sets in. But for Lacan the experience of perceiving one's own image in the mirror as distinct from seeing one's image in mother's eyes is an exciting and jubilant one. For the first time the baby perceives himself as separate from mother, as having another face, as it were. But even more important is the fact that he perceives himself not as a helpless creature who can hardly sit up if not held by mother, but as a human whole, and he applies to himself a human Gestalt which, in the previous stage, he had already acknowledged as his own through mother. But at the 'Mirror stage', as Lacan calls it, he is human and he sees himself as more complete than he actually is; he is the image of what he is going to be when his body will enable him to stand up and do things for himself. The mirror is an orthopaedia of human power and beauty, in other words Narcissus falls in love with his own image. But unlike Narcissus, the baby recognises himself in that ideal human image and he identifies with his image. There is a disparity between the baby's dependence and lack of coordination and the imaginary precipitation into a complete and independent whole as perceived in the mirror. According to Lacan this is the origin of the Ego, that is, an identification with one's own specular image as an illusion of mastery and bodily coordination which has not yet been reached, and a further alienation from mother's gaze into one's own image. This further split between one's own fragmented being and its reflection in the mirror constitutes a new psychic stage in the dialectic of separation/unification. The mirror doubles as well as splits, to come back to Narcissus. The world is no longer an extension of the infant but is doubled; the other becomes a double of oneself. This relation with the double always provokes conflict, because if the other is a double of oneself he is also a rival. The mirror inaugurates a rivalry with oneself; the object of identification also becomes an object of hatred and aggression. This is very obvious in paranoia where the loved person, the one the paranoid is identified with, becomes the persecutor who wants to get rid of him and vice versa. This is the phenomenon of transitivism, where the child who strikes another then claims that it is he himself that has been struck. An example from literature is Edgar Allan Poe's William Wilson who, by destroying his own double, only destroys himself. These are the various facets of Narcissus.

But the double is not always there, in the same way that the breast was not always there in earlier infancy, when its absence was either received with the cry or denied by hallucinating it (or rather the satisfaction/pleasure derived from it), or by substituting one's own body for it (Ivana used either her fist or thumb), or by substituting any other object or person at hand (Ivana sucking my thumb while mother was finishing her breakfast). Even though Freud did not set up an infant observation seminar while carrying on his discoveries, he could not help observing. He observed his grandchild, whose mother was absent for a while, and he was struck by his solitary game with a cotton reel with a string attached to it. By throwing it under his cot he would make it disappear, and then by pulling it back he would make it appear again. The child was one and a half and could hardly say but a few distorted words, but would utter the sounds *'fort'* when he threw the reel away and *'da'* when he pulled it back; Freud deciphered these sounds as the German words 'gone' and 'back'. The toddler was dealing with his mother's absence by devising a game where he was in control of the presence and absence of the object, in other words, by becoming master of the situation. Even if Freud had been wrong in his interpretation of the sound uttered by his grandchild, the latter was certainly symbolising the comings and goings of the loved object through his game. What struck Freud was the fact that the child was symbolising, that is, he was acknowledging the absence of mother by representing it in his play. Lacan saw in this observation a crucial moment in the psychic development of the infant, the moment when separation is articulated, not by the other, but by the child himself in the other's absence. In this example it is not the inarticulate cry that expresses his demand for unity, but the child's meaningful sounds and playful actions . The 'fort/da' phase, as Lacan calls it, inaugurates a new dialectic of presence/absence where the latter finds psychic representation; it is separation raised to a psychic function, where an empty place finds a voice in the subject. The world of language starts here where words substitute for the missing object , and a cotton reel can assume the function of a symbol. When Lacan calls this the symbolic order, he not only means an order which structures the ineffable and helpless world of infancy, but also an order which brings up to date the inarticulable infantile experience. That is the Freudian 'deferred action' where what happens later reinterprets and shapes what had happened before. For Freud, as for Lacan, psychoanalysis is the reinterpreting and reordering of one's own history, one's own trauma and one's own destiny through the power of language. This is the heart of the psychoanalytic rite.

Language is the exclusively human way of representing what is not there. Not only do words come in the place of things , they are also part of a system which has its own independent relation to the world of things. In common with Wittgenstein, Lacan thought that it was thanks to the world of language that we have a vision of the

world which , although it is never perceived and understood directly , at least it is perceived through a mediation of physical and mental agencies. Philosophy, science and psychology have always tried
to establish the categories which determine the comprehension of
the world; space, time, consciousness, the senses, the nervous system, affects and so on. Psychoanalysis, as conceived by Freud, discovered that the Unconscious is a system of symbols representing
something which cannot be said by consciousness directly, but only
through dreams, slips of the tongue, negations and so on. For
Lacan, what cannot be said by our consciousness is this lack and
this unspeakable desire for absoluteness which reveals the very limits of life and our being. It is a relation to death which cannot be
said, rather than a relation to an object. Even if Klein doesn't spell it
out in theory, her system is also a triangular one in which the psychic process of the child unfolds through the conflicts which go
beyond the enclosed pre-verbal world of mother and child.
Kleinians have dismissed the importance that Freud gave to the
father, identifying the key to later mental states in the early stages
of development. Lacan reintroduces the father and the importance
of the Oedipus complex as the founding moments of the introduction of the child to the other, which is outside the mother-child
enclosure. The father functions as a symbol, the symbol of the limit
to a one-to-one relation. In the symbiotic relation there is the illusion that the world closes up in this pre-verbal self-sufficiency of
breast and mouth to be fed, closes up around the presence of the
desired object which is all we need to accomplish our mental stability; this illusion is broken by the intervention of a third element,
represented by the father. We have already said that the mother too
is subject to the law of absolute demand. In the same way as the
child she is subject to the separation from the other. This is like saying that she also desires something beyond her own child in the
same way that the child desires something beyond mother, and
without this 'beyond' they are trapped with each other in a position
where the devouring and aggressive fantasies (even if for too much
love) become reality. We can say that Lacan does not deny pre-
Oedipal encounters with the world mediated by the presence of
mother and her partial objects, but each new encounter has an effect
on and enriches the previous one rather than the other way around.
Consequently the Oedipal stage determines the position that the
subject will take in relation to his incestuous desire for mother (a
further version of his desire of unification with her), and the prohibition against this desire. The Oedipus complex is the milestone of
this conflict between language, where the subject is called to articu-

late and take responsibility for his desire, and his unarticulated desire to possess and be possessed by mother.

Often childhood neurosis is only the effect of the difficulty, for everybody to a greater or lesser extent, to navigate their way through this passage. This more or less painful attempt to achieve the development of Oedipus that Freud called 'infantile neurosis', is not an obstacle to the child's development, as popular belief would have it. The effects of not having developed and overcome the Oedipus stage already imply an adult neurosis.

But from a clinical point of view, neurosis proper sets in when the Oedipal phase can either find no solution at all, or only solutions in precarious forms, such as denial, evasion, false acceptance of its effects, and so on. The regression to previous infantile stages takes place in analysis in connection with, and as a result of, the Oedipal struggle. When an adult is said to regress to oral or anal stages this does not mean that he has not moved from the Oedipal stage and is still like a four year old or an infant, but it certainly indicates where a false step was made. He has moved, but without resolving the puzzle of Oedipus; he has moved by leaving a question unanswered in the Unconscious. But the insistence of the unanswered question is indicated where the mental gap has found its compensation. Regression does not tell us much about the actual infantile stages, but about the infant's encounters with the world's demands and offerings, as well as missed encounters. Regression gives us a sign of the point at which a resistance to give up one pleasure for another takes place; it shows us where desire stops moving and gets stuck every time in a repetition, not answering for its choices. For Lacan, the Unconscious is an ever open question which is silenced by the symptom. A silence which is only compensated by the excessive noise that the symptom makes. It is up to the analyst to hear the noise of the open question, behind the regressive demands and invocations of the analysand. It is up to the analyst to recognize this open unsolved question.

[1] This is a shortened and modified version of an article published in 'The British Journal of Psychotherapy' Vol 5 No 3, Spring 1989.

DISCUSSION OF PAPERS ON CHILD PSYCHOANALYSIS

Q: In the psychotic there is always a dyadic relationship with the Other and we find in the clinic there is also a dyadic relation. You said there is a function of the father, but not a specific function. The question is - is there is a contradiction in the suggestion that the function could be either father or mother.

Benvenuto: In psychosis we don't identify the primordial Other of the infant as the mother. We are always talking about the functions, for example the caring function, and in more and more cases it is the father who raises the children and it is therefore he who is the primordial function; but the breast is not an object - or the bottle - it is a function. There is a cry and the mother interprets 'You want the breast.' The child is not asking for breast but for 'something' that is gone.

Q: I'd like to ask about the structure of the sessions and how frequent they should be, in relation to Winnicott who gave access on demand. What thoughts are there on the theory behind the structure of sessions?

Rustin: As I think I said, I don't think you can do *analytic* work outside a strict recognised structure. That does not say you cannot use psychoanalysis to do other things creatively as Winnicott did in his occasional consultations, but I don't think it is *psychoanalysis*. It is not manipulative - it can be quite an inspired kind of contact but it is not analysis. It is something the child wants that is different from an ongoing relationship, where I think analysis depends on the transference and counter-transference being the locus of the whole endeavour and you cannot just have it whenever.

Benvenuto: Psychoanalysis is a contract between two people - even with children! If it is not the child who makes a demand for analysis the preliminary interviews can last for years, so that you can make sure you have a clear contract for the specific work... Winnicott didn't use psychoanalysis on demand as a rule. He would not make a rule out of it.

Q: Would both speakers comment on a possible parallel between the idea of containment in Kleinian thought and the symbolic in Lacanian. What came over clearly in Margaret Rustin's talk was that containment was very strongly linked with the Lacanian idea of the symbolic. When the patient - the boy - got down from the cupboard he came down at the point when you were talking about *time* - about holidays, etc. What puzzles me about Kleinian thinking is the lack of theory about speech content! There has to be something unusual about his writing his name all over the place - on the wall. His name must be problematic. Either he has a name or he takes on the name of his adopted parent. You spoke about the biological mother of the child but said nothing about the situation in which he was living apart from the fact that he was adopted. However little this child knows about the circumstances of his upbringing and his father...

Rustin: Obviously I was trying to give a clinical example, since it is a clinical paper. I don't feel I work in a way which precludes the father - anything but. It is true there are no particular examples in that session of this. I think your starting point is the importance of the shift in the session in relation to time. Father is always represented within the therapist because father is phantasised by the child to be always inside mother - because of the structure of the sessions. The Tavistock Daddy says the session must end!

In this boy's treatment he had had therapy prior to the start of his work with me which had to end as the original therapist was ill and I took him on from her. In the work with her the boy's violence had been so extreme that it was only possible, to make the session work at all, if his own father sat outside the room - so the notion that there is no father in Kleinian work is mistaken.

My thinking on this is that father is always inside the mother for the child from the beginning. You can think about the nipple - the hard bit of the breast - as the penis, linked to father in addition to the soft receptive mother. But it is not mother all the time. Mother is not always there, not always providing. I very much agree with Bice that for the child mother is also always not there!

Benvenuto: The father's penis (and this is different in Lacan where 'penis' and 'phallus' have very different meanings!) inside the mother is not the father function but the opposite one - it is the persecutor. The penis inside the mother is the thing that causes the break in unity with the good. It isn't always the enemy; the thing is inside the mother, it remains inside the empire of the mother's body. I think the function of the lift man in the Tavistock and the names of the friends which Tim writes refer to the Name-of-the-Father, which is missing from the session. Still he wants his friends' names to appeal to something else. There is a difference on how the father is viewed between the Kleinian and Lacanian perspective; for Lacan, he has to be symbolised - he cannot be seen as something *ex machina*, but as something that makes order. The father's penis is real and part of the paranoid-schizoid state: the phallus is a named element that changes the psyche.

Q: I was going to say that the father has many functions and one is a protective function. We can say the lift keeper is a tyrant or someone helpful who can ensure Margaret sees the patient next week or something.

I would like to say something about the relationship with the father and the idea of the object. I enjoyed both papers and found them so rich but I feel we need a trialogue. The comparisons you both made would be well. discussed in relation to the Freudian bridge and ideas of development. I get the sense that where the discussions are missing each other at some point is around the issue of psychic reality and what it means to talk about the reality of internal objects.

As I see it both traditions are saying it is not the same as external reality and there is not a simple kind of sucking in of the outside world which gets fixed. Both of these rest fundamentally on the notion of absence and work in relation to absence of being. Maybe symbolic function could be influential to enable symbolic rather than syncretic function. What is the nature of internal reality that Kleinian tradition is trying to describe? One idea I had was around terminating the analysis and I wondered what kind of considerations would go into determining whether or not a child was ready to finish the therapy - of course, there are special considerations for children. They go on growing and can always come back again. Has this child enough to travel with? In the material Margaret gave us she did not put things into the child's head in terms of interpreting what went on in his unconscious but there was a lot of containing there and the child put together various things. The child surprisingly came out with a kind of integration - a sorting out - 'we will start with sorting the room out - clean it up!'. He says he is going off skating. What is the significance of this skating? Going out skating you have to stand on your own feet; you have to be able to stop slipping about too much. It takes much courage to step on ice. Perhaps there is an object there which is good enough to take those risks and in fact he has consolidated it in the course of this session and it has both paternal and maternal aspects in terms of being able to step out on to the ice. This is a good-enough object and is not based on the particular prior experiences of that boy.

Benvenuto: I don't know about the good object, but I see that he is constructing a possibility for the future and certainly the question of time is crucial at that point where he is almost doing a baptism of himself through the name - and baptism gives a name to the subject. There is a sense of leaving but there is also denial. Actually a lot of denial - it's not walking on the real earth, in skating on ice the construction that has been made is fragile. Ice is something exciting - not working on earth, but it is certainly a possibility for this child;

it is like having ice put on the horrible paranoid-schizoid - it could melt at any moment. At least he has managed this kind of operation. The therapy is finished in itself and it is finished for this child, but my thought is that the therapist knows it is on ice.

Q (Robert M. Young): I've been pondering on the question of time in respect of the setting - the analytic frame. This is a question to Bice. There is a lot of loose talk about short sessions in the Lacanian paradigm. I feel very strongly about the regularity of sessions: in the context of child therapy I cannot imagine anything less than regular sessions. I could not actually conduct my day and the my practice without regularity. I believe it may be a satirical thing to talk of shorter sessions; I have never heard anyone speak of it and I wondered if you would.

Benvenuto: It is not shorter sessions, it is a question of sessions of variable time. There is a contract. But what contract? A contract is something you agree with others It's true that in the Kleinian tradition there is more emphasis on technique. In the Lacanian tradition technique is still a theoretical problem. Freud's papers on technique are quite highly theoretical - in the analyses of Anna Freud, Balint, Klein and Winnicott there are clinical strategies *behind* the technique. Let us say that the variable session is one Lacanian technique - a strategy for the opening of the Unconscious. Other schools will have their own strategies for opening the Unconscious.

Variable time is not a matter of having a set time. I agree that there is an importance of the setting in terms of the regular session that have been agreed on as part of the contract with the patient, in which you do certain work. Within 50 minute sessions there is a problem of time - subjective time: you can't predict how that will be. This is not a matter decided by the analyst alone but in the contract with the analysand. If I have made a contract for there to be a fifty-minute session, I don't suddenly kick someone out of my consulting room - that would certainly be something to analyse for the therapist!

When variable time becomes intrinsic to the analytic work then the patient knows that the Unconscious cannot wait for the last 10 minutes of the session to open up and must open from the beginning because the session can close at any time. To close it *could* be traumatic - it can repeat trauma, so that someone could go away and throw himself under a train....

Robert M. Young: ... or throw the analyst under a train (*laughter*).

TECHNIQUE AND INTERPRETATION IN KLEIN

Catalina Bronstein

In the Introduction to Freud's papers on technique, Strachey makes an important point. He states that 'rules could be of value only if the grounds for them were properly understood and digested'. He also stresses that 'Freud never ceased to insist that a proper mastery of the subject could only be acquired from clinical experience and not from books'. Clinical experience here meaning not only clinical experience with patients but 'also and above all, clinical experience from the analyst's own analysis' (Strachey, 1958).

Clinical work was of the utmost importance to Klein, being the basis on which she developed her theories and technique. When I was invited to give this talk, I asked whether I should bring clinical examples, a case? I was told that all Kleinians seem to ask the same question! I decided to compromise by approaching the discussion of today's subject from a theoretical point and then illustrating it with a small clinical vignette.

Klein's development of her play technique in the treatment of children was concurrent with the development of her theories. Her technique allowed her to analyse very young children, some under the age of three. She regarded play in children as the counterpart of free association in adults (Spillius, 1994) and thought that children, as well as adults, developed a transference-neurosis (Klein, 1932). She therefore concluded that the analysis of children should be no different from that of adults, in terms of the latters' aims and the importance of interpreting unconscious phantasies. Klein was critical of analysts who introduced other elements such as education or reassurance in their work with children. I will briefly describe the technique she developed in the analysis of children. She provided them with a number of small and simple toys which she described as 'little wooden men and women, cats, carriages, trains, animals, bricks and houses, as well as paper, scissors and pencils' (Klein, 1932). She also felt it was important to have a wash-basin with running water. She would provide some spoons, glass tumblers and some vessels. She thought that games with water gave the analyst a deep insight into the fundamental pre-genital impulses of the child, as well as offering a means of illustrating his sexual theories.

Klein felt that, for some children, their state of anxiety on coming into the room and throughout their time with her was so great that it was necessary to start interpreting immediately. She described how this reduced the child's resistance, enabling the child to go on playing. She also emphasised that transference could be understood and interpreted in children as well as in adults and that it developed in child analysis in a similar way to in adult analysis. Her experience of the analysis of children led her to emphasise the importance of destructive impulses, which she generally described as sadism, and of the anxieties and defences activated by them. Klein strongly opposed an analysis based on emphasising the positive transference. Her point of view contrasted and conflicted with that upheld by Anna Freud. Klein asserted that her theories were closely based on Freud.

Klein's experience with children also influenced the way in which she formulated interpretations, in that she tended to use bodily-based part-object language.

Interpretation

Given that interpretation is inevitably linked in Klein to the concept of transference, I would like to say something about both transference and counter-transference. This subject is discussed in another lecture so I will be brief.

For Klein the concept of transference was linked to her notion of unconscious phantasy which underlies all thought (conscious and unconscious) and which was described by Susan Isaacs as the mental representation of instincts (Isaacs, 1952). Therefore, the emphasis on the pervasiveness of transference is derived from this concept of unconscious phantasy. This notion of transference moves away from Freud's use of the concept of transference as resistance and is thought of not just as a repetition of old attitudes and conflicts from the past but as an externalisation of unconscious phantasy here and now in the analysis.

In *The Origins of Transference* (1952), Klein describes the importance of early anxieties in the relation to the object (paranoid anxiety in paranoid-schizoid position and depressive anxieties in depressive position) as well as the defences that went along with them. Klein was mainly interested in the content of these anxieties and in the mechanisms that the baby used to deal with them, such as the primal processes of projection and introjection. This paved the way for the development of the concept of projective identification as the basis on which transference operates. I will return to this later when I touch on projective identification in Klein and its importance for understanding what she means by a transference interpretation.

Klein, also states that 'it is my experience that in unravelling the details of transference it is essential to think in terms of total situations transferred from the past into the present as well as of emotions, defences and object-relations' (Klein, 1952). Her theory of 'positions' as different from a developmental theory allows us to understand the notion of acting out these anxieties in the transference. Thus, it is not just based on a concept of regression to an earlier developmental stage but the expression of unconscious conflict in the here and now. It is the here and now that is the route to understanding past experiences. The oscillations between the paranoid-schizoid and the depressive positions underlie the process of working through. The relation to the original objects is then re-lived in the analytic situation. According to Klein, all free associations that come to the patient's mind can be referred to the transference (Hinshelwood R, 1991). This idea of transference as a total situation and the patients' acting-out of their unconscious phantasies (impulses and defences, etc.) in the analytic situation has been later explored and developed by other Kleinian analysts such as Betty Joseph (Joseph, 1985).

In 1952 Klein stressed that 'her conception of transference '...entailed a technique by which from the whole material presented what will be deducted are the unconscious elements of the transference.'

Even though the importance of understanding the transference is paramount in Kleinian analysis, in the last thirty years there has been some change in the development of Kleinian technique, well described by Spillius (Spillius, 1994). For example, the early emphasis on destructiveness, which was the consequence of the development of Klein's idea about innate envy and the death instinct, gave way to a wider understanding of both hate and love and the importance of the wish for or possibility of reparation of the object that has been attacked and destroyed in phantasy. The notion of the attack on the object - the breast - was combined with the wish to repair this damage and be able to mourn the loss in the depressive position.

There has also been a move away from interpreting at a part-object level, using part-object language. Klein developed a very concrete language of part-objects and bodily functions in her work with small children. This language became rather ritualised and was felt by many analysts as 'forcing' patients into accepting the analyst's preconceptions. Even though there are still some Kleinian analysts who do interpret unconscious phantasy in part-object language, and this might still be relevant in the case of small children and psychotic patients, most Kleinian analysts would now interpret the patient's immediate experience in the transference, that is, the content of the anxieties and defences as expressed through dreams, free association, etc. However, some Kleinian analysts do not simply interpret the transference in the here and now. According to Hannah Segal: 'A full transference interpretation (and though we cannot always make a full interpretation, we aim eventually at completing it) will involve interpreting the patient's feelings, anxieties and defences, taking into account the stimulus in the present and the reliving of the past' (Segal, 1973).

From this we can see that some Kleinian analysts would make a link between the transference interpretation in the here and now and the patient's past experiences while others prefer to formulate their interpretations mainly in the here and now.

Klein's notion of transference developed concurrently with her understanding of the mechanisms of projection and introjection. Internal object relations are mobilised by projection onto the analyst and then modified through interpretation and experience as they are reintrojected. But what gets projected is not just a 'whole' object (for example the analyst being experienced as the abandoning mother), but also parts of the self that feel unbearable to the patient. For example, the analyst can be experienced by the patient as containing the envy that the patient has split and projected onto the analyst, who is subsequently experienced as an envious object, from whom the patient now feels he has to protect himself.

I will now bring in a clinical vignette to illustrate some of these points on technique and interpretation. A patient, a 30 year old man who had been in analysis for several years and who felt unable to work or lead an adult life (he did not work, he had a girlfriend but there was virtually no sexual relationship between them, etc.) and with a history of a possessive phobic mother to whom he was devoted, came to one of his sessions 10 minutes late. He started speaking very anxiously, even before he lay down on the couch, and very fast: 'Don't ask me why I am late because I don't know'. He went on to tell me a dream: He was with a 'girl' and he liked her and they were going to meet again. He could see his mother in the background. They were at a party. When the girl was parting from him she said they would meet again. He was so happy when he woke up that could not get out of bed in time to be on time for his session. He stopped there and seemed unable to produce any associations.

The range of possible interpretations is vast. If one moves away from the question, 'when should one decide to make the first interpretation?', and decides to interpret, what will one say?

The question of when and why one decides to start interpreting is an important one. In my opinion, Kleinian analysts probably interpret far more than Lacanian analysts. I decided to make an interpretation based on my awareness of the anxiety that prevented him from producing any associations to the dream.

What could I take up? One could say that there is Oedipal material, the mother in the dream, maybe the analyst in the transference, elements that remind the analyst of his past, etc. Actually, there were two things in the dream that struck me, one being the use of infantile language, the use of the word 'girl' instead of woman. The other was the notion of parting.

I thought the interpretation should be directed at his experience of himself and me in the session. This was where his anxieties and defences came together in connection with his unconscious phantasies. If I had taken up his desire for a woman, and the possibly forbidding and forbidden mother in the background, it might quickly have become intellectualised and used by him as a story he could tell himself which would have had no therapeutic impact. Now, he had started by telling me (through his double negative, 'Don't ask me because I don't know') that he knew something about himself that had made him miss the first 10 minutes of the session. What he knew had to do with his sexual desire. He felt that, with me, he could not use ordinary adult language. What sort of object was I now in his mind ? Why did he need to appease me ? Maybe he felt he had actually attacked me by having this dream. Here I am trying to convey the possible questions that I might have formulated to myself, possibly not fully consciously. The dream then, would not have been just a dream expressing unconscious desire for a woman but would have been part of the total situation as seen in the transference.

I said to him that he wanted me to know what he secretly knew, which was that he was a man capable of having an erotic dream about a woman but that this knowledge made him very anxious because of his fear of my possible response to it.

He then said that he had woken up with an erection. He had then hugged his girlfriend but did not tell her his dream. He remembered that after leaving his session the previous day, he had just gone home and did nothing for the rest of the day. He had been mindless as usual, and just watched TV.

I said that when he left the day before, he had prevented himself from knowing how he felt about parting from me because he could not allow himself to know that I was a woman who would not be just waiting for him in the background.

In relation to this material, one could say that he had projected into me an image of his own internal objects and now I had become the persecuting object who could not accept his sexuality (here I am leaving aside all other possible ways of understanding the material, such as the Oedipal sexual interest in me, etc.), and who might be envious of his potency that he had now to keep secret from me.

Interpretation of his anxiety and his defence (his need to placate me by saying he did not know), allowed him to reintroject a less persecutory object, as well as to feel able to realise that in those ten minutes that he had kept me waiting he was acting out the denial of how he had felt after leaving the previous day's session.

One could say that his need to attack his capacity to think (and he actually became a mindless sort of voyeur, watching TV for the rest of the day) might have had to do with his need to kill the awareness of a separate me, who would be engaged in intercourse with others after he left. His projected hatred and jealousy turned me into a potential attacking object. At the same time, even though it had to be disguised, the patient also wanted me both to know why he was late and that he actually knew it himself.

Now, I have spoken of transference interpretations but not about counter-transference. Klein was rather uneasy about Paula Heimann's extension of the concept of counter-transference and linked this term more closely to the analyst's own reactions and feelings brought about by his own experiences and difficulties. Nowadays, I believe, most Kleinian analysts use the concept more widely, to cover 'a state of mind at least partly induced in the analyst as a result of verbal and non-verbal action by the patient, thus giving effect to the patient's phantasy of projective identification' (Spillius, 1994). The counter-transference is used by the analyst as a tool to help him understand the patient's projections.

Setting

In order for a process to develop there has to be a setting in which to contain it. The basic features of Klein's technique have been derived from Freud. Some of them (Spillius, 1994) are: the rigorous maintenance of the analytic setting, so as to keep the transference as pure and uncontaminated as possible, an expectation of five sessions a week, an attitude of active receptivity in the analyst, the interpretation of anxiety and defence together, the importance of understanding and interpreting the transference, as well as avoiding any other sort of communication, such as suggestion, reassurance, sharing of the analyst's feelings, exchange of presents, etc.

Possible Differences Klein-Lacan

One issue I could imagine coming up in today's discussion is the difference between a fixed time - say, 50 minutes - compared to the open-ended session. I think it is important to keep the duration of the sessions constant, to protect the stability of the setting. If the analyst introduces changes into the setting it might be more difficult to understand what is being communicated by the patient. It might lead the analyst to act out his counter-transference and this often becomes conscious to the analyst once the patient has left. The analyst should be very careful not to act out what might either have been projected by the patient or be based on his own personal conflicts.

Moving on to the issue of interpretation, and I should say that my knowledge of Lacan is very limited, I think that one of the criticisms that Lacan makes of Klein, while he evidently respected her work, has to do with his view that she worked mainly in the field of the Imaginary, possibly introducing the Symbolic Register but without realising it. Eric Laurent, in his comments on Melanie Klein (in Laurent, 1992), stresses this as well. He also asserts that Klein's work centres on the Imaginary and he equates Kleinian transference interpretation with a sort of paranoia centred on the analyst.

I don't believe this to be the case. If one considers Klein in the light of the developments of Bion and Segal, one could say that the capacity to think, that is, the capacity to identify the patients' anxieties, register their projection onto the analyst, and then put them into words, is a complex phenomenon, not dissimilar to the capacity to see the object as a separate whole object who can relate to another separate whole object in the Oedipal triangle. Thus, if I am presenting the patient with a space to think about his anxieties, by not identifying myself with his projections and acting them out, that is by not being a 'living mirror' (Lacan,1955), I am introducing the Symbolic Register. If I had gone along with my patient's projections and, for example, reacted angrily at the fact that he was late, or had gone along with his need to appease my supposed envy and jealousy by talking of 'girls' instead of women, I should have kept him and me in an imaginary, narcissistic identification, possibly akin to Klein's description of the search for the Ideal object of the paranoid-schizoid position. In that case he would have not been able to remember that he had woken up with an erection or his decision about not to talk about it.

INTERPRETATION

Bernard Burgoyne

Psychoanalysis is a response to human suffering. While there are other forms of intervention that aim to bring about a shift in the way that a human being relates to his or her suffering, this one in particular, unlike those proposed by psychiatry and medicine, operates not with chemicals and surgery, but with words. That words can bring about such effects is however something that demands explanation, and Freud never ceased devising theories of this kind throughout his lifetime. Words constitute the basic vehicle of the psychoanalytic situation: they are the means by which a symptom and its underlying structure are analysed, and as a result they are at the heart of the question of interpretation.

Analytical work starts when someone comes to the analyst with a demand, with a complaint that they want the analyst to do something about: this complaint is usually about work or about love, or about both. The intending analysand has had enough of repeating the same kind of failure or the same kind of pain, and they want something changed: generally, however, they do not want to change their opinions about sexual love - what they want changed are their symptoms. The aim of much of the preliminary work in analysis is for the analyst to be able to convince the analysand that the symptoms follow from the opinions, that one cannot be changed without the other: but how is the process of the analysis to bring about such a conviction?

The analytical relation is a situation that has been brought into being by the analysand being asked to speak in a very particular way - in a way that he would not ordinarily allow to himself. Correspondingly, the analyst's side of this contract is to agree to listen to what is said and alluded to, while subtracting from this listening any response determined by the analyst's own personal interest. Psychoanalysis therefore puts forward a very peculiar relationship - a peculiar way of talking and listening, not encountered in everyday relationships - as the agency of change. So how is it that a change of sexual opinion, a change of sexual phantasy, can be brought about by this commitment to try to speak about what previously could not be put into words? The answer to this question demands some consideration of the unique ways of speaking which, as Freud pointed out in 1926, build up the material that constitutes the analytical relationship. The "powerful instrument" of language which can do "unutterable good" and also "cause terrible wounds" is given a new setting in the analytical relationship. From the beginning Freud had been determined to keep this problem of the functioning of words at the centre of the technique of analysis, and in this way to organise the themes of psychoanalytic theory and practice around the problem of the workings of language in the human soul.

The problem Freud faced was this: by what means can a particular way of talking bring about a change of opinion? There is a long-standing solution to this problem that stems from the time of Socrates, a solution that Freud knew much about, and whose articulation requires a prior look at Greek theories of how language functions as a toxin in the human soul. The school immediately preceding the development of the research programme of Socrates was that of the grouping that called themselves "orators". They are usually known by the name of Sophists. Despite the bad press given to this group of philosophers by Plato, many of their hypotheses were agreed with by Socrates. In particular, there is in a text written by the Sophist Gorgias which claims that language functions not as a neutral instrument of thought - in the vision later widely propagated in England - but as a form of poisoning. In his investigation of whether or not Helen is guilty of bringing about the state of war at Troy, he puts forward in her defence the argument that her actions were brought about by her having been poisoned by two factors that all human beings are subjected to: the poisonings of language and the poisonings of love. "Speech" he says "is a powerful master, and achieves the most divine feats with the smallest and least evident body": "the power of speech", he continues, "has the same effect" on the body "as the disposition of drugs". Human beings, says Lacan, are poisoned by language, condemned to negotiate their desires through the medium of words.

The Sophists see the human condition as one which demands an intervention into the way in which people stumble from one opinion to another, with no orientation, either in the sphere of work or in the sphere of love. The effects of speech "cause pain ... benumb and bewitch the soul". This field of language which influences everyone from the moment of their birth brings people into a state of universal depressed inactivity for which the Sophists see only one solution - that there be a class of orators whose function is to speak well. The orators will activate individuals and groups by the power of rhetoric, engaging them in projects that will give an otherwise lacking direction to their lives. The Socratic response to this was an agreement to the diagnosis of confusion and misdirection, combined with a refusal to agree that the only response to it lay in the field of suggestion and rhetoric. The new solution proposed by Socrates was to claim the existence of a new way of speaking, one in which each party is attempting to alter the opinions of the other, not by an imposed force, but by leading the other to see that absurd consequences follow from the opinions they maintain. The aim of this new form of dialectic is then to induce the other to give up or weaken their attachment to certain opinions. Freud translated an extensive account of this theory of Socratic dialectic into German in 1879, and there are indications that he intended this dialectic to be the structure at play in at least the early work of analysis. Without going into the wider philosophical influences on Freud - particularly those stemming from the Scottish Enlightenment - at least the early work of analysis can be formulated as the introduction of a Socratic dialectic: the analyst is trying to get the analysand to loosen their attachment to certain sexual opinions. This view of things has been repeatedly stressed by Jacques Lacan, and represents the first orienting point in his theory of the work of interpretation.

The problem of interpretation is related to this functioning of dialectic. For both Freud and Lacan, chains of signifying terms, and more particularly, the networks constructed by their intersections, form the material within which interpretation operates. The correctness of an interpretation is judged by whether or not it facilitates the production of more material; not by whether it has other effects on the analysand, whether the analysand refuses it or agrees to it, or whether the analyst is pleased with it. That is, it is effective only if it overcomes to some extent the resistance. In the Socratic relation between the analyst and analysand, a dream or a part of a dream will often be a response to a previous interpretation, whether made by the analyst or by the analysand. Several questions can be raised about this functioning of interpretation in relation to the production of material. Who associates best to the dream? The answer is: the analysand. Who interprets best? The answer is: the analysand. The reason for this is that it is the analysand, and not the analyst, who knows the particularities of the psycho-sexual history of the analysand, even if it is known at first only in a way that is inaccessible to consciousness. The way that Lacan reads Freud here is that the analyst interprets relatively little: there are many periods of the analytical work where the analyst needs to interpret hardly at all. But in all of this, the function of interpretation is the production of pathways that approach unconscious desire.

Resistance, Lacan would frequently say, is always on the side of the analyst. If the analyst is not adept enough to wrong-foot the ego, catch the ego by surprise, then he is failing to listen to what is not said: to what is said only between the lines. One of the main forms of interpretation that Lacan recommends is equivocation: the function of equivocation is to confuse the ego, which while it catches hold of one drift of meaning allows the other to escape. This gives a reason for why a joke is usually very effective as an interpretation: Lacan also indicated that an enigmatic interpretation can function in the same way. Any linguistic term that plays a role within the tapestry of associations that translates the Unconscious naturally functions equivocally: the term that Freud used to designate such a property of dream elements is "over-determined" - that is, more than one thread of meanings is attached to them. This problem of equivocal signifying terms and their translation raises the question of the functioning that Freud assumed for representations and signs. The antecedents of this problem of sign and signification in Freud and Lacan would include Helmholtz and Peirce - there is no time here to go into the details of this, except to say that it is something that one would not be impelled to suspect, starting from Strachey's translation of Freud and many Anglo-Saxon commentaries on Lacan. A very early theory put forward by Freud is that the action of repression - the fundamental defence operative in neurosis - is brought about by the question of translation between systems of signs, repression being the direct result of a failure of such translation. Another early Freud theory that one would have expected not to have been ignored by most clinicians is that speech-signs compose the most articulate form of representation available within psychic structure. So where did this stress on language in Freud become lost in the development of the psychoanalytical movement?

Lacan describes what he takes to be a series of deviations from Freud's work. Freud's original programme was to equate analysis with the analysis of material. By the time of the First World War the notion had become current in the analytical movement that resistance forbade access to such material, and a new theory was proposed to the effect that first one analysed resistance, and only later moved on to the analysis of material. In the 1920s, a further idea was proposed to the effect that by the time that you have analysed resistance then you have already analysed everything there is to analyse: so psychoanalysis was then taken to be analysis of resistance and nothing else. Reich's idea of character analysis is a form of this further shift away from Freud. By the 1930s this latest deviation from Freud was being interpreted in terms of the analysis of resistance being equivalent to analysis of the ego's defences, and the final deviation in this line produced during Freud's lifetime was that analysis of the ego replaces analysis of material as the directing orientation of psychoanalytical work. Much of Lacan's work in the 1950s is aimed at criticising formulations of interpretation as working between "ego to ego". Drawing on the distinction between two, three and four person psychology introduced by Rickman and Balint, Lacan instead puts forward as the aim of interpretation the reconstruction of the subjective history of the analysand. For Lacan interpretations are not addressed to the ego, but to the subjectivity which is constituted by the functioning of words.

Klein, in a paper published in 1927 ("The Importance of Words in Early Analysis") stressed the importance of words in her version of psychoanalysis: "The word ... is the bridge to reality, which the child avoids as long as he brings forth his phantasies only by playing". As if to avoid any misunderstanding, she adds an emphasis: "It always means progress when the child has to acknowledge the reality of the objects through his own words". The phantasy emerges, according to Klein, within a dialectic of question and response: she is at times very explicit about this dependency, and from the beginning of her work she drew on a fairly explicit theory of language in order to demonstrate it. This is very clear for instance in *The Psychoanalysis of Children*: "The *form* of an interpretation", she says "is also important ... I endeavour to express the contents of the unconscious phantasies in as clear and plainly spoken a way as possible. In doing so I lean on the concrete way in which children think and speak". Her theory of the nature of a child's language is much more explicit than the much more taken-for-granted ideas that she has of the language of the adult: on the one side in Klein there is an incisive study of phantasy, on the other common-sense assumptions about laws of meaning. Her account of the functioning of a child's language allows her to formulate what she takes to be a relationship between the functioning of phantasy and the functioning of words: "A child ... analyses a word in terms of its vivid descriptiveness ... and in terms of the phantasies for which (the word) is a go-between.". In spite of the difficulty of this relationship, she time and again explains away the problems by means of her theory of language: "If we want to gain access to the child's unconscious in analysis (which, of course, we have to do through the ego and through speech), we shall only succeed if we ... use plain words. The language of the Unconscious", she says "is concrete and graphic", and in making interpretations to a child she formulates her interpretations by means of such plain and direct words. There are many important problems raised here about the nature of interpretation, and about the functioning of words in relation to the Unconscious, but they are problems that are not addressed and that are certainly not resolved, either by her, or by the development of her school.

The question of how words function in psychoanalysis is a topic that together with the themes of the body and identification, determines the central concern of Lacan's work. These themes are developed in Lacan's text of 1958 which he finally decided to call *The Direction of the Treatment, and the Principles of its Power*, after having lightly suggested to Winnicott that an English version of this title might be *The Rules of the Cure and the Lures of its Power*. One of the many ideas proposed by Lacan in this text is that the function of rectification - alteration of the analysand's relation to reality - is not relegated to the end of the analysis, after the work of transference and interpretation, but rather that the functioning of a Socratic dialectic at the start brings about this aim of altering both the way in which analysands position themselves in the surrounding world and also the ways in which they relate to others. There are also other effects: the dialectic introduces a brokenness into the sexual opinions of the analysand, and this brokenness is evocative of the broken love relationships of childhood. The Socratic dialectic evokes the Oedipal love relationships that remain otherwise repressed, and this brings into being the production of the transference. There are other such effects of evocation of past loves: a psychological effect discovered in the Berlin research school of Kurt Lewin in the 1920s, is that broken or interrupted tasks are remembered much more significantly than assignations that have been allowed to run to their end. This "Zeigarnik effect" in Lacan's formulation allows the analytical dialectic to augment memory - one of the central aims of the analytical situation. Lacan's introduction of a variable length of session is in part based on the same principle: both Socratic dialectic and the variable session evoke the love relations of childhood. Some of the relations between tranference and interpretation can be seen to be at play within these structures. The moment of the transference is when some aspect of the analyst - or of the analyst's environment - is taken into the body of the otherwise repressed love relationships of the analysand. This introjection starts to produce the experience of there being ways through, where previously the analysand had experienced only impasse and an inability to solve problems in their love relations with others. That this subjective rectification introduced at the start of the analysis is also a form of interpretation for Lacan has been stressed by Eric Laurent in his seminar on identification at the "Section Clinique" in Paris. The direction of the treatment according to Lacan moves from this initial subjective rectification, this Socratic form of interpretation, to the production of the transference, and then to interpretation within the transference relations, where the analysand is "plunged into an interpretative space where the analyst, even when silent, is interpretative". These considerations provide the second and third orientations to interpretation in Lacan.

Of all the signifying terms that are produced during the analysis, some have a particularly important role. The whole class of terms that construct the symptoms and sexual life of the analysand can be reduced, it seems, to a smaller number of terms. This 'compactified' class of terms has a particular relation to the way in which language relates to the body: this small class of terms is also the framework on which fundamental phantasies are constructed. A late phase of analysis consists in the search for these terms, the terms which resound in the body of the analysand. Classically, this late work is called the construction of the phantasy, and Lacan claims that you need previously to have worked through a great number of signifiers to be able to compactify in this way. His claim also is that it is only in this way that the analytical work can construct the phantasy, and move towards the end of the analysis. The final shift, the analysand being able to engage with a sexual life no longer dominated by the functioning of the symptom, presupposes the lengthy elaboration of the phantasy during the middle and end phases of the analysis.

Klein had thought that you can recognise the phantasy structure at a much earlier stage, and, as has been mentioned already, she was led to this because of her view of the nature of language. Her theory of the interpretation of the child's anxiety in fact presupposes an idea of how words function, and how they relate to the structure of phantasy. Many of these problems are addressed in Lacan's work, and until after the Second World War there was an extensive region of common ground between Lacan's work and Klein's. It is in this period when the Schools finally diverged, the Kleinian School having by then decided on the banner "the Unconscious is structured like a phantasy", while the Lacanian school adopted its own competing banner "the Unconscious is structured like a language". Much of the criticism and debate that took place during the period of the "Controversial Discussions" within the British Psycho-Analytical Society concern the nature of the functioning of words. It was at this time that Susan Isaacs tried to investigate the question of the existence of a period of "pre-verbal" construction of phantasy in the life of a child. She was very clear that the limits of such a supposed period cannot be determined by the moment of a child's first steps in talking, since the understanding of often quite complicated series of words "long antedates their use". She also argued that the length of time between a "comprehension" and a "usage" of words can be quite long: "as much as one year". Using a variety of methods of argument, and drawing heavily on psychology texts (of her time), she finally concluded that there must exist a period during which there can be no comprehension of "the phonetic form of ... words", and this period - of the first six months of life - became the matrix of the supposed "pre-verbal" period where the child's experiences are "independent of words". She produced these conclusions despite her agreeing to the facts that a child will often utter "several clearly defined syllables" at six months, that most children are speaking by the age of 12 months, and that the "time-lag" that she had discovered between this moment and the comprehension of words can be as much as one year. She also talks of the existence of "linguistic play" during the first half-year of life; but despite all of this, the notion of a "pre-verbal" stage subsequently became deeply entrenched in the assumptions of British analytical practice. Lacan however insists that a child is being influenced by the words used by and to its mother long before any of the periods described by Susan Isaacs - it is being influenced and affected in this way even before it is born. There is much that is valuable in these discussions; it is a pity that their influence was allowed to wane, to be replaced by the establishment of received opinions about structuring by speech.

It is not only Klein's school that wants to distance itself from the functioning of words; since the 1930s it has become almost a hallmark of a claim to success for a new style of psychoanalysis to pretend to give a place to the structure of words that is demonstrably very subordinate. Whichever Freud case you look at - Dora, or the Rat-man, or Hans - you will find that a great number of signifying terms emerge as the work gets under way. By comparison, Klein thinks that she can interpret without waiting for the production of such a battery of terms, relying only on the vocabulary that she thinks is already constituted in the world of everyday relationships. But in fact, in order to be able to move to what lies beyond the signifying structure, the particularities of the psycho-sexual history of the analysand need to be brought into the analytical relationship; these particularities are the terms that have been directing the conflicts of the analysand's love relationships since earliest childhood. Freud was able only to start the construction of these terms in the case of Dora, but in his analysis of her case "Hof" would have been a preliminary term, linking the family complex with her sexual life. "Friedhof: Bahnhof: Zwingerhof: Vorhof" is a chain that associates the dream representation of the dead father to the question to her mother about her father's sexuality; it links an Art Museum in Dresden to her young suitor via a bodily cavity which forms an entrance to another. This process of deciphering and decrypting applied to the staging posts that construct a dream provides a determination of the body of terms within which the analysand constructs the reality of their own body. Interpretation clearly comes into play in relation to this body: "give me a notion of a body", one could say "and I will give you a corresponding notion of interpretation". Lacan comes back several times to this question of various styles of interpretation in relation the theme of incorporation; he does so in particular in relation to the detail of an analysis presented by Ernst Kris - in a case that he had taken up from Melitta Schmideberg. There are a series of references by Lacan to this case: the first is in Lacan's Seminar One, as part of Lacan's reply to Jean Hyppolite's presentation of Freud's paper "Die Verneinung (Negation)". A second is in "The Direction of the Treatment , and the Principles of its Power" and a third can be found in Lacan's Seminar of 1966-67. This chain of references from 1953 to 1967 seems to indicate that Lacan took it that there was something to comment on. We might follow up an injunction which Lacan gave to the audience of his Seminar in the session of 8th March 1967, a recommendation to read the Kris paper, and also the original Schmideberg article where the case was first presented[1].

Schmideberg presents this case only after first relating a series of fragments of her work with other analysands. First a schizophrenic, a woman for whom anything of real value could be experienced only as "food stolen between meal times"; then a second analysand, a man who "prized knowledge only ... if he acquired it in secret, 'stole' it". This man's main anxiety, says Schmideberg, was that a woman would devour his brain. She used the Freud-Ferenczi notion of symbolic equation in order to set up a series of equations in this case between "knowledge" and "the contents of his head" and "the contents of his body". In the case of the analysand later to see Kris, she says of him "in his eyes activity was bound up with theft, and scientific work with plagiarism". It is clear from her comments that she would analyse this "bound up" also in terms of symbolic equations, but, as is usual in the Kleinian tradition, she does not at any moment propose ways of analysing the functioning of such symbolic equations by means of results taken from the study of the structure of language. Instead, she takes for granted that such a symbolic functioning is in place, and rather than focus on any problem of interpretation within the tapestry of this structure, she proceeds to interpret the case in terms of part-objects and the relation to the mother. Not only in this case, but in all the cases she presents in this report, Schmideberg gives a direction to her work by means of this mythology of the body of the mother. In neither of the published versions of this paper does she makes any reference to any separate functioning of the father, except, surprisingly, at the end of her English version, where "father" is its last word.

Kris's analysand "a young scientist in his early thirties" came to him after this earlier analysis with Schmideberg: he asked for this second analysis to be kept a secret from his first analyst, lest she be hurt by his wish that he now be analysed "by a man". A major symptom of the analysand was "an impulse to use somebody else's ideas"; during the analysis he found that he was working on a piece that he feared he had plagiarised - he even informed his analyst of the source that he thought that he has stolen it from. Kris's response to this was to inquire into the context of the work referred to, and to check in detail that the fear of plagiarism was in fact groundless. Kris further decided that in reality the "young colleague" with whom the patient worked closely and whose ideas he took himself to be stealing was in fact actually using the analysand's ideas without acknowledgement. In placing himself in this position, Kris assumed that he had access to what is real in the material presented to him, via the reflections of his own ego. There is little reflection in his account of the case on the associative chains present in the material - no interpretation is presented which is based simply on this network and on what it alludes to, that is, the constitution of desire. Kris felt himself to be facing two sets of issues: the first, the existence in the material of what he calls a series of "expressions with a connotation", and the second, the corresponding existence of "typical patterns of behaviour" in his analysand. Faced with these two sets of data, he gave priority to interpreting the second. The way he did this was to take the phrase "I am in danger of plagiarising" to be a feeling, and to set it within what he established as "patterns of behaviour", rather than of meaning. Such elision of meaning will generally lead to an acting out; if Kris had been aware that "expressions" come with equivocal meaning, and even with a series of "connotations", than he may have been alerted to the complexity of the problem of meaning, and to its centrality in the analytical relationship. Instead of which, any reference to the functioning of desire in "getting new ideas" has to come to Kris by means of an action outside of the analytical setting.

There is in Kris's work however, a central reference to the father, which puts the style of interpretation adopted by Schmideberg into a new light. The plagiarism complex, says Kris "reproduced conflicts of his earlier relationship to his father". In fact, Kris is prepared to go back further than this: his analysand's grandfather had been an important scientist, and in this field where the grandfather had succeeded, the father had failed. Kris reports a dream in which his analysand battles with his father using books as weapons, and in which "conquered books were swallowed". It is an Oedipal dream, he says, and the analysand is identifying with his father. If this is so, then he is fighting the grandfather, and wanting to eat the book that is a measure of the grandfather's success. But this instrument of success is not his father's: he has to take it from someone else. The terms that construct the scenario of this family's history across three generations were sufficiently available to Kris, but he did not draw on them for his interpretation. He proposed instead an interpretation of the dream "as a wish to incorporate the father's penis". This style of interpretation often requires amplification, and Kris linked it to something more palpable from his analysand's history: his going on fishing expeditions with his father, to see who can catch the bigger fish. Taking fish, comparing fish, stealing fish, stealing ideas: this network was traced by Kris through "many ramifications and disguises during latency and adolescence". But what he took himself to have traced in this way was "details of behaviour", rather than the network of terms that constituted his analysand's relation to the father. Eventually he put to his analysand his conception of the point at which this behaviour towards the father "was displaced onto ideas": "At this point of the interpretation" says Kris, "I was waiting for the patient's reaction. The patient was silent, and the very length of the silence had a special significance". A psychoanalyst more concerned with words than with behaviour would have been looking for a response rather than a reaction, but a reaction is what Kris got: the patient informed him at this point of what he often did after leaving the sessions at lunch time in the wake of an interpretation such as this - he went out to eat his "preferred dish - fresh brains".

Lacan, Schmideberg, and Kris all agree that this man's desire is organised around taking something from someone else. But where Kris assumes the network that constitutes this desire to be produced by behaviour - and shaped by displacements - Lacan directs the analysis rather in terms of a network of signifying chains that are at work in shaping the history of the young man. In this context, Lacan says that Kris is right to have chosen to take up the signifier "grand" from grandfather, and from the games of catching a bigger fish than the father. But Kris italicises this "grand" rather awkwardly: "a *grand* father" he says. The account that Lacan gives in French of the switching use of this term "grand" doesn't translate into English either - "grand-père" and "le plus grand poisson pris à la pêche" do not translate into English as terms at a cross-roads in this analysand's history. Let us assume however, that the analysis was of someone who at least in his youth spoke German: there is some probability that this was the case, and this assumption allows the question of the functioning of these terms to escape from the difficulties that seem to surround them in English. The relation of rivalry between the analysand and his father expresses itself in terms of a "big" fish - "Gross" in German. The relation between the child and his father involves the grandfather - "Grossvater" in German. So "Gross" then becomes a signifying term in the child's history. It answers Kris's question: how did the displacement from stealing food to stealing ideas happen? The analysand had started by stealing sweets: this term "Gross" links the grandfather's books with the father's fish, providing a channel connecting food and ideas. In terms of this term "Gross", it may also be worth noting that the German for brain - "Hirn" - has a compound "Grosshirn" for the brain proper, the cerebrum. "Gross'" is then the term for the father who has ideas where his own father was without them: it is the link between stealing, eating, and plagiarising, as well as being the term which introduces lack, which brings into play the functioning of desire.

The question of exactly which signifying terms are missed by Kris is now a question of finding the ways in which he skips over the functioning of language. What follows from this then, for the question of interpretation? In order to interpret in a more Lacanian or Freudian way within this material that Kris reads as behaviour, all you need to do is to accentuate the term "Gross". There are many different ways of doing this - there is no standard interpretation to bring to bear. This does not mean however that any old interpretation will do, but only those that are directed towards the construction of desire. "Gross", for instance, is a possible interpretation: "A father with little fish" is another. "A father with little fish, and a grandfather (Grossvater) with ideas" is a third: or try the interpretation introduced by Lacan - "Your father was not blessed with ideas: didn't your grandfather sicken him of them?". Notice how Lacan's interpretation moves back to the theme of the incorporation of the oral object centralised by Schmideberg, and continued in the dream recounted by Kris.

Lacan says two things about Kris's interpretation of this material: the first is that it is worth its salt ("une interprétation valable") -
if salt is something that you can put onto fresh brains. The second
is that it leads to an acting out. An acting out is always a consequence of a lack in interpretation: the lacks in Kris's interpretation
are (i) the focusing on the actual text of the proposed plagiarism,
and (ii) the walking straight past a signifying chain - unlike his
patient who did not walk past the shop with the brains. Kris is effectively questioning him on the object of his desire. The reply given to
Kris in this dialectic presents him with the object on a plate: but
given the inability of the interpretative threads to approach this
object, an action does it instead. The context that generates an acting out is that of a weakness or insufficiency in the analyst's interpretation: where something is not being interpreted, not entering
the network of the signifying material of the analytical work, a
reply is given by means of an action instead of by means of a
response. Lacan, in order to give some clarity to the term, looks at
the English usage of the phrase "acting out" - it is, after all, surprisingly, a term which has entered the analytical vocabulary in its
English form. Webster's dictionary may seem an unlikely place to
find enlightenment on this issue, but Lacan is quite good at picking
up cues from backgrounds that are seemingly unlikely: he takes up
the term as Webster describes it in relation to a play - to act out a
play is to "to represent ... in action ... as opposed to reading". Here
then there is an allusion to acting against the background of a lack
of attention given to a text, of a lack of response to the functioning
of words. A play is merely acted out against the backcloth of a
faulty interpretation: an infantile drama remains within analysis if
enough attention is given to what is being said.

An investigation into the functioning of language in the young
child was conducted by René Spitz in 1957. Psychoanalytical investigations such as this are rare, and he comments explicitly on this in
his introduction to his text. "Verbal and non-verbal ... communication", he says, together constitute the instrument of psychoanalysis,
and he adds that it is surprising that references in the psychoanalytical literature since the First World War to problems of language
are so sparse. It is still rare in Anglo-Saxon contexts, nearly forty
years after Spitz's comments, to find the structure of language
investigated explicitly. Lacan's School was cognisant of Spitz's
work from the time of its appearance, and particularly of his work
on the effects of the intervention of the function of "no" in the life
of the child. Spitz thinks that all the necessary elements needed for
the solution of these problems may lie in Freud's Project, published

in the early 1950s, but written in 1895, more than a hundred years ago. A hundred years is a long time for a problem to lie dormant in any science, let alone in a field that is barely one hundred years old. Since 1950, Lacan's orientation has been precisely to wager that all incapacity in human relations stems from the inability to negotiate desire in terms other than those of language. One half of the world's psychoanalysts now work within this orientation: one half do not, and they have a tendency to ignore those that do. There are therefore rich outcomes to be had from a debate between the schools of Lacan and Klein. It is high time for such work to be developed, and hopefully these discussions will begin to undo the effects of standardisation on the world of speech.

[1]Schmideberg's paper had originally been presented in English at a meeting of the   in September 1933. Lacan bases his comments on the German version, later translated into English by Jacqueline Rose. A slightly different version of the paper has appeared as "Intellectual Inhibition and Disturbances in Eating", in the International Journal of Psycho-Analysis in 1938; my quotations are from this early English version, described by Schmideberg as a "part" of the paper delivered to the British Society.

DISCUSSION OF PAPERS ON INTERPRETATION

Robert M. Young: I'd like to take up a point early in Bernard's presentation. You said the purpose of interpretation was to keep the material coming. This reminds me of a story of a patient of Klein's who came 10 minutes late for a session and Klein said 'You've missed the first interpretation!' and another story about Ernest Jones who only spoke twice during sessions, once to say 'Hello' and once to say 'Goodbye'. One of my patients is a schizophrenic with multigenerational delusional system and if I don't break into it he will go on forever. There is another patient who exhibits a feature Betty Joseph writes about called 'chuntering': there is plenty of material but it's not about anything - it's all on the surface and if it has any purpose it is defensive and that too one has to break into. I've always thought of the purpose of interpretation in the Kleinian approach being to reach as far as one can into the primitive anxieties and, if you are right, to assuage the anxiety by virtue of hitting the target - not just to keep the material flowing!

Burgoyne: I'll answer the second point first. Yes - of course there's a lot of bla bla bla... The analyst functions so as to judge whether the material is there...

Robert M. Young: ... so 'material' is a judgment of quality?

Burgoyne: ... There is a direction to the analysis moving into whatever is repressed. A lot of talk is there to avoid that. The analyst helps this move towards unconscious material through making links within what has been said. But first a point needs to be made: everything I am saying is intended to be within the context of classical analytic theory of work with neurosis; the place of the analyst in work with neurosis is very different from when working with a psychosis. Lacan claims a person has either a neurotic or psychotic structure and it is the task of the analyst to make hypotheses early in the analytic work, to judge that at the outset and to decide where to place themselves. The place of the analyst is more the position of being a witness with the psychotic, rather than that of using questioning and Socratic interrogation. The neurotic doesn't know what's going on, and the Socratic questioning is directed towards this: a psychotic knows *very* well what is going on. Unlike the assumption made a lot in Britain and America that everybody is a bit mad and that one is bound to encounter some psychotic strata in everybody, Lacan says that there are some people whose structure is neurotic and some people whose structure is psychotic. With the schizophrenic, with psychotics in general, there would be no point in following the Socratic dialogue.

Robert M. Young: How about my question about penetrating as deeply as possible to allay anxieties?

Burgoyne: The theory of anxiety is complex. Unlike the Anglo-Saxon tradition where affect is relied on with some confidence, Lacan feels he is taking up Freud in showing that all affects are displacements, with the exception of one - anxiety. If you hate a man it may be because you love his wife. There is displacement in all feeling except anxiety, which has a very fundamental function in the structure of the Unconscious. It would take a long time to go into this theory of the relationship of anxiety to various aspects of analytic work. The main difference in Klein is that she believes that words are accessible and that they lead to meanings fairly directly, and that you can interpret anxiety from the beginning. For Lacan the idea of a symbolic equation is replaced by a more structured field of symbolism and that idea is totally unanswered in Klein's school, where it is assumed that you can rely on the ego and commonsense. For Lacan nothing in the ego structure is to be relied on - all you can rely on is that there are surface symptoms and there are various methods and ways of getting from one of those shifting surfaces to underlying unconscious material. Pathways created by free association are very narrow passageways which are to be constructed and facilitated in analysis. For Klein you can do it more easily.

Bronstein: Now I think that for Klein it is possible to analyse psychotics using the same technique. I don't think Klein is saying we could all go mad, but I think she would say that within all of us there are possibilities of going not into psychosis but into the positions and it depends on the dynamics of the Unconscious phantasies. For somebody in psychosis one would say the split is part of the self - splitting the object, for attacks on linking prevent object relation - and then outside becomes a bizarre object containing the hatred plus part of the self that has been projected, which is a part of himself that he wants to get rid of. I think the cases would not be too dissimilar.

Q: I wanted to ask Catalina about your case because I can hear from the way you reported it that it's about persecution, and linking it back to the question of the child, of relationship to language - *woman* rather than *girl*. By introducing the question of sexuality and sexual desires you place him somewhere else; seemingly you are using *symbolic* in a developmental way and comments you have made confirmed that - insofar as you see development from the paranoid-schizoid to the depressive position. But I cannot see how you could deal with the criticism of forcing the analysand back into a dual relation because in the end you come down on one side: *woman* rather than *girl*. A Lacanian would have said, 'Girl?' Why do you want to take a position? Why do you not want the analysand to produce his own material in order to establish what his position is?

Bronstein: I think that I was getting the idea that at first he was unable to say 'woman' - his associations stopped him. I think it was more important to understand his anxiety; I am not sure he would have got there if I had just said 'girl'. There was also the link between the girl and the party, and linking girl and party in connection with the last session. I think that when I made the interpretation it produced more associations with the reduction of his anxiety. The matter of his feelings could then come up and it was then that he produced the association that he had had an erection. I think the interpretation diminished paranoid anxiety and he was less anxious about himself and more able to come up as a man rather than a boy and go on to talk about what happened after that session ended.

Q: Why is that not a form of reassurance done in an interpretative way?

Bronstein: I don't think it is a question of reassuring him whether he was a man or not. He could not be a man if he could not allow me to be a separate object. I am not reassuring him that he can be a man; I am letting him know he is attacking me and projects himself into me. I don't think that's reassurance.

Burgoyne: There are similarities between your style of interpretation and the interventions that Lacan would use. There is a signifying thread between these terms 'girl, 'woman', 'party'. This is related to sexual rivalry and to affects and anxieties and certainly to sexual rivalries in adult life - affects and anxieties concerned in and going back to the Oedipal relations of childhood. For Lacan the signifying terms are wrapped around the series of affects which are given a place within signifying structures. The two schools are not disagreeing on what terms are pertinent in the life of the analysand. Our positions are different in terms of what one can rely on in terms of directing the analytic work. There are differences in ideas of development, of notions of common sense, ideas of reality, and in the Lacanian insistence that only the construction of the signifying terms will give you a platform from which the Unconscious can be discerned.

Q: I was interested in your comment at the beginning about the setting and interpretations within the setting. Two things you said - one about the breaks. I wondered about precisely the kind of thing that's been aired - about the way that there could be an acting out by the analyst within the session, but I was also interested in what you said about jokes, because it seems to me that a lot of these things have a kind of double edged significance: that on the one hand clearly jokes are going to go beneath the defences and yet they could very easily become a seduction. I'm wondering, in the same way whether forcing breaks can become an acting out and either a seduction or a rejection, what would be your comments on that?

Burgoyne: There are some technical difficulties about how one chooses to define 'acting out' - I don't think the analyst can act out in the session. Your question is about power. The analyst has great power as a consequence of the analytical disposition, how the set up is arranged. If the analyst uses that power in any way, then the work is hindered; if he uses it more than a little bit the work is brought to a complete stop. The power is there - part of the ethic, the obligation on the analyst in terms of his commitment, on his side of the contract, is just to listen and to facilitate the listening to what is trying to be said. It's not to use that power! And if they make mistakes about it they can only hope to correct some of the consequences.

The end of the session shouldn't be forced: it should be on some material that is part of the problems being faced by the analysand in trying to give words to things. In that sense the problems faced by the analyst are exactly the same in choosing when and how to end a session as when and how to interpret - exactly the same. An analyst can force an interpretation, an analyst can give an interpretation which gives the analyst power. An analyst needs to have filtering mechanisms to get rid of such a tendency. For instance, if you are an analyst, considering an interpretation, and if there is the slightest response of 'no' from you before you've said it, for whatever reason - even if you haven't the slightest clue as to why there's a 'no' - then , almost always, it should not be said. It is the analyst's responsibility not to be using or exploiting that power.

Q: I am not sure if this is a question - more a reflection of what you were saying. I was thinking of this idea of psychoanalysis as a response to human suffering - I was aware in your presentation of repeated references to the Oedipal situation and to 'the father' and very aware that Freud in a way neglected the role of mother and I was sitting here pondering on the notion of the whole of the symbolic order and something about the male which is powerful in the your Lacanian presentation. I was thinking about the fact that Klein was a woman and is undermined on that score; something about not just dealing with the symbolic order but with something else that might be in the realm of what might be called the female. I think I'm seeking some kind of response from you on this.

Burgoyne: Lacan focuses and formulates Freud in terms of a centralising of the Oedipus complex and the Castration complex within the structure of the Unconscious. That raises questions about how one deals with material which is sometimes called pre-Oedipal and questions about whether one agrees with the existence of what is often called the preverbal. For Lacan a child is being affected by language before birth whilst being carried in womb, in terms of directly feeling strong emotions which are the result of the mother's passion and agitation in relation to her lover.

The formulation that Lacan gives to these questions from around 1950 onwards constitutes a breaking from common terrain from Klein - for 20 years before that Lacan in many ways is quite close to Klein. Even in the 1930s he is trying to formulate ideas about images - imagos and the unconscious functioning of images - that in many ways closely parallel Klein's formulations. What there isn't at that stage is Lacan's subsequent decision that the functioning of language is dominant over that of images. So throughout the 1930s and until World War II there are Lacan and Klein, struggling in many similar ways with very similar problems.

It's not until around 1948-50 that Lacan finally decides that image functioning is subordinate to the functions of language: if you like, images - including unconscious images - take up their home, build their nest in the structures provided for them by the framework of the symbolic. And it's at that point that he stresses the priority of the symbolic and introduces the trinity of the Symbolic, the Imaginary and the Real, the Real being something that's very difficult to gain access to. It's certainly different from reality as constructed by the ego, and it is something that in part tries to grasp the notion of 'impossible to assimilate' that Freud put forward in his explanation of trauma. It is then that you get these classical Freudian problems addressed by Lacan in increasingly different ways from the ways in which they had been addressed by Klein's school, although for instance in the 1930's there are many parallels between the arguments of Susan Isaacs about the structuring of experience by means of unconscious phantasies, and Lacan's contemporary arguments about the structuring of reality through a functioning of imagos and identifications. But Lacanians are not saying that what Kleinians discovered about archaic and fundamental phantasy is wrong. Once you have actually produced the phantasies they are related to symbolic functioning - they are related to phrases. The inability of those phrases to completely represent the structure of the phantasy introduces the register of the Real.

I take it that, with feminine sexuality and masculine sexuality, the problem came out of Freud's theory of Oedipal love - questions about how the Oedipal relations are traversed and how one moves out of these situations in analysis. One finishes up with a sexual identity as a result of the negotiation of the Oedipal relations: the whole review of feminine sexuality in Lacan is based on the study of the different pathways of people who will become men and people who will become women.

There's a kind of catch-phrase which is current concerning what Lacan says it means to be a woman: he's saying that what it means to be a man is to be entirely caught up within the effects of the signifying structure. A woman is also caught up in that, but a woman has resources that go further. Lacan's slogan is "a woman is not all": not all of her life is going to be determined by the symbolising structures and their phallic function. I have recently seen something published where Lacan is described as saying that woman "fails in her taking up of the symbolic order". It's not like that at all. He's saying that a woman is quite adept at confronting the symbolic order.

Bronstein: I was thinking about the question of the role of the woman and the preverbal and I think Klein would stress that there are unconscious phantasies that don't necessarily have to wait for the development of language. Of course access is only through language, so we don't know what happens before that, but this two-year-old girl sees mother feeding a new baby, looks at her mother's breasts and says 'those are what you bit me with'. Is it that her phantasy at that moment was structured through and by language or was it an earlier unconscious phantasy that can now be put into words?

Someone who also thought a lot about this was Bion. He would say that babies from very tiny have pre-conceptions and anxieties and the mother has the capacity to pick up this raw material - which he calls beta-elements - and interpret it, put the anxiety into words. Mother introduces speech and language that will help the baby with the raw anxiety, which might have to do with anxiety about annihilation and falling to bits; by being named by mother they are transformed into alpha elements. It is in that primary interaction that in some way a child could begin to develop. So I think there are these differences between Klein and Lacan.

PHANTASY AND PSYCHOTIC ANXIETIES

Robert M. Young[1]

One of the illuminating distinctions that post-Kleinian psycho-analysis has given us is that between knowing and knowing about. In psychoanalysis, knowing about something often operates as a defence against knowing it in a deeper, emotional sense. I well recall my first, greatly-valued supervisor, Bob Hinshelwood, saying once in a self-deprecating way that if you don't understand what the patient is on about in the session, you make a clever interpreta-tion, and if you aren't inward with the patient at all, you can always write a paper.

The things I shall write about in this essay are not new. Most of my sources were published between the year of my birth and 1955, when I was a second-year undergraduate and began reading psy-choanalysis seriously. I have known about much of the literature on unconscious phantasy and psychotic anxieties for some time, hav-ing read some Klein and Bion before and during my own analysis. There is, however, a sensible bias against reading too much during one's clinical training, so one rarely studies a topic in a systematic way. As a consequence, it is only now, some years post-analysis, that I am beginning to feel (and I do not wish to exaggerate the extent to which I feel it) that I might take in these matters properly. I like to think that I am in the foothills of knowing it. One of my pur-poses in essaying about these issues is exegetical - an attempt to bring these things together for myself to see if they cohere for me.

Of course, what one comes to know one knew all along, as I shall illustrate, and knowing about it can be as much a barrier as a cata-lyst to being able to think about that tacit knowledge. I have known all along about the normality and ubiquity of unconscious phan-tasies and psychotic anxieties, but I am beginning to be able to afford to realise it and to reflect upon some of the consequences of the omnipresence of primitive, unconscious phantasies for life, cul-ture, politics and the theory of knowledge.

Having completed a reconsideration of the literature on uncon-scious phantasies and psychotic anxieties, I have two tasks. The first is to try to describe and give some emotional meaning to the kinds of phantasies against which we - as individuals and in groups and institutions - spend so much of our energy defending ourselves. Second, I want to gather together and draw attention to the impli-cations of Kleinian and neo-Kleinian ideas for how we think of human nature, by which I mean, with respect to individuals and all other levels of culture and civilisation. It turns out that defence against psychotic anxieties is offered by Kleinians as a deeper explanation than the incest taboo as the basis of that thin and all too easily breached veneer that constitutes civility and stands between what passes for the social order, on the one hand, and chaos (or the fear of it), on the other. This turns out to be a mixed blessing, since our defences against psychotic anxieties act as a powerful brake on institutional and social change toward less rigid and more generous relations between individuals and groups.

I first heard of psychoanalysis nearly forty years ago on my first day at university, where new students from very different backgrounds were thrown together as room-mates. One of mine cackled when he learned that I had never heard of Freud, whom he described as 'the guy who thought all doorways are cunts and all neckties are dicks'. In the early 1950s psychoanalysis connoted sex to American undergraduates and smutty sex, at that. I quickly learned the close connection between these matters and violent, mad feelings such as murderous envy when, only a few weeks later, that same roommate tried to stab me with a Swiss army knife because he couldn't bear it that I had a girlfriend, and he didn't.

I offer this anecdote for several reasons. First, Freud's theory of civilisation drew attention to the taboo against violent sexual competitiveness and rapaciousness as the corner-stone of civilisation. The polymorphously sexual patriarch was said to have been killed by the primal horde, thus establishing the incest taboo, the basis for all other taboos and the system of custom and legality that gave birth to civilisation and culture, terms Freud refused to distinguish. He constantly emphasised that man is a wolf to other men, that the veneer of civilisation is thin and under threat from moment to moment and that all of life is a constant struggle conducted in the fraught space between erotic and destructive instincts. For Freud the basic conflicts occurred at this level of the psyche (see Young, 1994, ch 2). As Meltzer describes it, Freud's world is 'a world of higher animals', 'creatures seeking surcease from the constant bombardment of stimuli from inside and out'. He contrasts Klein's world as 'one of holy babes in holy families plagued by the devils of split off death instinct' (Meltzer, 1978, part 3, pp 115-16).

This is not merely a difference of emphasis. As the shocking example from my college experience shows, matters which may appear on the surface to be about genital sexuality may also turn out to be about much more primitive psychological levels of distress. Similarly, the difference between the worlds of Freud and Klein may be described as one of *level* of explanation and of causality. Bion put the point clearly in the conclusion to his essay, 'Group Dynamics - A Re-view', which, as Menzies Lyth points out, was more explicit about the Kleinian inspiration of his ideas than his better-known collection of essays, *Experiences in Groups* (1961). Bion says, 'Freud's view of the dynamics of the group seems to me to require supplementing rather than correction' (Bion, 1955. p 475). He accepts Freud's claim that the family group is the basis for all groups but adds that 'this view does not go far enough... I think that the central position in group dynamics is occupied by the more primitive mechanisms which Melanie Klein has described as peculiar to the paranoid-schizoid and depressive positions. In other words, I feel... that it is not simply a matter of the incompleteness of the illumination provided by Freud's discovery of the family group as the prototype of all groups, but the fact that this incompleteness leaves out the source of the main emotional drives of the group' (ibid). He then summarises the notions of 'work group' and the 'basic assumptions' that assail them - 'dependence', 'pairing', 'fight-flight' - and suggests that these may have a common link or may be different aspects of each other. 'Further investigation shows that each basic assumption contains features that correspond so closely with extremely primitive part-objects that sooner or later psychotic anxiety, appertaining to these primitive relationships, is released. These anxieties, and the mechanisms peculiar to them, have already been displayed in psychoanalysis by Melanie Klein, and her descriptions tally well with the emotional states of the basic assumption group. Such groups have aims 'far different either from the overt task of the group or even from the tasks that would appear to be appropriate to Freud's view of the group as based on the family group. But approached from the angle of psychotic anxiety, associated with phantasies of primitive part-object relationships... the basic assumption phenomena appear far more to have the characteristics of defensive reactions to psychotic anxiety, and to be not so much at variance with Freud's views as supplementary to them. In my view, it is necessary to work through both the stresses that appertain to family patterns and the still more primitive anxieties of part-object relationships. In fact I consider the latter to contain the ultimate sources of all group behaviour' (p 476).

In Bion's view, then, what matters in individual and group behaviour is more primitive than the Freudian level of explanation. The ultimate sources of our distress are psychotic anxieties, and much of what happens in individuals and groups is a result of defences erected *against* psychotic anxieties, so that we do not have to endure them consciously.

I'll say something about the term 'psychotic' and then turn to the concept of phantasy and the anxieties which primitive phantasies generate. To most of us 'psychotic' refers to psychosis, a primary disturbance of libidinal relations with reality, and psychotic symptoms are an attempt to restore the link with objects (Laplanche & Pontalis, 1973, p 370). When I was trained as a psychiatric aide in a state mental hospital in the 1950s, we were taught a small number of things about psychosis, and they seemed adequate in those pre-Laing and pre-Goffman times. Psychotics were 'out of contact with reality' for much or all of the time. They heard and saw things that were not there - hallucinations - and wildly distorted things that were - delusions.

I want to turn now to the mechanisms in question and their evolution from the asylum to the nursery. Klein described schizoid mechanisms as occurring 'in the baby's development in the first year of life characteristically... the infant suffered from states of mind that were in all their essentials equivalent to the adult psychoses, taken as regressive states in Freud's sense' (Meltzer, 1978, part 3, p 22). Klein says in the third paragraph of her most famous paper, 'Notes on Some Schizoid Mechanisms', 'In early infancy anxieties characteristic of psychosis arise which drive the ego to develop specific defence mechanisms. In this period the fixation-points for all psychotic disorders are to be found. This has led some people to believe that I regard all infants as psychotic; but I have already dealt sufficiently with this misunderstanding on other occasions' (Klein, 1975, vol 3, p 1). Meltzer comments that 'Although she denied that this was tantamount to saying that babies are psychotic, it is difficult to see how this implication could be escaped' (Meltzer, 1978, part 3, p 22).

Kleinian thinking evolved in three stages. As in the above quotation, Klein saw schizoid mechanisms and the paranoid-schizoid position as fixation points, respectively, for schizophrenia and manic-depressive psychosis. Then the paranoid-schizoid and depressive positions became developmental stages. Her terminology included 'psychotic phases', 'psychotic positions' and then 'positions' (Klein, 1975, vol 1, pp 275n-276n, 279). Thirdly, in the work of Bion and other post-Kleinians, these became economic principles and part of the moment-to-moment vicissitudes of everyday life. The notations 'Ps' and 'D' were connected with a double-headed arrow to indicate how easily and frequently our inner states oscillate from the one to the other and back again: Ps <—> D (Meltzer, 1978, part 3, p 22).

In Bion's writings on schizophrenia an ambiguity remained as to whether or not the psychotic part of the personality is ubiquitous or only present in schizophrenics, but Meltzer concludes his exposition of Bion's schizophrenia papers by referring to the existence of these phenomena in patients of every degree of disturbance, even 'healthy' candidates in training (p 28). Going further, he and colleagues have drawn on the inner world of autistic patients to illuminate the norm; Frances Tustin has essayed on autistic phenomena in neurotic patients, while Sidney Klein has described 'autistic cysts' in neurotic patients.

So much for bringing 'psychotic' into the realm of the normal and neurotic. Turning now to 'phantasy' I'll begin by pointing out that a full page of the index to *Developments in Psychoanalysis* (Klein et al, 1952) is devoted to this single term, and the entry fills half a page in the historical account of *The Freud-Klein Controversies 1941-1945* (King and Steiner, 1991). The essays in *Developments in Psychoanalysis* are versions of the papers which formed the basis for the Kleinian position in that controversy. Many things were at stake, but at the heart of it, in my opinion, was the question of the primacy of the inner world, as opposed to the more interactive, adaptive framework of ideas which came to be associated with ego psychology and, in our own time, contemporary Freudianism. Anna Freud rebuts the claim that she 'has an inveterate prejudice in favour of the modes of external reality ... and of conscious mental processes' (King and Steiner, 1991, p 328), but I think it is a legitimate demarcation between Kleinian and Freudian orientations and became even more so at the hands of Hartmann, Kris, Loewenstein and the American school epitomised by the systematising work of David Rapaport.

As a part of the issue over the primacy of the inner world, I believe that people were genuinely spooked by the sheer craziness and nastiness of the inner world as described by Klein and her supporters. Indeed, there is a protest along these lines by Michael Balint, who drily comments in the discussion of Susan Isaacs' fundamentally important paper (to which I shall turn next) that 'perhaps Mrs Klein is laying undue emphasis on the role of hatred, frustration and aggression in the infant' (p 347). Fairbairn, in contrast, seemed to feel (at least at that time) that Kleinian accounts of phantasy were so successfully descriptive of the inner world that he proposed dropping 'phantasy' in favour of 'inner reality' (p 359).

I begin with the elementary point that 'phantasy' refers to 'predominantly or entirely unconscious phantasies', as distinct from the sort of conscious fantasies or imaginings we associate with, for example, Coleridge's explorations of the imagination (Isaacs, 1952, pp 80-81). Joan Riviere appeals to Freud's hypothesis that the psyche is always interpreting the reality of its experiences - 'or rather, misinterpreting them - in a subjective manner that increases its pleasure and preserves it from pain' (Riviere, 1952, p 41). Freud, according to Riviere, calls this process 'hallucination; and it forms the foundation of what we mean by *phantasy-life*. The phantasy-life of the individual is thus the form in which the real internal and external sensations and perceptions are interpreted and represented to himself in his mind under the influence of the pleasure-pain principle'. Riviere adds that 'this primitive and elementary function of his psyche - to misinterpret his perceptions for his own satisfaction - still retains the upper hand in the minds of the great majority of even civilised adults' (p 41).

This general function is repeated in Susan Isaacs' definition: "This mental expression of instinct *is* unconscious phantasy... There is no impulse, no instinctual urge or response which is not experienced as unconscious phantasy. The first mental processes... are to be regarded as the earliest beginnings of phantasies. In the mental development of the infant, however, phantasy soon becomes also a means of defence against anxieties, a means of inhibiting and controlling instinctual urges and an expression of reparative wishes as well. ... All impulses, all feelings, all modes of defence are experienced in phantasies which give them *mental* life and show their direction and purpose.". (Isaacs, 1952, p. 83).

When we turn to the content of the phantasies a problem of communication arises: 'they are apt to produce a strong impression of unreality and untruth' (Riviere, 1952, p 20). This is because when we write or speak about them we are clothing preverbal and very primitive mental processes in the language of words in dictionaries. My way round this is to share some images and experience from my own clinical and personal experience. Phantasies are rendered as black holes, nameless dread, part-objects, offal, shit, urine, a patients' dreams of wet cinders or barren desert mindscapes, pus, slime, feelings of being overwhelmed, engulfed, disintegrated, in pieces, devoured, falling through empty space, spiders, bugs, snakes. Language drawn from work with autistic patients includes dread of falling apart, falling infinitely, spilling away, exploding away, threat of total annihilation, unintegration (*as distinct from* the disintegration of schizophrenia), experiencing a missing person as a hole (rather than 'missing' them as not present).

When I cannot find a piece of paper or go to a room and cannot recall why, I don't just think of age and preoccupation. The fabric of reality is rent asunder, and I feel in imminent danger of dying, of disintegration, of unendurable panic. When I was a boy there was a nearby grand house, set in large grounds in a gully, with walls and a gate with a heavy chain and a wrought iron sign: 'DRIVERDALE'. I could not go near it without intense anxiety. (It was a feat of my adolescence to drive my motor-bike at high speed through the grounds.) The same intense terror was experienced with respect to a green house we had to pass on the way to the swimming pool, and we called the woman who lived there 'the green witch'. I believed in and feared the Bogeyman and could not go to sleep unless the door of my wardrobe was shut. I was mortally afraid of the Frankenstein monster and the Mummy (of the movie, 'The Mummy's Curse'), and until I went away to university I could not go into the kitchen without first reaching round the door jamb and turning on the fluorescent light, which took an age to go on. The same was true of the back porch, while going into the back garden after dusk was simply out of the question. My childhood and adolescence were filled with terrors, imaginings, fantasies and some activities about which I would blush to tell - all rending the fabric of civilised society. Prominent among the terrors was the sheer horror of hearing the word 'Terrell', the name of the nearby state mental hospital. I cannot recall a time when this word did not conjure up an unpicturable hell, into which my depressed mother and I were in imminent danger of being tossed as a result of my transgressions, in particular, my inability to be sufficiently respectful of my father. A version of this terror still overcomes me when I am in the grip of an argument and cannot let up. Behind these conscious experiences, I now know, lay psychotic anxieties.

I offer these reports, somewhat shyly, as a way of inviting you to make similar searches of your memories to glimpse the tips of the icebergs of your own phantasies and psychotic anxieties. They are my version of what Klein calls 'a cave of dangerous monsters' (Klein, 1975, vol 1, p 272). My general point is that if you ask the question, 'What is a psychotic anxiety when it's at home and not in the pages of an implausible and nearly unfathomable text by Melanie Klein?', you'll be able to be less sceptical if you interrogate the fringes of your own memories and distressing experiences and, of course, your dreams. I shall offer more illustrations anon, but for the present I want to assert that psychotic anxieties are ubiquitous, underlie all thought, provide the rationale for all culture and institutions and, in particular cases, help us to make sense of especially galling ways of being. I have in mind at the moment Meltzer's idea of the claustrum (1992), wherein dwell ultra-ambitious and survivalist conformists who live in projective identification, which he takes to mean that their dwelling place in the inner world is inside the rectum, thus confirming the colloquial description of such people as 'arseholes'. His analysis shows that this degree of use of projective identification is a defence against schizophrenic breakdown. This suggests that many of our chief executives and leaders live perpetually on the verge of madness. No wonder that they *must* get their way. Greedy ambition is running scared.

Klein's views on these matters are based on Freud and Abraham's notions of oral libido and fantasies of cannibalism (Gedo, 1986, p 94). She refers to sadistic impulses against the mother's breast and inside her body, wanting to scoop out, devour, cut to pieces, poison and destroy by every means sadism suggests (Klein, 1975, vol 1, p 262). Once again, the projective and introjective mechanisms of the first months and year give rise to anxiety situations and defences against them, 'the content of which is comparable to that of the psychoses in adults' (ibid). Orality is everywhere, for example, in the 'gnawing of conscience' (p268). Riviere says that 'such helplessness against destructive forces within constitutes the greatest psychical danger situation known to the human organism; and that this helplessness is the deepest source of anxiety in human beings' (Riviere, 1952, p 43). It is the ultimate source of all neurosis. At this early stage of development, sadism is at its height and is followed by the discovery that loved objects are in a state of disintegration, in bits or in dissolution, leading to despair, remorse and anxiety, which underlie numerous anxiety situations. Klein concludes, 'anxiety situations of this kind I have found to be at the bottom not only of depression, but of all inhibitions of work' (Klein, 1975 vol 1, p 270). It should be recalled that these are prelinguistic experiences developmentally, and sub-linguistic in adults. It is a characteristic of the world view of Kleinians that the primitive is never transcended and that all experiences continue to be mediated through the mother's body. Similarly, there is a persistence of primitive phantasies of body parts and bodily functions, especially biting, eating, tearing, spitting out, urine and urinating, faeces and defecating, mucus, genitals.

Having said that, I shall offer an example of undiluted Klein. She is in the middle of an exposition of the part which the paranoid, depressive and manic positions play in normal development (Klein, 1975, vol 1, p 279) and offers two illustrative dreams, which I shall not quote. (I should emphasise that I am quoting a passage from the middle of an exposition and interpretation which is six pages long.) I want to convey the flavour of the primitive phantasies which I have been discussing. Here is part of the interpretation: 'The urination in the dream led on to early aggressive phantasies of the patient towards his parents, especially directed against their sexual intercourse. He had phantasied biting them and eating them up, and among other attacks, urinating on and into his father's penis, in order to skin and burn it and to make his father set his mother's inside on fire in their intercourse (the torturing with hot oil). These phantasies extended to babies inside his mother's body, which were to be killed (burnt). The kidney burnt alive stood both for his father's penis - equated with faeces - and for the babies inside his mother's body (the stove which he did not open). Castration of the father was expressed by the associations about beheading. Appropriation of the father's penis was shown by the feeling that his penis was so large and that he urinated both for himself and for his father (phantasies of having his father's penis inside his own or joined on to his own had come out a great deal in his analysis). The patient's urinating into the bowl meant also his sexual intercourse with his mother (whereby the bowl and the mother in the dream represented her both as a real and as an internalised figure). The impotent and castrated father was made to look on at the patient's intercourse with his mother - the reverse of the situation the patient had gone through in phantasy in his childhood. The wish to humiliate his father is expressed by his feeling that he ought not to do so' (Klein, 1975, vol 1, p 281). And so on for another half page. A similarly daunting example could be drawn from Meltzer's account of the dream materials which can be attributed to unconscious phantasies of anal masturbation (Meltzer, 1988, esp. pp 104, 106-7).

This is veritably hard to bear, hard to credit, hard to follow. Klein is operating well and truly in the most primitive parts of the inner world, where dream symbolism meets up with primitive bodily functions and body parts. Her way of describing these phantasies is easy to caricature and becomes wooden when adopted in a parrot-like fashion by inexperienced acolytes. In the subsequent history of Kleinian psychoanalysis, however, her outlook on unconscious phantasy has continued to prevail. Elizabeth Spillius reports that this is one of Klein's concepts which has been 'very little altered' by subsequent Kleinians.

However, many Kleinians (though not all, for example, Donald Meltzer) have altered their language and have become more likely to make interpretations in terms of functions rather than anatomical part-objects. Edna O'Shaughnessy has suggested the notion of 'psychological part-objects' as an analogy to bodily part-objects. Spillius takes this up and argues 'that we relate to psychological part-objects... to the functions of the part-object rather than primarily to its physical structure. It is the capacities for seeing, touching, tasting, hearing, smelling, remembering, feeling, judging, and thinking, active as well as passive, that are attributed to and perceived in relation to part-objects'.

Spillius concludes her remarks on this change in emphasis in technique by relating it to Klein's concept of projective identification. The functions 'are frequently understood as aspects of the self which are projected into part objects' (Spillius, 1988, vol 1, pp 2-5; cf. vol 2, pp 8-9).

Klein was untroubled by being called an 'id psychologist' (Gedo, 1986, p 91). She unrepentantly conceived the analyst's task to be to confront the patient with the content of the Unconscious. She eschewed 'corrective emotional experience', did not encourage regression and the reliving of infantile experiences, or explicit educational or moral influences, and kept 'to the psycho-analytic procedure only, which, to put it in a nutshell, consists in understanding the patient's mind and in conveying to him what goes on in it' (Klein, 1975, vol 3, p 129). She felt that confidently articulating interpretations of very primitive material in the face of resistance diminishes the patient's anxiety and opens the door to the Unconscious. Nor did she shy away from such deep interpretations or transference interpretations from the beginning of analytic work with a patient (Klein, 1975, vol 2, pp 22-24; Gedo, 1986, p 92).

Why is all this such an innovation? Riviere points out that anxiety was of great significance to Freud, but that much of his rhetoric was physiological. He did not concern himself with the psychological *content* of phantasies. By contrast, 'anxiety, with the defences against it, has from the beginning been Mrs Klein's approach to psycho-analytical problems. It was from this angle that she discovered the existence and importance of aggressive elements in children's emotional life... and [it] enabled her to bring much of the known phenomena of mental disorders into line with the basic principles of analysis' (Riviere, 1952, pp 8-9).

From that point, Kleinians went on to propose elements of a general psychology, including the claim that there is 'an unconscious phantasy behind every thought and every act' (p16). That is, the mental expression of primitive processes 'is unconscious phantasy' (ibid). It is not only a background hum, as it were. Isaacs claims that 'Reality thinking cannot operate without concurrent and supporting unconscious phantasies' (Isaacs, 1952, p 109). And again: 'phantasies are the primary content of unconscious mental processes' (pp 82, 112). 'There is no impulse, no instinctual urge or response which is not experienced as unconscious phantasy' (p 83). 'Phantasies have both psychic and bodily effects, e.g. in conversion symptoms, bodily qualities, character and personality, neurotic symptoms inhibitions and sublimations' (p 112). They even determine the minutiae of body language (p 100). The role of unconscious phantasy extends from the first to the most abstract thought. The infant's first thought of the existence of the external world comes from sadistic attacks on the mother's body (Klein, 1975, vol 1, p 276; vol 3, p 5). 'Phantasies - becoming more elaborate and referring to a wider variety of objects and situations - continue throughout development and accompany all activities; they never stop playing a great part in mental life. The influence of unconscious phantasy on art, on scientific work, and on the activities of everyday life cannot be overrated' (Klein, 1975, vol 3, p 251; cf. p 262).

These anxieties are not only ubiquitous: they interact in complicated ways. As Riviere points out, 'It is impossible to do any justice here to the complexity and variety of the anxiety-situations and the defences against them dominating the psyche during these early years. The factors involved are so numerous and the combinations and interchanges so variable. The internal objects are employed against external, and external against internal, both for satisfaction and for security; desire is employed against hate and destructiveness; omnipotence against impotence, and even impotence (dependence) against destructive omnipotence; phantasy against reality and reality against phantasy. Moreover, hate and destruction are employed as measures to avert the dangers of desire and even of love. Gradually a progressive development takes place... by means of the interplay of these and other factors, and of them with external influences, out of which the child's ego, his object-relations, his sexual development, his super-ego, his character and capacities are formed' (Riviere, 1952, pp 59-60).

Turning to the bearings of these ideas on groups and institutions, I want to begin with two points. The first is that the move is a simple one. Bion says, 'My impression is that the group approximates too closely, in the minds of the individuals composing it, to very primitive phantasies about the contents of the mother's body. The attempt to make a rational investigation of the dynamics of the group is therefore perturbed by fears, and mechanisms for dealing with them, which are characteristic of the paranoid-schizoid position. The investigation cannot be carried out without the stimulation and activation of those levels... the elements of the emotional situation are so closely allied to phantasies of the earliest anxieties that the group is compelled, whenever the pressure of anxiety becomes too great, to take defensive action' (Bion, 1955, p 456). The psychotic anxieties in question involve splitting and projective identification and are characteristic of the paranoid-schizoid and depressive positions, now as group processes (p457). The move from the individual to the group does not raise new issues about explanation. He says a little further on, 'The apparent difference between group psychology and individual psychology is an illusion produced by the fact that the group brings into prominence phenomena which appear alien to an observer unaccustomed to using the group' (p 461).

My second point is that those of us who have tried to change institutions, and have learned that there are (as Bruce Springsteen says) 'things that'll knock you down that you didn't see coming', will be relieved to have this illumination and to be better informed about what we are up against. I remember with some chagrin the occasion when Bob Hinshelwood (who has since published the best book on groups: Hinshelwood, 1987) insisted that I train in group therapy and go to a two-week residential Leicester Conference on group relations (Miller, 1990). I was offended by his saying I'd had no experience of groups, since I'd spent the Sixties and Seventies in all sorts of collectives, co-ops and even a commune. I felt he was being dismissive of some of my most painful scar tissue, and we had a blazing row about which of us was being arrogant... Looking back from the vantage point of a number of years of conducting and being supervised on group therapy, as well as trying to assimilate the experience of a Leicester Conference (which all acknowledge takes years), I gratefully (and only residually resentfully) say that unless we understand the psychotic anxieties Bion is on about, we will never know what we are up against in human nature and in trying to change things. Bion says that falling into the forms of basic assumption functioning which he describes is instinctive, involuntary, automatic, instantaneous and inevitable (pp 449, 458).

Elliot Jaques and Isabel Menzies Lyth are also very sober and stoical in their assessments of the barriers to change. Jaques begins his essay on 'Social Systems as a defence against Persecutory and Depressive anxiety' by reiterating that 'social phenomena show a striking correspondence with psychotic processes in individuals', that 'institutions are used by their individual members to reinforce individual mechanisms of defence against anxiety', and 'that the mechanisms of projective and introjective identification operate in linking individual and social behaviour'. He argues the thesis that 'the primary cohesive elements binding individuals into institutionalised human association is that of defence against psychotic anxiety' (Jaques, 1955, pp 478-9). He points out that the projective and introjective processes he is investigating are basic to even the most complex social processes and directs us to Paula Heimann's argument that they are at the bottom of all our dealings with one another (p 481, n.). His conclusion is cautionary and points out the conservative - even reactionary - consequences of our psychotic anxieties and our group and institutional defences against them. He suggests that as a result of these reflections on human nature 'it may become more clear why social change is so difficult to achieve, and why many social problems are so intractable. From the point of view here elaborated, changes in social relationships and proce-dures call for a restructuring of relationships at the phantasy level, with a consequent demand upon individuals to accept and tolerate changes in their existing patterns of defences against psychotic anx-iety. Effective social change is likely to require analysis of the com-mon anxieties and unconscious collusions underlying the social defences determining phantasy social relationships' (p 498).

I turn, penultimately, to the investigator whose work strikes me as the most important body of writings on the social bearings of psychoanalysis, Isabel Menzies Lyth, who built her research on the shoulders of Bion and Jaques. She has investigated a number of fraught settings, for example, the fire brigade, motor-cycling, chil-dren's institutions, as well as a number of industrial ones, and most recently the tripartite group structure of the Institute of Psycho-Analysis in London.

The piece of research which has deservedly made her world-famous is described in a report entitled 'The Functioning of Social Systems as a Defence against Anxiety'. It is a particularly poignant document, which addresses the question why people of good will and idealistic motives do not do what they intend, that is, why nurses find themselves, to an astonishing degree, not caring for patients and leaving the nursing service in droves. It would be rep-etitious to review the mechanisms she describes. They are the ones discussed above. What is so distressing is that they operate over-whelmingly in a setting which has as its very reason for existence the provision of sensitivity and care. Yet that setting is full of threats to life itself and arouses the psychotic anxieties I have outlined. She says, 'The objective situation confronting the nurse bears a striking resemblance to the phantasy situations that exist in every individ-ual in the deepest and most primitive levels of the mind. The inten-sity and complexity of the nurse's anxieties are to be attributed pri-marily to the peculiar capacity of objective features of her work sit-uation to stimulate afresh those early situations and their accompa-nying emotions' (Menzies Lyth, 1988, pp 46-7).

The result is the evolution of socially structured defence mechanisms which take the form of routines and division of tasks which effectively preclude the nurse relating as a whole person to the patient as a whole person. 'The implicit aim of such devices, which operate both structurally and culturally, may be described as a kind of depersonalisation or elimination of individual distinctiveness in both nurse and patient. For example, nurses often talk about patients not by name, but by bed numbers or by their diseases or a diseased organ: "the liver in bed 10" or "the pneumonia in bed 15". Nurses deprecate this practice, but it persists' (pp 51-2). She lists and discusses the reifying devices which reduce everyone involved to part-objects, including insight into why the nurse wakes you up to give you a sleeping pill (p 69). There is a whole system of overlapping ways of evading the full force of the anxieties associated with death, the ones which lie at the heart of the mechanisms which Klein described (pp 63-64; cf. Riviere, 1952, p 43).

Menzies Lyth also draws a cautionary conclusion: 'In general, it may be postulated that resistance to social change is likely to be greatest in institutions whose social defence systems are dominated by primitive psychic defence mechanisms, those which have been collectively described by Klein as the paranoid-schizoid defences' (Menzies Lyth, p 79). In recent reflections on her work and that of her colleagues, she has reiterated just how refractory to change institutions are (Menzies Lyth, 1988 pp 1-42, and personal communications).

The Leicester Conferences on group and organisational behaviour, with particular emphasis on authority and leadership, have been held at least once a year since 1957. They are heir to the traditions discussed above, especially the work of Klein, Bion, Jaques and Menzies Lyth. (Other influences are mentioned in Miller, 1990, pp 165-69.) One among several interrelated ways of characterising the two-week residential conferences is that they are so arranged as to facilitate experiential learning about the ways in which group processes can generate psychotic anxieties and institutional defences against them (p 171). The struggles that ensue in the members' minds between individuation and incorporation, as a result of the conference group events, is hard to credit by anyone who has not taken part in a Leicester Conference or related 'mini-Leicester' events. Similarly, descriptions of events and feelings are likely to seem odd to anyone not familiar with the sorts of events around which the conferences are structured. I believe, however, that the relevant emotional points will be sufficiently clear without a (necessarily) long description of the conference rubric.

My own experience involved feeling continually on the edge of disintegration as a result of behaviour in the various group events (ranging in size from a dozen to over 100 people) which I found appalling and from which there seemed no escape, while efforts to persuade people to behave well produced flight, sadism, collusive lowering of the stakes or denial. The potential of the group for uniting around (what was called on occasion) 'cheap reconciliation' or for cruelty, brought me to the point of leaving on several occasions, and I frequently had the experience of having to use all my resources to hold myself together against forces which I experienced as profoundly immoral, amoral or pathetically conformist. No appeal to standards of group decency was of much avail.

I ended up forming a group in my mind which consisted of all the people I admired in history and in my lifetime, e.g., Socrates, Lincoln, Gandhi, King, Bonhoeffer, Marcuse, Mandela, who had stood up to intolerable social forces without quitting the field or having their spirits broken. I dubbed this 'The Ps <—> D Solidarity Group' and, armed with their mandate, managed to talk my way into a meeting with the staff, for the purpose of mounting a critique of the rubric of the exercise. I felt contained by the inner solidarity provided by my imagined group, while I was, in truth, actually on my own in the phenomenal context of the conference events. I had blown out of a group in considerable distress, because it had utterly failed to live up to its self-designation of advocating and practising decency and civility among its members and urging such standards on the larger group of conference members.

Just as I was on the point of sitting down to confront the staff group in the name of my inner world group (vainly hoping they would show some interest in its name, membership and values), a representative of the group I had left appeared and bestowed 'plenipotentiary powers' (one of the designated forms of delegation of authority) on me, freeing me from the dreaded status of 'singleton'. A singleton is a person with no role status in the large group (see Miller, 1990, p 179 and Turquet, 1975, where the plight of the singleton is insightfully and poignantly described). I had felt unutterably alone, almost totally in the grip of paranoid persecutions, holding on for dear life to my hallucinated historical group. The bestowal of my conference group's trust reincorporated me into the social whole on terms I could accept.

My confrontation with the staff group, acting in this exercise as 'Management', was predictably without issue, but I went away feeling that I had spoken my piece without suffering the humiliation that many others had experienced. I had offered my analysis of the situation and their role in it, one dimension of which was that they *would* - as a part of the exercise's point - continue to behave as they were doing, i.e., act as an immovable object on to which the groups would project their phantasies about authority and (hopefully) begin to take responsibility for themselves. I felt that I had done that and negotiated my own rite of passage - just. Having gone some way toward resolving my own temporary insanity (though not my omnipotence) I was only able to bask pleasantly in group member-ship for a few minutes before members of another group, who had sought refuge in being regressed and silly (they called themselves 'The Potty Training Group'), stormed into the room where the staff/Management group were holding court. The person whom I had considered to be the mildest member of that group physically attacked a German member of staff with shouts of 'fascist' and other violent epithets. He was aided and cheered on by other mem-bers of his group, until one, a woman I felt sure was a Jew but I now recollect was probably not but was a German, broke down sobbing and shouted for all this to stop.

The descent from work or task-oriented groups to groups in the thrall of psychotic basic assumptions is, as Bion pointed out, spon-taneous and inevitable, even in a situation which all concerned know to be temporary and 'artificial'. I continue to find this pro-foundly sobering. I also continue to ruminate it and am far from having digested the experience, though I have found it increasing-ly helpful in my work and related activities.

After canvassing the literature on unconscious phantasy and psychotic anxieties and reflecting on it and my own personal and clinical experience, I am left with a daunting sense of the power of the inner world and an awesome awareness of how very deep, primitive, abiding and alarming its nether regions are. The anxieties I have attempted to outline (and, to a degree, evoke), exist through-out human nature - in all of life from the cradle (some say earlier) to the grave, in all of play and culture, and act as a brake on benig-nity and social change which it is hard to imagine releasing, even notch by notch.

The history of psychoanalysis has left us with a small number of ideas about the veneer of civilisation. Freud said it was thin and under threat. One reading of those who still speak in his name and quote his slogan: 'Where id was, there ego shall be. It is a work of culture - not unlike the draining of the Zuider Zee' (New Introductory Lectures on Psychoanalysis, S.E.XXII, p 80), takes this to mean that the result can be dry, flowering land, i.e., that there can be a 'conflict-free sphere of the ego'. A second, rather disparate, group proffer a continuum extending from Reich's advocacy of desublimation and a promise, of a return to Eden, to the Winnicottian position that eschews Klein's undoubted stress on the power of thanatic, destructive forces, and sees rather more decency and hope in liberal society.

I dare say that Klein said rather less about the other side of human nature - the constructive or erotic impulses - because she found herself in mutually critical dialogue with colleagues who she felt overemphasised those aspects. Finding the twig bent, as she thought, too far one way, she bent it the other way, perhaps to leave it straight for those that followed. A third group are orthodox Kleinians and point out that the veneer of civilisation is very thin indeed and that the maelstrom beneath is perpetually and rather pathetically defended against. It can be argued that this provides the basis for an optimism of the will, coupled with a pessimism of the intellect and a belief that it is essential to know what is bubbling away underneath the surface if we are to have any hope of cooling some of the crust.

I also believe that this position is consistent with a careful reading of Freud's *Civilization and Its Discontents,* written half way through his sixteen-year struggle with cancer. He says there that the history of civilisation is 'the struggle between Eros and Death, between the instinct of life and the instinct of destruction, as it works itself out in the human species. This struggle is what all life essentially consists of... And it is this battle of the giants that our nurse-maids try to appease with their lullaby about Heaven' (S.E. XXI, p 122).

[1]This is the revised text of a talk given to THERIP (The Higher Education Network for Teaching and Research in Psychoanalysis) in November 1991. It has subsequently served as a basis for an essay on 'The Ubiquity of Psychotic Anxieties' and a chapter in *Mental Space.*.

PHANTASY IN KLEIN AND LACAN

Darian Leader

Rather than asking 'in what way did Melanie Klein fail to write Ecrits?', why not pose the alternative question: 'Given that Lacan was steeped in the work of Melanie Klein in the late 1940s and early 1950s, why don't we have a theory of phantasy in his texts from this period?'. He had supposedly been working on a translation of *The Psychoanalysis of Children*, he makes several references to the theory of internal objects, so why does this crucial concept fail to make an appearance? To answer this question, it is worthwhile asking a related one: 'If there isn't a theory of phantasy, what is there instead?'. And the answer to this is somewhat clearer: there is a theory of what Lacan calls the 'permanent modes' through which the subject constitutes its objects, a notion which gives a privileged place to the power of the image.

Certain images will have a special value for the subject. They will captivate him and literally hold him prisoner. When the chain of free associations is blocked, it is due to the inertial, disruptive power of such images which block the dialectic of analysis with their stagnatory presence. They function as the resistance to the unfolding of speech. An example might be the image for Dora of tugging on her brother's ear lobe while sucking her thumb. A memory like this can function both to block further associations and the production of other memories, and as a 'permanent mode' through which Dora will construct her relations to the opposite sex. Each relation with a man might be forced into the primitive mould of this captivating image. Lacan's idea implies that the sexes can only relate to each other through some kind of filter, something which would order and regulate what we would call in this country object relations. Already we can see the germ of the later theory of phantasy as a frame through which the subject maintains his relation with his object.

What is singular about this early conception in Lacan is the idea that these 'permanent modes' are, strictly speaking, identifications. If the ego is itself made up of a series of imaginary identifications, the material to be worked on will be just these strata of the ego: analysis would aim, initially, at a sort of decomposition of the ego, an unspooling of its central identifications. This perspective makes sense in the context of Lacan's notion of neurosis as a question : the subject can ask a question using its ego, that is, using an imaginary identification. Thus for Dora, if her question is 'what is it to be a woman?', she can identify herself with either her father or Mr K in order to have access to the one who incarnates the mystery of womanhood, Mrs K. Lacan elaborated this view in detail in the early '50s and we could compare his remarks in the famous 1953 Rome speech with the contemporary comments of Paula Heimann on interpretation at the Geneva Congress. Heimann says that 'The question the analyst has to ask himself is: "Why is the patient now doing what to whom?"'. The answer to this question is analytic interpretation. Lacan, however, puts the emphasis on something slightly different: 'To know how to respond to the subject in analysis, the method is first to recognize the site of his ego... in other words, to know by whom and for whom the subject is posing his question'. Thus, the one term Heimann leaves unquestioned, 'the patient', is exactly the term that Lacan wishes to see challenged. The question of who is speaking must be addressed in order to find out what is being said. In contrast to many of his analytic contemporaries, Lacan shows a profound sensitivity to the problem of identification.

Now, before continuing our survey of the concept of phantasy in Lacan, we can simply stress two features of the early formulations. First of all, we can see the presence of a disparity of elements: the ego consists of imaginary identifications, which will function as resistances or barriers to the progress of free association, and which act in opposition to the symbolic circuits of speech. And secondly, we see the presence of an inertia: the imaginary elements do not want to give themselves up, they persist in opposition to the analytic work. They exert their silent pressure, and it is up to the analysis to reintegrate them into the dialectic of speech. These two features - disparity of elements and inertia - remain constant in Lacan's later formulations of phantasy and its structure.

By 1958 there are two crucial additions to the theory of 'permanent modes'. It is now not simply a question of being captured in an image, of being enslaved to the captivating powers of something alien to the organism. Lacan has introduced the dynamic of the subject and what he calls the action of the signifier. It is thus no longer simply a matter of the image but of the image plus a subject, a link which implies the presence of a scenario. There is an activity of the subject in organising his phantasy rather than the passivity of capture in an image. Lacan defines phantasy now as 'the image set to work in the signifying structure', and he rebukes Klein and her followers for confusing phantasy with imagination: they would avoid this misconception if they were alert to 'the category of the signifier'. In order to situate this criticism in a clinical context, we can examine some of the examples Susan Isaacs privileges in her famous paper on 'The Nature and Function of Phantasy' to see if and how this 'category of the signifier' can clarify and make sense of the material. Isaacs' article is of particular importance in the history of psychoanalysis because she provides a detailed exposition of the Kleinian theory which is lacking in the work of Klein herself. Commentators have often debated the meaning of the phrase 'phantasy is the psychical representative of the drive' but here the real problem is in the representative function of Isaacs' paper. It is astonishing that whenever a scholar is attempting an exposition of Klein's ideas, when it comes to the theory of phantasy, we read something like 'Isaacs provides a clear account of Klein's theory so we will quote from her'. This practice is so widespread that one may even pose the question: did Melanie Klein herself really have a theory of phantasy anyway? Any access to this is blocked by her psychical representative, Susan Isaacs.

Isaacs supposedly provides the metapsychological foundations of a Kleinian theory of phantasy. She argues that phantasies express 'the specific content' of the earliest 'urges' and 'feelings' of the infant. They provide an 'affective interpretation of bodily sensations'. So, for example, if a child feels anxiety, he might feel 'I shall be bitten or cut up by mother'. Isaacs claims that such phantasies are 'implicit meanings', significations which are latent in impulses, affects and sensations. 'Comprehension of words', she continues, 'long antedates their use'. Meaning thus comes before words. 'We know', she says, 'from our own ready and intuitive response to other people's facial expression, tone of voice, gesture, etc, how much implicit meaning is expressed in these things, with never a word uttered, or in spite of words uttered.' This is a peculiar statement for anyone who has worked with very young children, where one might argue for exactly the opposite: that an expression has little value before it is linked to some kind of articulation. Likewise, the very idea of an implicit meaning, subtracted from language, is a suspect one. Meanings, Lacan would claim, are generated by linguistic elements. Language does not have to be speech here, rather, just any system of differentiated units. Expressions and gestures can form a language as long as they are different from each other: the child learns their code from the perception of the distinctions between them. This side to Isaacs' argument thus makes the confusion of identifying language and speech.

A child is in a linguistic world well before it can use speech. It is still in a world of differences.

This may be seen with infantile autism. There is often no reaction to different people being in the room, moving through the visual field, other children playing or toys being presented. In other words, in the world of the autistic child, there are no differences: to react to a toy or the presence of a newcomer, these must be perceived as different. Instead of this, the autistic child is in a world of continuity. Now, if difference is a result of language, since the definition of a linguistic system is simply a system of differences, one could say that the autistic child has not incorporated the structure of language. Hence he does not know difference. But what are autistic children frequently so sensitive to? Precisely to shouts, clapping, abrupt noises: that is, to things that suddenly break continuity. They are attracted to the sudden emergence of discontinuity, a fact which may be observed empirically with little difficulty. This shows the sensitivity of the youngest and most troubled infant to the dimension of language, to that which makes differences, discontinuities and breaks. It is thus crucial to stress the presence of linguistic structure - difference - from the earliest age, but linguistic structure to be distinguished from speech as such. Isaacs' examples testify to this presence of the preverbal, in the sense of pre-speaking, but not to the pre-linguistic.

When Isaacs first presented her formulations in the 'Controversial Discussions' in the British Psycho-Analytical Society in 1943, her suppositions about meaning and language were taken up by her critics. Her notion of phantasy rested on the supposition of meaningful but nonverbal experiences. Her opponents said, why not just say states of well-being or discomfort? Why refer to meanings? Isaacs' particular philosophical constitution made her insist on the term, while separating it from the register of words, which she believed were secondary. Phantasies, she says, 'are not experienced in words'. 'Words are by no means an essential scaffolding for phantasy'. This attitude was so fundamental to her position that Marjorie Brierley, one of her colleagues, suggested doing away with the word 'phantasy' altogether, and putting the term 'meaning' in its place.

The interest of Isaacs' paper lies to a great extent in her effort to give a scientific status to the concepts of Melanie Klein, since this involves an appeal to philosophical authorities. If Klein was influenced, for example, by Cassirer, she doesn't tell us anything about it. But Isaacs does, to a certain extent, put her cards on the table: the key references for her are James Ward and John Locke. From Locke, she quotes approvingly, 'We have no ideas at all, but what originally came either from sensible objects without, or what we felt within ourselves.' Now, if one disagrees with the Lockian philosophy, it will be necessary to reformulate some, at least, of the theory of phantasy.

Here are three examples from Isaacs of the function of phantasy. 'A little girl of one year six months saw a shoe of her mother's from which the sole had come loose and was flapping about. The child was horrified and screamed with terror'. Later, at two years and eleven months she says to her mother in a frightened voice: 'Where are Mummy's broken shoes?'. The mother replies that she had sent them away, to which the daughter comments, 'They might have eaten me right up!'. Now, Isaacs adds the following commentary herself: 'The flapping shoe was thus seen by the child as a mouth, and reacted to as such, at one year and eight months, even though her fear could not be named. Here then we have clear evidence that a phantasy can be felt and felt as real, long before it can be expressed in words. And does it not seem likely that in seeing her mother's shoe as a threatening biting mouth, the child was expressing her fear of a phantastic vengeful mother, who would bite her up in retaliation for her own biting impulses?'.

We might differ from Isaacs in her interpretation of the material here. Doesn't the focus on the flapping sole indicate exactly the opposite of her thesis, that in fact the child has succeeded very well in pinpointing or expressing her fears? She has succeeded, after all, in distinguishing the sole from the other elements in the world around her, and she has been even more precise in linking her fear to the sole that flaps. Thus, she has transformed anxiety into fear: anxiety is vague in its attribution and for this reason, all the more unsettling. One does not know what it is linked to. But fear represents a development of anxiety since one is afraid of something. The anxiety has become coordinated to a representation or signifier, in this example, the flapping sole. Whatever the child might imagine about the biting properties of the sole, it serves nonetheless to introduce an organising element into her relation with the mother: it is not just mother and child, but mother, child and sole. There is thus a third term through which the girl can mediate her relation to the mother, a signifier distinguished from all the other elements surrounding her.

In the second example, a 16 month old girl refuses food, screaming in protest unless she was allowed to have two or three spoons on her tray which she could hand to her mother between the spoonfuls of food which she took. As Isaacs says: 'She thus alternated taking food herself with the giving of imaginary food to her mother, and showed by her screams and inability to eat if not allowed to do this, how important it was to her.'. Isaacs goes on to link this with an earlier episode in which the mother had temporarily left the child. She had refused her food both at that time and on the mother's return. Isaacs comments: 'From what we know of the refusal of food in older children, it seems likely that the child's resentment and anger at her mother's absence had poisoned the food which had been left for her to take, and even when her mother returned, still distorted her perception of her.'. The example, however, suggests another interpretation. The child is introducing a third term into her relation with the mother. The mother is trying to feed her and she is insisting on certain conditions being met first. The game with the spoons shows that what matters is not the biological nourishment of the body, but the signifying relation with the mother. As she had been at the mother's mercy during the earlier absence, now the tables have been turned. Precisely by repeating the game with the mother, it takes on value as a signifier, a ritual which puts a symbolic game before the food: the priority is with the ritual, not with the food. A triangle is present: mother, daughter and game, the symbolic accent of which is stressed by the imaginary spoonfuls of food. The register of the signifier is what can make the food disappear, and is itself the principle of so many children's games.

In the next example, a boy of about the same age has a favourite game of shooing imaginary ducks into a corner of a room, driving them from one corner to the next. 'He showed that they were ducks by saying 'Quack quack', although his language was ill-developed and he said nothing else in this game'. The boy experiences night terrors at this time, often waking screaming in the night. Later, he would put the content of the nightmare into words: 'White rabbit biting my toes'. Isaacs finds it hard not to resist the conclusion that the 'white rabbit' represented 'in part, at least', the mother's breast, which he feared would bite him as he had bitten it, or wished to, when it frustrated him. (Note that this interpretation supposes a sophisticated theory of abstraction, linking 'milk' to 'white' and so on, which Isaacs does not comment on.) The play with the ducks then represents his attempt to overcome his fear of the biting retaliatory breast. A duck is well suited to represent a breast since it is a white creature with a prominent mouth. Once again, the category of the signifier proves useful if one is not convinced by the rather tentative nature of the explanation. The boy is a little Wittgenstein: he has transformed a duck into a rabbit. What testifies to the presence of the signifier is precisely this transformation. Language is what makes substitutions possible. Words, as everyone knows, do not have intrinsic relations with objects, but refer to objects due to their place in the network of language. What matters is the difference between the terms. To show the split between a word and the image usually associated with it, to turn a duck into a rabbit, is to show that one has registered the real nature of the structure of language. Children demonstrate this all the time, often to the exasperation of adults. A boy runs around calling many things a 'tractor', including all the things which are anything but farm vehicles. He is thus showing a registration of language, the lack of any necessary link between a word and its referent, and the priority of the linguistic element itself. The word 'tractor' will organise his reality at that time, not the real vehicle. Things are divided up by the word 'tractor': it is the signifier which organises the world of the child in this example. It is thus a positive sign that a child has really understood something about the nature of language when he starts to make 'mistakes'.

Lacan's recentering of the debate on phantasy around this category of the signifier is echoed in the similarity of the title of Isaacs' paper on phantasy and his own famous Rome discourse in which he sets out the agenda for a programme of analytic research founded on linguistic considerations. Where Isaacs had written 'The Nature and Function of Phantasy', Lacan put his 'Function and Field of Speech and Language': Isaacs' 'phantasy' is thus replaced by the linguistic register, and the term 'nature' disappears, the linguistic 'field' slipping into its place. Where Isaacs had put phantasy, Lacan put language.

Lacan's idea of the role of the signifier here owes much to his study of phobia, particularly his rereading of the case of Little Hans in 1956/7. He shows how a phobia gives a privileged value to a certain element (a horse, a dog...), but to stress its separation from its supposed referent. A child might complain of a fear of dogs all day long, without showing much reaction when confronted with a real dog. 'Dog' is a signifier, a linguistic element used to reorganise the relations of the child with those around him or her. It matters in fact precisely because of this detachment from the register of its referent: if a child can privilege a representation in this way, it shows that he has given an image the dignity of a signifier, something which does not have an intrinsic relation with its referent and hence may operate substitutions. When little Sandy, described by Anneliese Schnurmann, picks up a plastic dog and says 'pussy cat' towards the close of her dog phobia, it shows that she has understood this separation of registers, the autonomy of the linguistic over the image. Little Hans demonstrates the same thing, when he supplements his picture of a giraffe with another picture, this time on paper that is crumpled up. He calls it a 'crumpled giraffe', a possibility which is entirely dependent on the autonomy of the register of language: you can't find crumpled giraffes, after all, in a nature reserve. Lacan's examination of phobia is thus an important step in the definition of phantasy that we find in the 1958 text 'The Direction of the Treatment': 'once defined as an image functioning in the signifying structure, the notion of unconscious phantasy no longer poses any difficulty'.

To the condition of an image raised to the function of a signifier, Lacan adds a further characteristic of the phantasy: the presence of the subject. Susan Isaacs' definition of phantasy as the psychic representative of instinct entirely neglects the factor of subjective agency. Lacan's idea is that 'the phantasy, in its fundamental employment, is the means by which the subject supports himself at the level of his fading desire, fading to the extent that the very satisfaction of demand robs it of its object.'. The effort of the subject, it seems, is thus to maintain its desire, to keep desire present and unsatisfied at all costs. If a particular demand is satisfied, there is the threat that desire will be extinguished, due to the fact that desire is only desire due to not being satisfied.

What does this apparently abstract statement have to do with the experience of the child? It may be seen in the most concrete instance of a child's refusal to eat. As a mother demands that the child eat, she is met with a symbolic refusal, symbolic to the extent that the new aversion is not linked to any detail of the food itself. There is thus an attempt to maintain a desire, a dimension characterised by lack, and, furthermore, to situate this in relation to the mother.

If the mother continually makes demands on her child - even the implicit demands, listen to me, look at me - the child must find some way of showing that he is different and distinct from what comes from the adult. A child who conforms completely to the demands of a parent is like a robot, mechanical, waiting for the parental command before doing anything. To become properly human, to assume one's subjectivity, involves separating from the demands of the parent, introducing a margin into the signifying relations with the mother. The refusal to eat is one example of creating a lack.

In conditions such as autism a starker effort to make a gap is found: such children often try to remove the glasses or accessories from the care worker. The difference with the more common case of infantile anorexia is that whereas the latter involves creating a lack symbolically, in autism we see the effort to create a gap in the real, as if literally removing something linked to the body of the adult could have the same result and function. When Melanie Klein writes about the child's attacks on the mother's body, one may understand it in the simple sense of the attempt to make the body of the mother lack something, to emphasise the mother not as all-powerful and omnipotent but as lacking something. It is only once the child realises that it cannot satisfy the mother or complete her that the other side of the relation emerges: denying her lack altogether. It's as if the child is saying, 'if I can't fill your lack, you don't lack at all'.

Is this refusal of the child the same thing as phantasy? It involves, after all, the maintaining of desire. And if children can refuse things from the first few months, would that imply that Klein and Isaacs are right, that there is indeed phantasy activity from the tenderest age? The answer to this question must be negative. Children make many different sorts of refusals as they are growing up - refusals of food, of use of the potty etc - yet an unconscious phantasy has something of permanence about it. We could say that there is phantasy once a rhythm is established to these efforts to maintain desire, once a single formula is found to keep desire going. And it takes time for a child to find this formula. It isn't there from the first months of life. It will become constituted in the encounter with the desire of the mother.

The child might well be aware that the mother is making all sorts of demands, and to separate himself from these, he may offer some form of refusal. But the most terrible problem lies beyond this: what does the mother really want beyond her demands? Beyond what the child can understand of the mother's wishes, what else is there? This is the question of the ultimate value that the child has for the mother. It is the question of his existence, of what he represents. Lacan had the idea that language is incapable of replying to the question of one's existence. Words are not enough to tell us what we are. Instead, then, the response to the question comes from the register of the drive. An object - oral, anal, scopic, vocal - replies where language fails. This is what the subject is searching for in his world, and it gives the child a sort of compass with which to live. Does this mean that Susan Isaacs was right when she said that 'words are by no means an essential scaffolding for phantasy'? Lacan's argument implies quite the opposite: the object only takes on its value in relation to words. The whole question of the mother's desire may be introduced by what she says that the child cannot understand, and the absence of a linguistic response to the question of one's existence is so crucial precisely because it shows a breach in the linguistic network. In this sense, words really are the scaffolding of phantasy, even if, into this scaffolding, a non-linguistic object is inserted. Where Isaacs had posited a time gap between the child's understanding of words and their later use, Lacan bases his argument on the exact contrary: that a gap there certainly is, but this is between the words and the meaning which is left in suspense. The phantasy responds to what is not understood in the mother's speech, and it will supply a signification in terms of one of the phantasy objects only in a logically later time. Comprehension, then, always comes later.

The phantasy situates one's position in relation to the desire of the mother, and the particular object chosen will no doubt be linked to the preferences of the mother. It's like a little window through which the subject 's reality is filtered, and without which there is no relation to anything else. It is like a magnet which will attract certain images and words to it: this is the reason why you remember some things from childhood and not others. Certain memories have been given a special value because of their link to the phantasy. If in your phantasy you are identified with a rejected and worthless part of the body, then you might well have as your central memories scenes in which you are rejected and discarded as worthless. This phantasy magnet gives meaning to the world: it will serve to attribute a meaning to all the different things that can happen to you, giving a special form to the vicissitudes of one's existence. In this sense, we could agree with Isaacs' definition of phantasy as 'the subjective interpretation of experience': the difference would reside in the fact that for Lacan this is the end result of the formation of phantasy, whereas for Isaacs it is its original basis.

As well as organising the relation to meaning, the phantasy regulates the relation to the libido. Libidinal investment flows through it, so if another person is fitted inside this framework, they will become desired. If they step outside it, they will either not be recognised or they will fundamentally perturb the peace of the subject 's world. We see this at adolescence. The child has found some kind of solution, a formula, by which to situate himself in relation to the mother. The long years of the so-called latency period serve to consolidate it. And now, at adolescence, there is the possibility and pressure to engage in a sexual relation with another real live human being. The phantasy formula may prove robust enough to deal with the particularities of the other sexed being, but more often than not, it can't. After all, the other person has their own history, their own phantasy... there is no chance of a shared sexuality. Thus in adolescence the phantasy is tested in the encounter with a sexed being, and since it will probably prove ineffective in some way, incapable of absorbing all the sexuality of the other without leaving some disturbing remainder, the adolescent may well withdraw completely from the arena of sexual life. What becomes of paramount importance is simply preserving and safeguarding the phantasy rather than having a relationship with a member of the opposite sex.

Lacan describes two different ways in which desire is maintained in the phantasy. For the hysteric, desire is kept unsatisfied, for the obsessional, it is kept impossible. Thus, in hysteria the subject may deprive herself of what she apparently wants and, frequently, deprive the other also. For example, by exciting a man's desire and then leaving it perpetually unsatisfied. The obsessional also has unsatisfied desire, but what generates the lack of satisfaction is the condition of impossibility. For example, loving two different women and not being able to choose between them, or failing in love with a woman who is for some reason unattainable. A clinical example from Edmund Bergler provides another illustration: a man is most concerned about the poverty of his sex life and is prevented from sleeping by this thought - eventually, he finds a partner and sex life begins anew. But he still can't sleep, because now he is kept awake by the compulsion to imagine the sexual activity that had just taken place, to run through it once again in his thoughts. Thus both before and after the activity with the partner, the thought symptom generates an impossibility. Both the hysteric and the obsessional strategies suppose, in principle, an avoidance of the real sexual partner, keeping the latter forever at a distance. The phantasy could thus be defined as the way each human subject has of keeping their partner at a distance, of not encountering them, of keeping a screen in place.

Klein and Lacan share at least one conception of the role of phantasy here, giving it the role of that which organises one's reality rather than that which is opposed to it. Winnicott wrote a book called *Playing and Reality*, Charles Rycroft, *Imagination and Reality*, but Melanie Klein avoided this sort of conjunction. She shared with Lacan a basic suspicion of any attempt to contrast reality with phantasy, remaining to this extent true to Freud, who had stressed in his *Introductory Lectures on Psychoanalysis*, that the two terms should be equated rather than opposed.

Later in his work, Lacan went on to speak of what he called the 'logic' of the phantasy. The reference to logic is linked, at a certain level, to the earlier work on phobia. Taking an idea from the anthropologist Claude Lévi-Strauss, Lacan conceived of the development of a phobia as structurally similar to that of a myth. A myth is seen not as a solution to some fundamental problem (sex, existence), but rather as a way of formulating in new terms an initial contradiction or impossibility. In one of Lévi-Strauss' examples, the initial contradiction in the Oedipal story 'to be born out of the earth: to be born of a man and a woman' is expressed as another contradiction 'over-evaluation of a blood-tie: under-evaluation of a blood-tie' which we find in the familiar narrative of Oedipus the King. The first contradiction is replaced by two new terms which are self-contradictory in the same way. The contradiction between A and B is replaced by the contradiction between C and D. Thus a myth is less a solution to a first problem than a reposing of the problem: this 'working through' will sometimes have resolutive effects. A clinical example can illustrate this sort of functioning in the Unconscious. A woman has two dreams in the same night. In one, there is a savage battle with the father. In the other, the dreamer has killed someone, she knows not who. In the dream, she feels particularly guilty and is then confronted with her father. He turns to her and says, 'What you did was round'. Or, more precisely, 'You killed him in a shape that's round'. Now, rather than focusing on the various associations to the elements of the dream, let's approach it in a charitable, Lévi-Straussian way. The murder in the dream was no doubt that of the father, as many details indicated. Thus, there is the initial contradiction 'over-evaluation of a blood-tie: under-evaluation of a blood-tie'. This impossibility is then reciphered as a further contradiction or logical impossibility: to have killed someone in a shape that's round. The one contradiction is ciphered in the other, showing how logic is functioning where words are no longer adequate to express the complex structure of the relation at play. The lack of words or meaning of the initial impossibility is expressed in the form of the apparent absurdity, of having killed someone in a shape that's round.

Lacan's work on the function of logical relations in phobia was to prove important in his exact formulation of the phantasy. Lacan writes the phantasy: ($ <> a). The algebraic notation indicates first of all that it responds to a difficulty at the level of linguistic articulation. If phantasy involves the child's response to the question of his existence when language cannot give him an answer, it is only logical that its formulation should, in a sense, go beyond speech. The $ indicates the subject, the a the object and the <> the relation between the two. This relation may have a reversible quality.

Take the case of Sándor Ferenczi. We find again and again in his writings references to the work of the analyst as being like that of an obstetrician. The very frequency of these references may alert us to the presence of an unconscious dynamic. 'The doctor's position in psychoanalytic treatment recalls in many ways that of the obstetrician, who has also to conduct himself as passively as possible, to content himself with the post of onlooker at a natural proceeding, but who must be at hand at the critical moment with the forceps in order to complete the act of parturition that is not progressing spontaneously.'. The elements of a neurosis are even compared to a teratoma, to which 'no reasonable person would refuse to surrender on treatment to the surgeon's knife.' These analogies are focused on the idea of extracting something from the body.

Another current is also present, generating with equal frequency images of inserting something into the body of another. In his *Clinical Journal*, Ferenczi describes his fantasy of a corpse, the abdomen of which he is opening and into the open wound of which he is then being forced. He is thus in the place of the object that corks up the wound on the (woman's) body. In this context, he cites his memory of his mother's words to him 'you are my murderer', remarking that it was at this moment that he decided, against his inner conviction, to become a nice person. Now, what does all this material show? Entering the body to block up a wound but at the same time removing something from the body, he is himself the separable object which shifts from the one pole of the unconscious equation to the other. It is exactly the 'push and pull' that Ferenczi comments on in his famous paper on *Elasticity in Psychoanalytic Technique*: 'The analyst, like an elastic band, must yield to the patient's pull, but without ceasing to pull in his own direction.' The push ($<$) and the pull ($>$) are combined in the sign ($<>$) and the algebraic notation helps us to formulate what a standard sentence could not: how, after all, could we reconcile the two contrary propositions 'I want to extract something from the body of the other' and 'I want to push myself into the body of the other'? Lacan's solution to the logic of this problem at the end of the 1950s is basically a structuralist one. If it is impossible to formulate a signification as a proposition or as a sentence, it must be formulated as a relation. This is exactly the sense of the ($<>$), which sets out a relation between terms which includes a sign to index the relation of being contrary ($<>$).

I'll stop there.

KLEIN'S VIEWS ON SEXUALITY
WITH PARTICULAR REFERENCE TO FEMALE SEXUALITY

Jane Temperley

I became interested in the subject of Klein's views on women's psychosexual development when addressing another day conference years ago. I was sharing the platform at a public lecture at the Institute of Psycho-Analysis with Juliet Mitchell Rossendale. Her position then was a Lacanian one and I recognised, as I listened to her, how close it was to Freud's classical position. I also recognised, with surprise, how at variance with that position was the tradition in which I had been analysed and trained in the British Society. The audience, many of whom had had analysis or supervision in the British Society, found my account much more familiar than Juliet's. I realised that I was ignorant of the history of the divergence in the 1920s and '30s between the British psychoanalysts (led by Jones) and the Viennese, on the subject of the phallic phase and female sexuality. I subsequently became particularly interested in Klein's contribution to that debate.

André Green recently gave a talk entitled 'Does Sexuality have anything to do with Psychoanalysis?' - a very provocative title. His contention was that the sexuality which was so central to Freud's position has been lost sight of. Object relations theorists, he seemed to imply, tend to regard the patient's sexuality as a surface matter beneath which lie other more important issues. I think this misrepresents the object relations position and in particular it misrepresents Klein's. Klein greatly elaborated Freud's and Abraham's insights about internal object relations, but she remained an instinct theorist. In her view instincts express themselves always in phantasies about objects and these phantasies then structure the inner world. Klein followed Freud in seeing human nature as struggling with the tension between the Life and Death Instincts, and sexuality as a prime expression of the Life Instinct.

Another prevalent misapprehension - sometimes more a caricature - of Klein's position is that Kleinian analysis is primarily concerned with the mother-child dyad. In fact, since she dates the Oedipus complex as occurring in the first year of life, she gives the Oedipal father a much earlier significance in the child's development than does Freud. Klein pioneered the psychoanalysis of very young children and in her accounts of their play she describes their intense preoccupation with their parents' sexuality and with their own.

Klein wrote two major papers on the Oedipus complex - one in 1928 elaborating her view of its early dating and a second in 1945, "The Oedipus complex in the Light of Early Anxieties". In this later paper she gives a useful review of her differences with Freud on this subject. After 1945 she does not write works explicitly on the subject of sexuality or sexual difference: her attention moves to other matters. Whatever her subject, however, the unconscious phantasies, whose vicissitudes she considers, are concerned centrally with the patient's own sexuality and with that of other people around him, representing that of the parents.

One of the issues which I think may differentiate a Kleinian from a Lacanian perspective is the notion of the state in which the infant's psyche enters the human scene. In the Kleinians' view, the infant brings with him, because of his instincts and the phantasies in relation to objects in which they are expressed, an *active* contribution to the inner world which he then develops and which forms the core of his psychic life. I get the impression from Lacanian writers that their view of the infant is of a more passive seeking to meet the desire of the mother.

Klein originally underestimated the role of parental wishes and projections. This has been subsequently redressed by her followers. There is inevitably projection by the parents and this does affect the infant. Klein stresses, however, that one comes into the world with intense drives, drives of such fierceness that they are dealt with by projection and result in distortion and an intensely active subjective construing of reality. The effect of a person's drives on their perception of and relationship to the world around them is a very active process.

The British view of female sexuality that I became aware of in myself when I was sitting on the platform with Juliet Mitchell Rossendale, was an unreflecting adherence to a view that was heavily influenced by Klein's work on child analysis: it was also seminally influenced by Jones's disagreement with Freud about the phallic phase. Until 1923 when he wrote "The Infantile Genital Organisation: an Interpolation into the Theory of Sexuality", Freud held two different views on the importance of castration anxiety and the sources of female psychosexual development. As late as 1919 in "A Child is Being Beaten" - the paper in which he placed the Oedipus complex in its nodal position as the nucleus of the neuroses - there is no mention at all of penis envy and no mention of castration. The girl is assumed quite unquestioningly to start off from the female position. By 1923 he had jettisoned that point of view and gave explanatory prominence to the theory of phallic monism - i.e. that children originally believe there is only one genital, the penis - that they divide the world into, on the one hand, those with a penis, and on the other hand, castrates. Jones held that such a childhood belief was defensive: that unconsciously children know of sexual difference and of its meaning.

Little Hans is the only child case study reported by Freud. Despite being misinformed about the origins of babies, Little Hans recognised a pregnancy when he saw one and therefore knew how his sister originated. Freud describes an excited exchange between Little Hans and his father about forbidden spaces and what fun it would be to break into them. Freud himself suggests that the child recognises from the prompting of his own genital that there must be a corresponding space into which he wishes to penetrate - that the boy is beginning to imagine a vagina. Chasseguet-Smirgel has made the point that if Little Hans can begin to imagine a vagina, then little girls who actually have such organs are even more likely to have at least latent and unconscious knowledge of the vagina. The positing of latent and unconscious knowledge of sexual organs is one of the crucial differences between Klein and Freud.

In the most extensive of his case studies, known popularly as the Wolf Man, Freud considers the effect on the young child of witnessing the primal scene and the evidence for this. Finally, however, he pronounces that it is irrelevant whether his patient did or did not witness it. Human beings, he states, are patterned, whether or not we see our parents in the sexual act, to phantasise such acts. Bion argued similarly that there are certain innate 'preconceptions' which become 'conceptions' when the infant encounters the corresponding external event. The readiness to apprehend and recognise sexual reality, the nature of the genitals and their procreative potential, is innate. This reality is also very disturbing and for that reason is heavily defended against. What may look like dismay at a new understanding of sexual difference and its function is in fact the conscious recognition of what was unconsciously recognised in infancy.

Klein dates the early stages of the Oedipus complex in the first year of life. She based this dating upon her observation of the history, the symptoms, the behaviour and the play of very young patients. Her patient Rita was two years old. Klein made her observations on the analysis of these children in the 1920s. Their play, their response to her and to her interpretations led her to state, and to demonstrate in her accounts of her clinical work, that these children's inhibitions and symptoms were the product of intense phantasies concerning their parents' sexual and procreative activities.

In the Kleinian view there is not only a readiness to apprehend parental sexuality but a phantasy in the child that parental sexuality is always associated with conception and the possibility of new babies. It is recognised as a procreative pairing and for that reason is especially envied and disturbing. It is envied because the child cannot produce babies. It is disturbing partly because the parents can and might produce new siblings, ousting the child from his former position and stirring further rivalry and hatred.

This emphasis on the central importance of Oedipal phantasies, which she traced back in her patients' histories to the first year of life, has tended to be overlooked in non-Kleinian accounts of her work. I think this is in part due to the prominence she also gives to the child's first relation - to the mother's breast.

It was not until late in his life that Freud recognised the importance of the child's relation to the mother as the first object, e.g. "Female Sexuality", 1931. The child's view of the mother, as understood by Klein, is akin to a cornucopia, the source of all that is most desirable, comforting, interesting and provocative.

The mother's body, whether the child is fed from the breast or from the bottle, is the source of comfort, food and life. It is upon the fate of the child's relation to this desired, envied and extremely powerful figure that his/her subsequent development depends.

One of the child's reactions to the mother may be the phantasy of fulfilling the mother's feminine desire by adopting the position of the male lover. Freud laid great emphasis upon this phantasy in girls and so, I think, does Lacan. For Klein it was only one of many possible phantasies which the child adopts to defend itself from Oedipal reality and pain.

In Klein's view the negotiations of the paranoid-schizoid position and the establishment, to some extent, of the depressive position, is crucial to the outcome of the Oedipus complex. The child needs the mother's help in withdrawing the projections which originally produce a split perception of her as, on the one hand, ideal and, on the other, wicked and persecuting. Klein stressed the importance of the child's wish to integrate and to repair the object. When the relation to the mother has this more integrated, repaired quality, then the transition to the second object, the father, can be made from a more depressive position.

Oedipal rivalry is then less disturbing because the internal relation to the mother is to an object loved and in turn loving, an object which may be hated but which can forgive and be forgiven and be repaired. Where the paranoid-schizoid position is carried over into the relation to the father, the danger is that one parent is idealised and the other demonised or denigrated. In Klein's 1945 paper "The

Oedipus complex in the Light of Early Anxieties" both the children she describes have idealised, protective views of their mothers but their fathers are seen as dangerous. The child's own destructiveness and consequent fears of retaliation are projected onto the father and the child is arrested in the situation of having to protect mother and to see male sexuality as bad.

Frequently with girls the position is the reverse of this. Father is seen as wonderful and mother is discounted or demonised. There is on the surface a very positive heterosexuality but the unconscious identification with the mother on whom the girl's development as a woman depends, is with a denigrated, excluded object. Chasseguet-Smirgel pointed out the effects of the experience shared by both women and men of the original dependence on the life-giving, life-sustaining mother. Such dependence stirs enormous ambivalence. The danger, she contends, is that both men and women, in order to counteract that enormous power, can over-emphasise the power and significance of the penis. Men and male functions are then seen as what is really interesting and important. A problem then for women is that our confidence in ourselves as women, in roles that are specifically female such as child bearing, depends on our unconscious identification with our own mothers. We may find ourselves back in the role we so despised in our mothers - a background figure doing the washing up.

In the case histories she used for her 1945 paper Klein demonstrated, particularly with Richard, how, by being able to take up in the transference the aggression toward the mother, she was able to help him feel less frightened of this aggression, and so to take back projections from his father which had made him a feared and hostile figure. She frees Richard to make a more confident and potent identification with his father and to be less apprehensive about his own masculinity. In Klein's view of the inner world, the father and his penis can be seen as having a particular capacity to restore the mother. Girls do envy what they perceive as the father's capacity to restore the mother both in the pleasure of the sexual act and by giving her babies. In that sense there is penis envy but it is no more and no less significant than the corresponding envy, exemplified in the case of Little Hans, that the little boy feels of the girl's procreative role and capacities.

What then has happened to the centrality of the castration complex? I think the Kleinian view is that there is a crisis of development, but that it is less to do with giving up the idea that girls might have a penis or that boys might lose theirs: it is instead to do with the relinquishment of infantile omnipotence. The infantile phantasies, of supplanting the Oedipal rival or of controlling the parent, need to be relinquished. Klein's linking of the depressive position with the negotiation of the Oedipus complex has been particularly clearly elaborated by Ronald Britton in "The Missing Link: Parental Sexuality in the Oedipus Complex". He stresses how psychic control of the parental couple needs to be abandoned and how the child needs to accept his position in a triangular situation where he has relationships with both parents but must be reconciled to an outside position in relation to their intercourse. The capacity to think and especially to think creatively depends on the internalisation of a creative parental couple and this is interfered with if omnipotent phantasies denying sexual and generational difference persist.

Three last points. Klein differs importantly from Freud on the history and nature of the female superego. She contends that the girl has unconscious knowledge both of the vagina and of her latent capacity to bear children, The girl child not only attacks her mother's sexuality and the unborn babies within her but has phantasies of the mother's talion response. The origins of the Superego are, in Klein's view, laid down in the earliest paranoid-schizoid relation to the breast and are in the girl just as formidable as in the boy.

Secondly, according to Freud, the psychosexual development of the girl is particularly precarious because she has to relinquish an original idea of herself as a little man in relation to her mother and to reconcile herself instead to acquiring the longed-for penis in intercourse with a man and especially in the birth of a male child. Klein, on the other hand, sees the particular difficulty of female development as lying in the mother being both the first, essential object and yet, even at such an early stage, the Oedipal rival. In Freud's 1931 paper, "Female Sexuality", he refers, as he often had before, to the particular hostility which characterises many mother/daughter relationships (he alludes elsewhere in this paper to Klein's "Early Stages of the Oedipus Conflict" of 1928). It is only in this one paper that he suggests that the mother/daughter relationship is especially fraught because the relation to the mother is so early and involves such primitive ambivalence. Freud then asks himself why sons do not feel such intense ambivalence towards their mothers and he answers his own question by referring to the Oedipal constellation - the son, unlike the daughter in that situation, can divert the negative feelings onto the father. The daughter in the positive Oedipus complex must cope with sexual rivalry with the woman who is also her primary object.

Lastly, Klein wrote about the effect that the largely hidden nature of the female genital had on the development of the girl. The girl, unlike the boy, cannot resort to the physical and visual examination of the genital to counteract phantasies of the effect of her various attacks upon the parents and their imagined reprisals. The girl is more at the mercy of her phantasies and this may contribute to a diffidence in adult women which reinforces disparagement from more obvious social forces.

THEORISING THE COMEDY OF SEXES: LACAN ON SEXUALITY

Dany Nobus

Sexualism and Subjectivism

In his preface to the fourth edition of the "Three Essays on the Theory of Sexuality", dated May 1920, Freud observed that one of the main stumbling-blocks of psychoanalysis for the public at large is 'its insistence on the importance of sexuality in all human achievements and the attempt that it makes at enlarging the concept of sexuality.'. (Freud. S. S.E.VII). Freud deplored the fact that some people had characterised psychoanalysis as 'pan-sexualism' and had blamed psychoanalysts for attributing every human phenomenon to a sexual conflict.[1] However, and in contrast to what could perhaps be expected, Freud did not raise any arguments to counter this alleged psychoanalytic claim of a ubiquitous sexuality. Instead, he argued that the active sexual element behind all human realisations was not introduced by psychoanalysis, since it had already been acknowledged by the philosophers, and by Arthur Schopenhauer in particular.[2] In the same vein, Freud stressed that the ones reproaching psychoanalysts with their being 'oversexed' seemed to forget that the hymn of praise towards the omnipresent Eros had already been sung by a philosopher as unsuspected as Plato.

So, Freud did not intend to show that his critics had misjudged the central position of sexuality in psychoanalytic theory. He did not try to revise the concept of 'enlarged sexuality', but merely indicated that the critique of 'pan-sexualism' could as easily have been directed towards some philosophers as it was now addressed to psychoanalysis. Still, Freud considered 'pan-sexualism' to be a 'senseless charge', which leaves us with the question as to why he could easily agree with the idea of an omnipresent sexuality on the one hand, and continue to refute the reduction of psychoanalysis to sexuality on the other hand. One possible reason for this could be that, for Freud, those who considered psychoanalysis as an 'all-sex'-discipline were neglecting an enormous field of human potential and psychoanalytic operation. Indeed, Freud's 1920 discovery was that Eros, however important its influence may be, is not the only driving force in man. For its reign is continuously challenged by an equally powerful factor, namely Thanatos. This postulate of the death drive, as a companion to the sexual drive, introduces yet another Freudian dualism - besides biology and psyche, constitution and accident, pleasure and reality, etc. - but it also provides a good reason for the impossibility of regarding psychoanalysis as a pan-sexual theory. However, Thanatos seemed an even harder nut to crack than Eros, especially for Freudian psychoanalysts themselves. In this respect, post-Freudians like Hartmann and Loewenstein who rejected the death drive and replaced it by an 'aggressive impulse', can be said to have contributed in their own way to a theoretical drift of psychoanalysis towards 'pan-sexualism', since they replaced the Freudian binary by a system of adaptive forces that work together rather than being in conflict.

A remarkably similar process has affected the theory of Lacan, not so much implicating the role of sexuality, but principally concerning the place of the subject. One of the most widespread ideas about the Lacanian theory of psychic (dys)functioning, is that the subject occupies a crucial place in it. Numerous introductions to the works of Lacan emphasise that his theory is a major attempt to centre psychoanalysis around the subject, as such comprising a massive crusade against the rules of social adaptation professed by the representatives of ego-psychology. Those of you who have read some of Lacan's work in the original will probably have found this assertion very convincing, for there is hardly a page in Lacan's body of work which does not deal with the question of the subject. There is a real proliferation of the subject in Lacan, just as sexuality is a ubiquitous element in Freud's writing. Therefore, the overall presence of the subject in Lacanian theory could easily be used to qualify his theory as 'pan-subjectivism'. More often however, it is used to criticise other theories by saying that these theories largely neglect the importance of the subject. The classical Lacanian critique of non-Lacanian psychoanalysis is simply that it disregards the subject.

Just as with the assertion that Freudian psychoanalysis is pan-sexualism, there are some problems connected with the claim that Lacanian psychoanalysis is 'pan-subjectivism'. Firstly, the ease with which Lacanian psychoanalysts sometimes peddle their theories on the subject is neither an indication of the clarity of the concept, nor of the rigour with which it is used. Usually, one finds the following definitions: i) the subject is divided; ii) the subject is the effect of the signifier; iii) the subject is that which is represented by a signifier for another signifier; and iv) the subject is the prime focus of psychoanalytic treatment. From a Lacanian point of view, all these definitions are quite correct, but they do not fit the requirements of a clearly defined, operationalised concept, as we should also not be satisfied with the definition of a psychoanalyst as someone who practises psychoanalysis as a result of doing psychoanalytic training. Hence, claiming that Lacanian theory is subjectivist, whereas other psychoanalytic theories are not, or perhaps are less so, at least requires some precise idea of what Lacan has filed under this category, insofar as we are allowed to talk of a category in the first place.

However, there is a second, and probably more significant reason why it is difficult to present Lacanian theory as a psychoanalytic theory of the subject. For, as is the case with those who consider Freudian psychoanalysis as 'pan-sexualism', this statement neglects a whole area of Lacan's theorisation. Indeed, just as there is another Freud - the 'Freud of Thanatos' beyond the 'Freud' of Eros - there is beyond the 'Lacan of the subject ', still another Lacan, namely the 'Lacan of the object'. And again, this other side is a harder nut to crack. One could say that the subject, which has always been strongly connected to the signifier, represents the bright, Apollonian side of the theory, whereas the object represents its dark, Dionysian side.[3] Lacanian formulae belonging to the first side are generally more easy to grasp - and have not provoked much protest - unlike those belonging to the second side. For example, the Lacan of the subject and the signifier says that the Unconscious is structured like a language and operates through the basic processes of metaphor and metonymy. However, the Lacan of the object says that Woman does not exist, that loving is to give what one does not have, and that there is no such thing as a sexual relationship. The latter formulae are far more provocative than the former and give more rise to vehement discussion. This is why the Lacan of the object, who is also the Lacan of sexuality, is often neglected in favour of the signifying dimension. When sexuality is at stake, Lacanian psychoanalysts too often satisfy themselves by 'subjectifying' the Freudian positions on sexuality, at the same time clearly neglecting Lacan's own highly original and controversial ideas. Therefore, since it is a more challenging assignment to discuss Freud on the death drive than Freud on sexuality, strictly speaking it is a greater challenge to deal with the Lacanian positions on sexuality, than with those on the subject.

Signifying Sexuality

In his seminar *La Relation d'Objet*, Lacan stated that what caused so much scandal in Freud's theory, was less that it put sexuality centre stage, than that it claimed that man's sexual life is anything but a naturally designed process towards the harmonious unification

of two bodies: 'Analysis set off from a notion of man's affective relations, which I shall call scandalous. I think that I have already
underlined many times what, in analysis, has elicited so much
scandal in the beginning. It is not so much the fact that it has valued the role of sexuality and that it has played a part in sexuality
becoming a commonplace - in any case, nobody thinks about being
offended by it anymore. But it is precisely that it introduces, together with this notion, and even more than this notion, its paradoxes,
i.e. that the approach of the sexual object presents an essential difficulty, which is of an internal order.' (Lacan 1994 p59 my translation)

With this 'internal, essential difficulty' concerning the approach
of the object, Lacan referred to Freud's section on 'The Finding of an
object' at the end of his "Three Essays on the Theory of Sexuality",
(S.E.VII pp222-230).   There, Freud put forward the fundamental
idea that 'the finding of an object is in fact a refinding of it.' (Ibid
p222).   Thus he emphasized that the sexual object chosen by a
human being from the years of puberty onwards is merely a
retrieval of something that was already there in an earlier period,
but which was lost in the course of psychic development.
Moreover, it is not a retrieval of the lost object as such, but merely
of a substitute. So, on the one hand the sexual object has nothing
new about it, since it is approached according to the model of a lost
object, and on the other hand it is also completely inadequate,
because it is different from the lost one. The persistence of the lost
object as a model for object-choice in later life, is ascribed by Freud
to the importance of the child's primary experience of satisfaction
at the mother's breast. The inadequacy of the retrieved object is
attributed to the incest barrier, which makes it compulsory for a
human being to replace the mother('s breast) by something else. In
his seminar *La Relation d'Objet*, Lacan identified this whole process
as an 'impossible repetition'. (Lacan 1994 p15) Apart from this context of the (re)finding of an object, the 'essential difficulty' in man's
sexual life also appears in at least two other aspects of Freud's theory. Firstly, it is well-known that Freud substituted for the tradi-
tional biological notion of the instinct the new bio-psychological
notion of the drive, which is designed as a dynamic paste-up of four
different components - the source, the pressure, the object and the
aim - of which the organisation does not follow preconceived, natural patterns. For this reason, Freud called the drive a *Partialtrieb*,
literally a partial drive, a drive which is not one. (Strachey translates *Partialtrieb* as 'component instinct'). The drive does not constitute a unity, but is part of a oneness which only comes into being
if all the 'partial drives' work together. In this way, harmony is not

inherent to the drive as such, but is something that is dependent upon external factors.

Here we touch upon the second aspect. Freud assumed that the essential chaos of the partial drives is responsible for an original polymorphous sexual disposition in every human being. During sexual development, this polymorphous perversity becomes organised and curtailed through the Oedipus and castration complexes. However, Freud had serious doubts that such a normalisation was altogether possible, despite his distinction between a pathological and a normal sexual life, and although he tried to account for the normal development of masculinity and femininity. So much can at least be inferred from the following gloss, taken from Lecture 21 of the *Introductory Lectures on Psycho-Analysis*, on *The Development of the Libido*: 'From this time onwards, the human individual has to devote himself to the great task of detaching himself from his parents, and not until that task is achieved can he cease to be a child and become a member of social community. For the son this task consists in detaching his libidinal wishes from his mother and employing them for the choice of a real outside love-object, and in reconciling himself with his father if he has remained in opposition to him, or in freeing himself from his pressure if, as a reaction to his infantile rebelliousness, he has become subservient to him. These tasks are set to everyone; and it is remarkable how seldom they are dealt with in an ideal manner - that is, in one which is correct both psychologically and socially.' (Freud 1916-17 p337)[4] In their theoretical descriptions, the Oedipus and castration complexes are abstract figures of how the psychic apparatus is constituted under ideal, normative circumstances, whereas the actual processes are far more diverse and less streamlined.

These are the basics of Freud's conception of a strictly problematic sexuality; Lacan first reformulates the Freudian position by 'signifying sexuality', i.e, by putting sexuality under the aegis of the signifier. This Lacanian reworking of Freudian sexuality takes place by means of several substitutions (metaphorisations) and radicalisations (metonymies). The first and foremost substitution concerns the replacement of the biological by the lingual and this manifests itself on at least two different levels.

Firstly, in Lacan's view the drive is not partly rooted in 'an endosomatic, continuously flowing source of stimulation' - as Freud thought - but it is entirely produced by the functioning of the signifier. For Lacan, the drive is no longer a concept on the frontier of the organic and the psychic, but a purely psychic representation that stems from the action of the signifier. How are we to understand this? Contrary to Freud, Lacan posits that the newborn child is not a barrel full of unorganized drives, but simply a being in need. Already in his article on *The Mirror-phase*, one can read that the child suffers from 'motor incapacity and nurseling dependency'. (Lacan 1966 p94) The child is not capable of living without being given the necessary protection by someone who is willing to do so. This primary need is certainly a biological one, but it is the only strictly biological dimension Lacan acknowledges. The mere intervention of the 'one who is willing to satisfy the child's need', already introduces a different dimension. For this 'one', let us say this 'Other', is not a constantly present agency whose only job is to satisfy needs. This Other is a cultural agency with particular needs, demands and desires of its own, beyond the satisfaction of needs. Lacan contends that this Other constitutes the first presence of the symbolic order, because it is generally an Other who is part of a spoken world, but also because it is an Other who comes and goes, who is alternately absent and present, just like the elements of the symbolic order.

The symbolic action of the Other produces a gap in the status of complete satisfaction. It introduces a rift in the blissful status of a child whose needs are continuously satisfied by an ever present and fully adequate object. Like Freud, who stated that the origin of the drive is to be situated in an erogenous zone characterized by an opening in the body's integrity, Lacan also points out that the drive emerges from a gap, but in his opinion it is a gap produced by the symbolic action of the Other. The most abstract description of this process is to be found in Lacan's *Subversion of the Subject and Dialectic of Desire*: 'But although our completed graph enables us to place the drive as the treasure of the signifiers, its notation as ($ <> D) maintains its structure by linking it with diachrony. It is that which proceeds from demand when the subject disappears in it (*s'y évanouit*). It is obvious enough that demand also disappears, with the single exception that the cut (*la coupure*) remains, for this cut remains present in that which distinguishes the drive from the organic function it inhabits: namely, its grammatical artifice, so manifest in the reversions of its articulation to both source and object - Freud is unfailingly illuminating on this matter.' (Lacan 1960 p314) The starting point is the Other's demand, which Lacan writes with a capital D, to indicate that the demand is always an expression of signifiers - the demand indeed being one of the fundamental channels through which the signifier operates. In this demand of the Other, the subject is fainting, i.e. an incomplete subject is produced. Since the Other is demanding, the original, fully satisfied subject has to experience a lack. The subject is affected in its status of full satisfaction, because the Other does not merely satisfy needs and this lack remains when the Other's demand is no longer there. Indeed, the disappearance of the Other's demand does not entail the disappearance of the lack. From this perpetual lack the drive proceeds.

You will probably notice that the Lacanian conception of the drive is not very different from the Freudian view on the refinding of the object. In both cases, a process aimed at satisfaction comes into operation and in both cases it is controlled by an original lack. However, whereas Freud grounds the drive on the object, e.g. the mother's breast, Lacan establishes the drive on the signifier, e g the demand of the Other. As a matter of fact, this is probably the reason why Lacan 'places the drive as the treasure of the signifiers'.[5] Instead of an organic function, or a biological object to which the drive relates, Lacan moreover indicates its 'grammatical artifice', which he infers from Freud's recourse to active and passive tenses in *Instincts and their Vicissitudes,* in order to describe the drive's performance. (Freud 1915 pp 109-140)[6]

This specific cutting operation of the signifier on an existing harmonious condition, also appears on a second level. If the first level has to do with the relation between the child as a being in need, and the mother as a demanding Other, the second level has to do with the relation between a presupposed mother-child unity and the castrating father. In fact, this is Lacan's reworking of the Freudian Oedipus and castration complexes, and once again the basic principle consists of a substitution for the biological by the lingual. In Freudian terms, the male child has the task to give up his love relationship with his mother and to choose a love-object outside the community of family-members by identifying with the father. In Lacanian terms this decline of the Oedipus complex through the operation of the father's castration threat, has nothing to do with a certain social interaction between biological family members. The father at work is not a real father, a point which is stressed by Lacan in, for example, his seminar on *The Psychoses*: 'The notion of the father can only be supposed as provided with an entire series of signifying connotations which give it existence and consistency and which are a very long way indeed from merging with those of the genital, from which it is semantically different across all the linguistic traditions. [...] We're not here to develop all the facets of this function of the father, but I am pointing out one of the most striking of them, which is the introduction of an order, of a mathematical order, whose structure is different from the natural order.' (Lacan

(1955-56 [1993] p320).

It is important to observe that Lacan talks about the 'notion' and the 'function' of the father, and not, for instance, about the 'father figure'.[7] The reason is that a father figure should not be present for the Oedipus complex to unroll. In fact, for Lacan, there are no Oedipus and castration complexes whatsoever in the bio-psychological sense that Freud developed. For Lacan, castration represents the introduction of sexual difference and of the genealogical order in an undifferentiated condition, through the intervention of the symbolic law, which is the Oedipus complex itself. In his seminar *La Relation d'Objet*, Lacan stated: 'castration is essentially connected with a symbolic order as it is founded, and which comprises a long coherence, from which the subject in no way can be isolated. The connection between castration and the symbolic order is made clear by all our previous reflections, as well as by this simple remark - in Freud, from the beginning, castration has been connected with the central position that is given to the Oedipus complex, with the essential element of articulation for the entire evolution of sexuality. If I have written *symbolic debt* on the blackboard, it is because the Oedipus complex comprises from this very moment in itself, and fundamentally, the notion of the law, which can absolutely not be eliminated from it.'[8] In this way, castration is portrayed as a specific lack of object, which is the result of the intervention of the symbolic order and its cultural law. Lacan calls this lack of object a 'symbolic debt', by which he put forward that the symbolic order installs rules and regulations that can never be paid off by the subject. In other words, being subjected to the cultural law comprises the gift of subjectivity, but this produces at the same time a lack, because for this present, one cannot give anything adequate in return. On the contrary, the gift of subjectivity itself is based on the loss of an unclouded existence, due to cultural prohibitions, which means that settling one's debts would rather imply taking things back, than giving something in return.

Hence, the Freudian Oedipus and castration complexes are in Lacan's view disconnected from a certain family dynamics, and transferred to the dynamics of nature and culture in general. Furthermore, the operation of the cultural law produces castration indeed, but it is a castration that has nothing to do with the cutting of penises anymore. Castration is now the production of a gap, which is the result of the action of the symbolic on a unitary condition. The symbolic cuts something away, which is what Lacan calls *jouissance*. Applied to the operation of cultural laws, one could say that a human being has to hand in jouissance, if he or she wants to be part of culture. To enter the kingdom of culture, one has to leave one's jouissance at the gates. A culture cannot tolerate elements whose only business is to enjoy. It requires elements to be engaged, to be productive, to be relating to others in order to achieve a higher, unselfish goal. Culture puts a strain on sexuality, saying that is forbidden to have sex and nothing else, and saying that sex is limited to a certain number of actions with a particular sort of objects. In this way, sexuality becomes signified; it becomes an experience that is fundamentally connected with a prohibition and that is essentially characterized by a loss of jouissance.

Sexualizing the Signifier

Through the action of the function of the father, sexuality not only becomes signified for the subject, but the signifier also becomes sexualised. The final part of Lacan's metaphor of the Name-of-the-Father, as produced in *On a Question Preliminary to any Possible Treatment of Psychosis*, reads that the phallus is given a place under the Other as a result of the Name-of-the-Father. Again, Lacan emphasizes that the absence of a real father is perfectly compatible with the presence of the signifier.[9] But what exactly is this inscription of the phallus under the Other? In 'The Meaning of the Phallus', Lacan gives what is probably the most trenchant definition of the phallus: 'In Freudian doctrine, the phallus is not a fantasy, if what is understood by that is an imaginary effect. Nor is it as such an object (part, internal, good, bad, etc.) in so far as this term tends to accentuate the reality involved in a relationship. It is even less the organ, penis or clitoris, which it symbolises. And it is not incidental that Freud took his reference for it from the simulacrum which it represented for the Ancients. For the phallus is a signifier, a signifier whose function in the intrasubjective economy of analysis might lift the veil from that which it served in the mysteries.'[10] So, the phallus is not a fantasy, neither an object, nor an organ, but a signifier. It is a very special signifier though, and it seems that its function in psychoanalysis can teach us something about its function in the classical mysteries.[11] But what is this function of the phallus? According to Lacan, the function of the phallus is to pass for the signifier of the desire of the Other. As such, the phallus is inscribed in the Other as something which is inaccessible. Analogously to what is at stake in the mysteries, one could say that the phallus is the signifier that is hidden under a veil and around which the ritual of initiation is conducted. The organization of the signifiers, the ritualised, culturalised relations between the signifiers presuppose a special signifier that can be considered their organising principle. As such, the phallus is also the principle of difference. On a strictly linguistic level, it is only possible to organise the elements of a sentence because there is some space between them. If all elements in a system were the same, there would be no dynamic organisation. There can only be a dynamic organisation if the elements differ from each other and to differ, it suffices that they are separated by an interspace.

When Lacan says that the Name-of-the-Father gives a place to the phallus under the Other, this proposition can be interpreted as indicating that cultural laws inscribe the principle of difference within the Other. On a sexual level, this means that culture determines the difference between man and woman in language. In this respect, we see that Lacan defines man and woman in a different way than Freud. For Freud, man and woman largely remain biological categories, whereas for Lacan, man and woman are strictly signifiers, whose interrelations depend on a difference inscribed in language, through a process of culturalisation. For Freud, man and woman are largely determined by having or not having a penis. In Lacan's theorisations at the end of the 1950s, a human being's relationship to the phallus is considered crucial for the installation of the sexes. For Lacan, man and woman are indeed determined by the relationship to the principle of difference: 'But simply by keeping to the function of the phallus, we can pinpoint the structures which will govern the relations between the sexes. Let us say that these relations will revolve around a being and a having which, because they refer to a signifier, the phallus, have the contradictory effect of on the one hand lending reality to the subject in that signifier, and on the other making unreal the relations to be signified.'[12] The 'contradictory effect' has to do with the fact that being or having the phallus is a way to transform one's subjectivity into a meaningful reality, which is only possible by dressing up the existing subjective reality. Having the phallus is only possible by means of an 'appearing' (*paraître*). A subject can only act *as if* it possesses the phallus, by putting up a certain show. This can give the subject a phallic reality, but it is impossible for this reality to replace the existing one, for it is a mere simulacrum. Likewise, being the phallus is only realized through 'masquerade' (*mascarade*), which also functions as a kind of embellished veil - giving the impression of reality, but in fact being only a semblance.[13]

Continuing his train of thought in "The Meaning of the Phallus", Lacan suggests that when a woman enters into a relationship with a man, she depends upon the dynamics of being, whereas a man, in his relation to a woman, is dependent on the dynamics of having: 'Paradoxical as this formulation might seem, I would say that it is in order to be the phallus, that is to say, the signifier of the desire of the Other, that the woman will reject an essential part of her femininity, notably, all its attributes through masquerade. It is for what she is not that she expects to be desired as well as loved. But she finds the signifier of her own desire in the body of the one to whom she addresses her demand for love.'[14] In contrast to what feminists might perhaps understand, this does not mean that men are better off than women, the former having something the latter do not have, and the latter only being a phallic object in the eyes of the former. Lacan's statement merely implies that men and women are without common measure. Men are relying on the experience of possessing and not-possessing, and in this respect on being affected by difference. Women however are relying on the experience of being, and in this respect on being different. Therefore, a man is doomed to experience a woman as fundamentally inaccessible, while he is doing his utmost best to reduce his own difference and to present something to her of which he not only thinks that it is part of him, but also that she is interested in it. Therefore, a woman is doomed to experience a man as fundamentally deficient - he will never be as she would like him to be - while she is doing her utmost best to be as inaccessible as possible and to present something to him of which she not only thinks that it is really herself, but also that he is interested in it. Of course, the result is that the relation between the sexes is something very strange and at times highly funny. And this is probably the reason why Lacan, again in "The Meaning of the Phallus", writes that 'the ideal or typical manifestations of behaviour in both sexes, up to and including the act of sexual copulation, are entirely propelled into comedy.'[15]

Introducing the Object

Summarising our argument until now, we can say that Lacan introduces the signifier within the field of 'enlarged sexuality' conceptualised by Freud, and in this way reinterprets the notion of the drive, as well as the Oedipus and castration complexes from a lingual, symbolic, cultural point of view. The consequences of this reinterpretation are at least threefold:-

i) the problematic aspect of human sexuality becomes a structural, irreducible datum, considering the prohibition weighing on jouissance;

ii) man and woman are connected with the phallus as the principle of difference and therefore are implied in a relationship with something that is not 'available' as such;

iii) sexual relations are essentially based on a profound misunderstanding of subjective interests and ambitions by the ones involved.

The last consequence brings us to one of Lacan's epoch-making, though highly uncomfortable formulae of his later period, i.e. that there is no sexual relation[16]. How are we to understand this? Let us perhaps first try to explain what in our opinion should not be understood. Firstly, we should probably not understand this formula as the assertion that there is no such thing as sexual behaviour. Such an interpretation would turn Lacan into a complete idiot, for if we look around us it seems that the world is full of sexual behaviour. Furthermore, from a psychoanalytic point of view it seems that there is hardly any behaviour which is not sexual, for Freud has drawn attention to the fact that much behaviour that is apparently not sexual, insofar as it does not involve an obvious functioning of the sexual organs, is nevertheless sexual in nature. This is exactly Freud's definition of an 'enlarged sexuality'. Two copulating bodies are behaving sexually, but the same sexual element for example lies behind the transference that binds an analysand to the analyst. Secondly, we should probably not understand Lacan's formula as the assertion that there is no such thing as relationships. In fact, in the seventh chapter of the seminar *Encore*, entitled *A Love Letter*, Lacan points out that a speaking being is involved in at least three relationships. The first relationship is the one with the phallus, which is a privileged signifier because it is the signifier of difference. The second relationship is the one with a common signifier, belonging to the Other as language structure. At this point Lacan emphasizes that the language structure is always somehow lacking, making it possible for a speaking being to relate to a signifier of the Other, but not to the Other as a whole - precisely because there is no whole Other. In other words, there is a hole in the Other and therefore we cannot say the whole truth and nothing but the truth, neither about the Other, nor about ourselves. The consequence is that we can relate to and even identify with a signifier, e.g. the signifier 'mother', but not with language as a whole. The third relationship is the one with the object Lacan calls 'the object *a*'. This object *a* is a central concept of Lacanian psychoanalysis, but as is the case with many other Lacanian concepts, it is quite difficult to explain. On many occasions Lacan has indicated that the object *a* is at the same time a substitute object, the cause of desire and something intimately connected with jouissance. One way to understand this, is that the object *a* comes to fill the gap created by the operation of the signifier. We have explained above that the signifier is reponsible for a loss of jouissance, i.e. that it produces a cut in a presupposed original state of jouissance. In Freudian terms, the father bars the child's access to the mother as a sexual object and in this way deprives the child of a piece of jouissance. The object *a* is the substitute object for this lost piece of jouissance. In this way, it can temporarily restore the original experience of jouissance, but the problem is that it can never reinstall the original object. object *a* is an Ersatz; it is an object that is 'refound' but which can never adequately replace the original one. This is probably the reason why Lacan, in his later works, conceptualizes object *a* as 'plus-de-jouir', an object that is at the same time the supplier of *more jouissance* (than before) - because it replaces a loss - and the realization of *no jouissance anymore*, because it is only a substitute. This is probably also the reason why Lacan continues to consider object *a* as cause of desire. Object *a* will never be an adequate object; it will never provide complete satisfaction.

The function of object *a* can be illustrated by elaborating on the story of the highwayman who asks his victim: 'Your money or your life?'. In his seminar *The Four Fundamental Concepts of Psychoanalysis*, Lacan considers this to be an alienating choice, because the question does not present genuine alternatives.[17] If the victim chooses money, the highwayman will take her or his life, and even if he left the money after having taken the life, the victim will not be able to enjoy the money anymore. So, the victim is in a certain sense obliged to choose to live and leave the money behind. This is another example of the necessity to leave a piece of jouissance behind, in order to be able to live. Of course, after the victim has left money behind, he or she can try to repair the loss by accumulating new amounts of money, but this new capital will never be able to take the place of the old and lost capital. The new capital allows the victim to enjoy again, but it will not stop causing desire, because of the awareness that it is strictly not the same as what was left behind, and because of the awareness that, since lives can depend on money due to the highwaymen on the road, it can never be enough. This new capital, this substitute money could be called a figuration of what Lacan considers the object *a*.

Now let us return to Lacan's formula that there is no sexual relation. Since there are sexual behaviours and since there are relationships between speaking beings, signifiers and objects, what can this formula mean? Lacan himself gives some indications in his seminar *Encore*. For example, in the third lesson on *The Function of Writing*, he states that there is no sexual relation because it is impossible to write down a proportion between the sexes: 'If the worst comes to the worst, one could write *x R y*, and say that *x* is man, *y* is woman, and *R* is the sexual relation. Why not? Well lo and behold, it is a stupidity, because what is supported under the function of the signifier, of *man* and *woman*, are merely signifiers that are fully connected to the *courcourant* use of language current in courting."[18] Indeed we know that, on a strictly linguistic level, there is no way to write a privileged relationship between signifiers. It is essential to language that signifiers circulate and that they can be used in an unlimited set of combinations. Some new combination of signifiers is even considered poetry. In other words, between signifiers there is no such thing as a privileged, standard or ideal relationship; between signifiers there is nothing but difference, which accounts for the possibility of their being engaged in an infinite number of combinations. The same conclusion Lacan draws for the signifiers of the sexes. Between man and woman, there is no standard relationship, but only difference, which is responsible for the possibility of an infinite set of combinations - between man and woman, but also among men and among women. In other words, between man and woman, everything is possible because nothing is standard.

Lacan does not restrict himself to this fundamental statement of impossibility. He also tries to elaborate on the nature and the organisation of what is still happening between man and woman. In this respect, he claims: 'Since this is thus duplicated by the signifier on which basically it does not even depend, so it only ever relates as a partner to the object *a* inscribed on the other side of the bar. It can never reach its sexual partner, which is the Other, except by way of mediation, as the cause of its desire.'[19] What he aims at here, is that the impossibility of the sexual relationship can be masked by the introduction of an object. This does not mean that the impossibility is no longer there, but simply that it is no longer felt, due to the introduction of a mediating element that actually creates the illusion of a relationship. For a human being who is strictly adhering to the phallic principle, this object is nothing else than the famous object *a*.

To illustrate this, we can refer to what is enacted between Alcibiades and Socrates in Plato's *Symposium*. As far as Alcibiades is concerned, one does not have to be acquainted with the Lacanian propositions on having and appearing as the phallus, to perceive him as a phallic figure. Plutarch for example described Alcibiades as a cruel and merciless warrior, who played an active part in the genocide at Melos of 426 BC, and who caused great scandal in

Athens by begetting a child to a Melosian woman who was imprisoned after the assassination of her husband.[20] In his *Memoirs of Socrates*, Xenophon reported: 'Alcibiades [...] was courted because of his good looks by many women of rank, and, because of his prestige in the city and among the allies, he was pampered by many influential men and held in honour by the people, and enjoyed an easily won supremacy.'[21] Still according to Xenophon, Socrates' accuser considered Alcibiades as 'the most dissolute and arrogant of all the democrats.'[22] But see what fascinates him in the figure of Socrates! Not the reflection of his own image, but something else, namely that Socrates is hiding a little shining gem in the depth of his body. Behind the hideous figure of Socrates, Alcibiades locates an undefinable, elusive object, that never shows its nature, nor the material from which it is built. Alcibiades cannot define this object, but he sees that it shines and this makes Socrates extremely attractive to him. Of course, one could say that all of this is Alcibiades' fantasy and precisely so. It is in Alcibiades' fantasy that Socrates is granted the place of object, or, in other words, it is not Socrates as a speaking being who is involved, but merely the object that he is supposed to possess.

For a human being who is not strictly adhering to the phallic principle - and for Lacan this is characteristic of woman - the element mediating in the relationship between the sexes, is not an object, but a signifier.[23] This can be whatever signifier is available, and as such also the phallus. In the latter case, a feminine speaking being can engage in some kind of sexual behaviour with another speaking being and bridge the gap between them, by introducing the signifier of power and strength and by glorifying the difference between them. To illustrate this, we can once again refer to Plato's *Symposium*. Indeed, it is not only Socrates who is attractive for Alcibiades, but Socrates himself is attracted to another man, namely Agathon. As far as Socrates is concerned, nobody will doubt that he cannot be considered as the incarnation of the phallic ideal. It is even extremely difficult to consider Socrates to be the incarnation of anything whatsoever. In his seminar on *Transference*, Lacan says that Socrates is 'Atopos, an unclassifiable case, not to be situated.'[24] However, it is not because Socrates is not to be classified, or because he does not follow any category of people, that he is not involved in any sexual behaviours with other speaking beings. For Socrates, it is Agathon who is the chosen one. But here we should dare to ask ourselves why. Why would a speaking being, who is situated beyond any category, be attracted to a poet and a playwright like Agathon? Is it because Agathon had something shining for

Socrates, like he himself had for Alcibiades? Socrates does not say so, and Agathon was moreover a rather poor artist. In this respect, Lacan says that Agathon is a tragic poet, because he is only capable of producing very low quality verse.[25] In general, Agathon was not very bright. So what could have been so attractive in Agathon for Socrates then? There seems to be only one answer: difference. For Socrates, Agathon is draped in difference, for he is a playwright who has a particular place in society, who is not hostile towards philosophers as was the case with other playwrights, and who has even managed to gain recognition by producing an inferior kind of poetry. It is this difference which allows Socrates to be attracted to Agathon.

These are two situations, taken from the same classical text, to illustrate how speaking beings only relate to each other by the introduction of something that bridges the gap between them; we have deliberately chosen to explain these mechanisms by making use of relations between biological men only. Indeed, if Lacan says that from the perspective of a woman the phallus functions as a mediating agency between the sexes, this has nothing to do with biological females. It is a mechanism that can very easily come into operation between biological males, as is precisely the case in Plato's *Symposium*.

Sexuality in Clinical Practice

There is certainly a lot more to be said about these mechanisms, e.g. concerning the way in which they relate to jouissance, but we would like to conclude with some suggestions for dealing with sexuality in a clinical practice that is based on a Lacanian point of view.

A first directive for the treatment that can be inferred from these principles of sexuality, concerns the analytic repudiation of a hierarchical system of object-relations. In his seminar *La Relation d'Objet*, Lacan criticizes the object-relations theory of Maurice Bouvet, who roughly distinguished between two kinds of persons, pre-genital and genital ones. According to Bouvet, genitally functioning persons are in many ways superior to non-genital ones, among other things because their object-relations are more stable and they encounter less psychic problems. Conversely, persons with psychic problems are considered to suffer mainly from immature, non-genital object-relations. The consequence is that the analytic process is basically directed at the transformation of the patient's existing object-relations into more mature, genital relations.

Perhaps this seems to be an exceedingly simple line of reasoning, but it is still quite current in the practice of behavioural therapists and of psychoanalysts. In many countries, sex offenders are often treated by aversion therapy, in which an existing sexual practice - let us say transvestism - is first unlearnt and subsequently supplemented by the stimulation of genital and preferably heterosexual 'arousal'. Many psychoanalysts too consider genitality to be the ultimate realisation of a person's love life and the definite answer to a problematic sexuality. From a Lacanian point of view, there is no superiority of genitality, because genital sex is no less problematic than non-genital sex. On the contrary, perhaps genital sex is in itself more problematic than non-genital sex, because it comprises the most sustained illusion that there is indeed a sexual relationship. Thus, Lacanian psychoanalysis is not aimed at giving someone access to 'genital object-relations', if she or he has been keeping away from them, because genitality is everything but a benefit as far as psychic health and relational harmony are concerned.

For Lacan there is nothing to be written on the genital level and therefore nothing to presuppose, nothing to introduce and nothing to change. What *can* be written are the relations between a speaking being and the signifier, the phallus as its organizing principle, and the object *a*. The first relationship concerns the subject, the second concerns sexuation and the third concerns the fantasy and jouissance. These are the fundamental topics of a Lacanian psychoanalytic experience. On the first level, the one of the subject, the Lacanian analyst aims at something that is precisely the reverse of that what is aimed at by the ego-analyst. A Lacanian analysis is not directed at the construction of a strong ego, but at the deconstruction of the imaginary, alienating identifications through which the ego of the patient has been erected. A Lacanian analysis is not aimed at the better adaptation of the patient to his outside world, but at a disadaptation from the rusted lifestyle he or she has developed over the years. The idea is that with the identifications deconstructed and the lifestyle disadapted, the patient is given the possibility to start something new, in accordance with his or her desire. On the second level, the one of the phallus, a Lacanian analysis gives special weight to the fundamental question of gender, 'what does it mean for me to be masculine, feminine, both, or neither ?'. It is not the analyst's objective to make a man more masculine and a woman more feminine, but to allow the patient to find out in what way, for example, she established her femininity - on the basis of what kind of identifications - and what this femininity means to her. On the third level, and this is both the most important and the most difficult one, a patient is supposed to deal with his or her fantasy and with jouissance. This is probably the most difficult level, for two reasons. Firstly, the fantasy and jouissance are extremely difficult to bring into words. In fact, it is perhaps strictly impossible to do so, because the fantasy and jouissance have no strict symbolic contents. Their nature is mainly imaginary as far as the fantasy is concerned, and real as to jouissance. Secondly, to put the fantasy and jouissance under the power of words, implies that one is obliged to leave some parts behind, which entails another loss.

For all of this, we would like to characterise the process of Lacanian analysis by means of another of those formulae, which have always been so dear to Lacan. Analysis is gaining nothing and losing a lot. One loses plenty of money, sometimes plenty of time, but also the illusions of things that one has never possessed and *will* never possess: oneself, the Other and everything in between.

[1] The prominence of sexuality in Freudian doctrine had of course been one of the major points of dissension for Adler and Jung, who both developed a largely desexualised theory of psychoanalysis.

[2] In a letter to Lou-Andreas Salomé dated August 1, 1919, Freud wrote that he had started to read the work of Schopenhauer, in accordance with his recent interest in the theme of death. However, Freud did not discover the philosopher's ideas on sexuality during that particular period, for the reference to Schopenhauer's views on sexuality is already present in *A Difficulty in the Path of Psycho-Analysis*, which was published in 1917. In a remarkably detailed study of Freud's tributes to Schopenhauer, Paul-Laurent Assoun has shown that what Freud probably had in mind when he referred to the philosopher's emphasis on sexuality, is a passage from *Metaphysik der Liebe*, a supplement to Schopenhauer's magnum opus *Die Welt als Wille und Vorstellung* (1819), in which he stated that "the sexual instinct in general is merely the will to live." Assoun has also cogently put an argument for the proposition that Schopenhauer constitutes the "ideological model" of Freud's relationship with philosophy in general, i e that Freud read many philosophical works through Schopenhauer's perspective. Cf. E. Pfeiffer (Ed.), *Sigmund Freud and Lou Andreas-Salomé: Letters* (translated by William and Elaine Robson-Scott) (1966), London, Hogarth and the Institute of Psycho-Analysis, 1972, p 99; P-L Assoun, *Freud, la philosophie, et les philosophes*, Paris, PUF, coll. «Quadrige», 1995, pp 225-272 and pp 238-241 in particular.

[3] In a lecture at the First International Meeting of the Freudian Field in Caracas, 1980, Jacques-Alain Miller compared the reduction of Lacanian theory to the play of signifiers with the desexualisation of the libido by Jung: 'What else has happened with Lacan? Why have the philosophers, the men of letters, who have read Lacan and who have learnt from him to decipher Freud, exalted metonymy so much? Let us be clear: Proceeding from Lacan, they have found a way to desexualise desire. Yes, Lacan has been turned into a new Jung, the Jung of the signifier.' In our view, there is no reason to believe that psychoanalysts are exempt from producing this kind of reduction. Why would a psychoanalyst,

even a Lacanian one, be less reluctant to address the object than the philosopher or the man of letters? In *Television*, Lacan himself recalled that his Seminar on Anxiety and the object *a* affected his audience so much 'that someone from my circle got dizzy to the point (a repressed dizziness) of almost dropping - in the form of such an object - me.' To us, there is also no reason to believe that the subject is not implied in these kinds of reductive readings of Lacan. In contrast to the Lacanian object *a*, the subject is part of philosophical discourse, which makes it hard to believe that philosophers would only consider the Lacanian signifier, without dealing with the subject. J.-A. Miller, *D'un autre Lacan, Ornicar?*, janvier 1984, no 28, p 55 (our translation); J Lacan, *Television. A Challenge to the Psychoanalytic Establishment*, (Edited by Joan Copjec, translated by Denis Hollier, Rosalind Krauss and Annette Michelson), New York NY-London, W W Norton & Co, 1990, p 21.

[4]For a further comment on this passage in the context of Freud's theory on sexual development, see J Brenkman, *Straight, Male, Modern. A Cultural Critique of Psychoanalysis*, New York NY-London, 1993, pp 1-11.

[5]In the completed graph of desire in *Subversion of the Subject and Dialectic of Desire*, both the Other (A) and the drive (D) are directly connected with each other, from the lower level to the upper level.

[6] In his Seminar *The Four Fundamental Concepts of Psychoanalysis*, of 1964, Lacan elaborates on this particular interpretation of the Freudian drive, but without referring to his formula of 1960. Cf. J Lacan, *The Seminar, Book XI: The Four Fundamental Concepts of Psychoanalysis* (1964), Edited by J-A Miller, Translated by A Sheridan, Harmondsworth Middlesex, Penguin, 1994, pp 161-186.

[7]This is certainly not the only passage from the seminar in which Lacan insists on the importance of the 'function' of the father. In one of the previous lessons, he had stated quite significantly: '- there has to be a law, a chain, a symbolic order, the intervention of the order of speech, that is, of the father. Not the natural father, but what is called the father. The order that prevents the collision and explosion of the situation as a whole is founded on the existence of this Name-of-the-Father.' The notion of the 'Name-of-the-Father' was introduced by Lacan in a 1953 lecture entitled *The Neurotic's Individual Myth* and it appeared again in the famous *Rome Discourse* of the same year. It will gain full conceptual status in the years following the seminar on psychoses. Cf. J Lacan, *The Seminar, Book III, The Psychoses*, (1955-56) [1993], p 96; J Lacan, The Neurotic's Individual Myth (translated by M Noel Evans), *The Psychoanalytic Quarterly*, 1979, XLVIII, no 3, pp 405-425 & p 423 in particular; J Lacan, The Function and Field of Speech and Language in Psychoanalysis (1953), *Ecrits. A Selection*, p 67.

[8]J Lacan, *La Relation d'Objet*, p 61 (our translation). Some thirteen years later, in the seminar *L'Envers de la Psychanalyse*, Lacan returned to these formulations on castration, in order to relate them to his discourse theory. At that moment he also admitted that the Freudian Oedipus complex is strictly unusable. Cf. J Lacan, *L'envers de la psychanalyse* (1969-1970), texte établi par J-A Miller, Paris, du Seuil, 1991, pp 99-154 and p 113 in particular.

[9]J Lacan, On a Question Preliminary to any Possible Treatment of Psychosis (1957-1958), *Ecrits. A Selection*, p 200.

[10]J Lacan, "The Meaning of the Phallus" (1958), in J Mitchell & J Rose (Eds.), *Feminine Sexuality. Jacques Lacan and the Ecole freudienne*, New York NY-London, W W Norton & Co,

1982, pp 79-80.

[11]For discussions of Lacan's reference to the phallus in the mysteries, and more specifically in the fresco of the Villa dei Misteri, see C Hoffmann, "Mystérion, les deux jouissances", *Apertura*, 1991, V, pp 33-36; K Silverman, "The Lacanian Phallus", *Differences. A Journal of Feminist Cultural Studies*, 1992, IV, no 1, pp 84-115; B Benvenuto, *Concerning the Rites of Psychoanalysis, or the Villa of the Mysteries*, Cambridge, Polity, 1994, pp 129-146; D Nobus, El pudor ¿Un afecto feminino?, *Uno por Uno. Revista Mundial de Psicoanálisis*, 1993, no 37, pp 5-10. Freud's 'reference to the simulacrum' can be found for instance in S Freud, The Acquisition and Control of Fire (1932), *Standard Edition* XXII, pp 183-193.

[12]J Lacan, "The Meaning of the Phallus", op. cit. pp 83-84.

[13]For a further discussion of the dynamics of having and being in relation to the phallus, see P Adams, Waiving the Phallus, *Differences. A Journal of Feminist Cultural Studies*, 1992, IV, no 1, pp 76-83; C Soler, Qu'est-ce que l'inconscient sait des femmes?, *Psychoanalytische Perspektieven*, 1994, no 23, pp 25-35.

[14]J Lacan, "The Meaning of the Phallus", op.cit., p 84.

[15]Ibid., p.84

[16]Cf. for example J Lacan, *Encore* (1972-1973), texte établi par J-A Miller, Paris, du Seuil, 1975, passim; J Lacan, *Television*, op.cit., p 8; J Lacan, L'Etourdit, *Scilicet*, 4, 1973, no 4, pp 11, 20, 30 & 47.

[17]Cf. J Lacan, *The Four Fundamental Concepts of Psychoanalysis*, pp 203-215. See also J Lacan, Position of the Unconscious (1964) (translated by B. Fink), in R Feldstein, B Fink & M Jaanus (Eds), *Reading Seminar XI. Lacan's Four Fundamental Concepts of Psychoanalysis*, New York NY, State University of New York Press, 1995, pp 259-282 and pp 268-270 in particular.

[18]J. Lacan, *Encore*, p.36 (our translation).

[19]J. Lacan, *A Love Letter* , p 151. This statement is part of Lacan's gloss on the table with the 'formulae of sexuation'. For some recent discussions of these formulae, see: G. Morel, Conditions Féminines de Jouissance, *La Cause freudienne. Revue de Psychanalyse*, 1993, No. 24, pp 96-106; J. Copjec, Sex and the Euthanasia of Reason, in *Read my Desire. Lacan against the Historicists*, Cambridge MA-London, MIT, 1994, pp 201-236; E. Ragland, *Essays on the Pleasures of Death. From Freud to Lacan*, New York NY-London, Routledge, 1995, pp197-200.

[20]Plutarch, *Life of Alcibiades*, Oxford, Loeb Classical Library, 1941, 17.4-5.

[21]Xenophon, Memoirs of Socrates 1.2.19-27 (translated by H Tredennick & R Waterfield), in *Conversations of Socrates*, Harmondsworth Middlesex, Penguin Classics, 1990.

[22]Ibid., 1.2.8-19.

[23]This is not contradictory with the earlier statement that woman enters into a relationship with a man by being the phallus, since this assertion of woman being 'not-all' in the phallic domain, has nothing to do with the way she behaves and manifests herself for a man. It rather has to do with the feminine position in relation to jouissance.

[24]J Lacan, *Le Séminaire, Livre VIII, Le transfert* (1960-1961), texte établi par J-A Miller, Paris, du Seuil, 1991, p 126 (our translation).

[25]I bid, pp 129-130.

DISCUSSION OF PAPERS ON SEXUALITY

Audrey Cantlie: In listening to these two speakers, I have the same impression today that I had gained listening to previous dialogues between Kleinians and Lacanians. Jane Temperley reminded me of a woman who has just come in from the garden covered with earth. She knows the Latin names of the flowers to which she refers occasionally but her knowledge and experience is rooted in the plants she has been dealing with. When I listen to Dany Nobus, he reminded me of a man who works in a library reading books, in fact only one book - the book of Lacan, which is is a very difficult book. Like all Lacanian papers, Dany's serves as an exposition of what was in the mind of Lacan and what Lacan was thinking. I know that there is no such thing as pure perception and that what he perceives and how he perceives it depends on the theoretical frames and contexts of his ear. It's very important, indeed, to understand these differences. But it appears to me, that the two speakers are really talking about different things. They're not really, in a sense, engaging, although it may seem that they are.

My question, then, is really for Dany Nobus: you explained, in what I found a beautifully lucid and excellent paper, ideas of Lacan's on sexuality: what clinical implications do they have? How does this mean a Lacanian differs from a Kleinian in making a specific interpretation in the consulting-room?

Nobus: The first question is: where does Lacan get all his knowledge and material? And secondly, What are the implications of what he is saying and what he is elaborating for clinical practice. First, Lacan's theory is extremely rooted in clinical practice and one has the tendency to forget this, because his writings are so elaborated and so difficult and they have at times such a philosophical veil over them, that one does not have the impression that one is dealing with a psychoanalyst engaged in clinical practice. But one should not forget that Lacan, when he gave his weekly seminar, always gave another clinical presentation of which the text and discussions haven't yet been published; there was a continuous information between clinical material and theorising. It is difficult to show this, because there are only a few fragments published - Schneiderman published a very interesting presentation by Lacan with a psychotic man in Schneiderman (1993), in which you see that he develops his theoretical insights on the basis of what he's doing with that man. And the other way round - he's applying them, developing them.

What are the implications for clinical practice? First, let's start with the fact that, for Lacan, there is no such thing as the ideal relationship between man and woman. This implies that genitality is no less problematic than other forms of sex. In his seminar on object relations, he starts with a discussion of the object relations theory of Maurice Bouvet, who was making a distinction between pre-genital and genital persons. He said that pre-genital persons are those who haven't arrived at genitally mature object relations. For Lacan, this does not hold. He said that in practice we psychoanalysts should not try to understand someone's sexual problems in these kinds of terms. We should not try to make someone arrive at genital object relations, because there is nothing that allows us to say that genital object relations are more harmonious than, are less problematic, than others. At one point, in fact, he claims it to be just the other way round. When you engage with someone, and as long as you don't have genital sex, everything is OK; or perhaps less problematic than once you have engaged in genital sex *(laughter)*. We can discuss that, of course - it's a very provocative statement, but he means that, if we make someone a genitally functioning person, we don't have any reason to believe that he will encounter fewer problems, insofar as sexual relations are concerned. So, genitality - this form of sexuality - is not an aim; it's not something that is part of the finality of a Lacanian psychoanalytic treatment. He says: sexuality is problematic to the core. We should not therefore decide to transform an existing form of what we call a perverse form of sexuality into what we would call a harmonious genital, and preferably heterosexual, form of sexuality which would be less problematic. This is impossible.

The second point, to do with the way sexuality is dealt with in clinical practice from a Lacanian point of view, has to do with the question of when you have such a form of problematic sexuality. How is the psychoanalyst supposed to deal with that, if he is not supposed to transform it into genitality? He is still confronted with it, as is the patient. How can we relate masculinity and femininity - gender identity, the relationship with the object - in the light of the finality of the treatment? Now on that point, Lacan extrapolates his critique on ego psychology, saying that it's not a question of reinforcing the ego, of adapting the patient to reality, it's really a question of deconstructing the ego. So for him it's the other way round, as far as the ego is concerned. He says: ego analysts are trying to say that when someone has psychic problems, it's because he isn't well adapted; and Lacan says no - he's too adapted to his own identification. He's too adapted to the image he has of himself or herself as an ego. Our analytic process should be focused on deconstructing the identification. It's somewhat the same with problems of gender identity, which is based on an identification, on a relationship with the principle of difference. So the process of analysis is not reinforcing this identification, this relationship, or transforming it into another relationship, it's just questioning it. It's just deconstructing the existing relationship, deconstructing, for example, masculinity and femininity in the view of something else, which would be more in accordance, perhaps, with the patient's true desire.

Temperley: The difference between us, I think, listening to Dany, is to do with the question of the relationship to the body, which is absolutely central. I think you said that the drives are a function of the signifier. I fundamentally disagree with that: I think that they are part of human nature, as is the difference between the sexes. We agree that we have a polymorphously perverse disposition and partial sexualities, but they come together, if things go in a straightforward fashion - there is such a thing as normal development. Freud said there is a normal development, and these partial sexualities, he said, come together under the hegemony of the genitals in with the process of procreation. However prone to miscarriage that whole process is, there is a normal process involved, with all respect to the multifarious manifestations of our failure to achieve that. He says - and this is one of the points of difference between us - that there is inherent recognition of difference, which is terribly painful, and defended against by all sorts of omnipotent phantasies, but that there is a difference, and we are inherently capable of recognising it. We defend against the recognition of it.

As to what are analysts trying to do, putting people together in adult genital relationships which are often so fraught, so they are, but I think we're talking about the depressive position and its connection with the Oedipus complex. This means taking back various kinds of projection, coming out of projective identification with various sorts of objects. It is an exceedingly painful business - recognising what one has done to distort reality, one's attempts to reassert various kinds of omnipotent phantasy. It isn't something you arrive at, and everybody lives happily ever after. A lot of people find the actual process of arriving at the depressive position so painful they would rather remain with the limitations, with a more omnipotent frame of mind. No-one is talking about arriving at some wonderful genital heaven of mature heterosexual relations. One is talking about possibly being less prone to omnipotent phantasy and more able to relate to other people's difference, without the falsifying effect of one's own projections.

David Mayers: What about language, which I think is a meeting-point? Jane talks about men, women, boys, girls, penises, vaginas. and these are terms to which we come with a naive understanding. One thing which happens in analysis is that we in many ways develop and refine and extend the meanings that we put into such terms. Part of that process is the removal of misconceptions. They are, we could say, natural terms. Dany uses phrases like: the other, difference; in another category: the phallus, the object, the signifier. I think there are important matters of logical grammar here.

First, other and difference are adjectives, but they are adjectives which qualify concepts, not objects. I don't talk about another Jane, another Dany, but about another man, or another woman, or another penis, another place another time. And yet, when they are used without something to qualify them, it can sound as though they don't have that second order grammar, as if they have a first-order grammar. Let's take a phrase like the signifier or the phallus. Well, the mouse ran into its hole and the mouse is a rodent. Both have a phrase like the mouse in them, but their logical grammar is quite, quite different. I think that gets obscured when you talk as Dany has.

I wonder if there's a specific application here? The sort of logical grammar muddle that I think exhibits itself here is some sort of reflection of the confusion of sexuality and of understanding sexuality. When logical differences get swept under the linguistic carpet like this, it's because in some sense we want not to know about our sexual differences.

Nobus: It's a difficult problem because it touches on the epistemological basis of the theory. Every theory is founded in language, if you consider the very marvellous remark Freud made at the beginning of his paper on "Instincts and their Vicissitudes" - a metapsychological paper - that the difficulty in making a discipline is that you always have to rely on language. But there isn't anything else. So we are inventing a theory by relying on language, on the culture in which we live, by making elements of language into concepts, but there will always be a gap between those concepts and what we are talking about. In Lacan, this gap is even greater. because he says there is no direct route from language to reality, to the real. We are inventing a theory in which concepts are used and organised but you shouldn't think that this is the Real. This is language, this is theory, these are concepts, but it would be an epistemological mistake to think that these concepts are adequate. It was for a long time a philosophical criterion for judging between objective and subjective, that if the concept is adequate to the thing in reality, then you have an objective science. But Lacan said this is totally impossible. You are always using concepts and terms in a specific order that is part of a culture.

Another point: what Lacan shows is to do with speaking about the signifier and the phallus and desire, which are his concepts. Depending on the context in which these concepts appear and are used, they are granted different meanings, which makes it very difficult sometimes to understand Lacan, because he doesn't always use his concepts in the same way. For example, he speaks of the other, and you always have to rely on the context, to judge the context, before understanding what it means. But he said this is something which can be very useful for practice. Do we not, as analysts, if the subject uses a concept, uses a word, do we not too often understand immediately what he or she means? Wouldn't it be better to situate this word within its context, before trying to understand in the moment and from the outset what it means, and saying and believing that we understand it?

Temperley: Listening to you, it seems much clearer to me that Kleinian theory, like that of Freud, is much more based on the body, but maybe it's also much more based in the consulting-room. I feel you've given an over-emphasis to culture, and not enough to what I think are absolutes in the human condition: like that we are born, that we are differentiated by sex, and that we die; and that's not just a function of the way culture organises things. One of the things that your theory does not mention and that our theory would put a great deal of emphasis on, is procreativity, that sex is not just some curious getting-together that seems to involve misunderstanding and so on. It is perhaps the hegemony that both Freud and Klein would give to heterosexual adult union, that it is capable of producing new life. It seems to me from the way you talk, that it becomes divorced from the physical facts, the things that all of us will bring into life, irrespective of culture.

Nobus: You're compeletely right when you say that Lacanian theory is divorced from the body, procreation, and everything that's connected to that. He said that we psychoanalysts, we deal with the way these things are represented on the level of the psyche. We are not interested in the mechanism of procreation, or in the biological organisation of the body. We are interested in the way in which people experience procreation, experience their own bodies.

Temperley: Yes, so are we, but you take away the body from this. Importantly you said that Lacan does not agree with what Freud said about the drives: that they operate on the frontier. I think psychoanalysis operates on the frontier between the body and the mind, and that our minds are rooted in our physical lives and cannot be uprooted from them. The body would then be reduced to being some kind of currency, which it isn't. It's a source of the very psychic phenomena that we are dealing with.

Oliver Rathbone: In reply to David Mayer's point, I think you're being a little unfair when you say that Dany's language is more difficult to understand and less problematic than Kleinian vocabulary, in that Jane used words like paranoid-schizoid position, depressive position which are equally metaphysical concepts if you like, and don't actually have any reality, and the words Kleinians use to explain them would have to lead on to further definitions such as projective identification and so on.

David Mayers: But I was talking about grammatical form...

Oliver Rathbone: That applies to grammatical form also, the language that people are using is a function. The assumption is that people will know what paranoid-schizoid means, but won't know what objet *a* means, for instance. But why should that be? Dany is trying to describe what he means by objet *a* and Jane is proceeding on the assumption that we know what the paranoid-schizoid position is. My conception of it might be different from hers.

The other point I want to make about linguistic concepts is that there seems to be an implicit suggestion that when you talk about normal, it means correct; just because something is normal, doesn't also mean that it's correct.

Temperley: I take the point about language. I probably assumed that people would be more familiar with Kleinian concepts, given that Klein was a British analyst and that this is a British audience...

Nobus: I agree that it's essential, even when speaking to a Lacanian public, to question assumptions; we sometimes imagine that we are dealing with the same things in terms of Lacanian concepts, and we don't have any reason to think this. So why don't we ourselves try to explain what we think that Lacan is trying to explain every time anew and see how these concepts can be applied within psychoanalysis. This is basically a question of making and re-making theory. If you are a Freudian, and you think you know what Freud did, what he meant, if you are doing a Freudian analysis, and just applying your theory on whatever case presents itself to you, then theory won't evolve. That is the first thing; the second thing is that I think that Freudian theory does not allow that.

Temperley: And Freud himself was the greatest representative of someone who continually developed his theory and reviewed his opinions.

Vivien Bar: I was a bit surprised to hear Dany Nobus saying that Lacanians aren't interested in the body. I think that there's something - Jane Temperley spoke of the act of procreation itself - which is located in the body. There is a Lacanian interest in the body, but as something which is not a given, it is something which has to be constructed.

Nobus: I agree. Perhaps I was being too provocative. When I said that he isn't interested in the body, I meant that he isn't interested in the biological functions of the body as a given, he's interested in the way it's constructed for every human being in particular, in the way this human being experiences his or her body.

Temperley: I think you've located an important difference. The school of psychoanalysis to which I belong does not think that sexual difference is the result of social construction. There is innate readiness to recognise sexual difference at a psychic level; and it is our struggle with our bodies and our sexual phantasies, phantasies rooted in the body, that we explore in psychoanalysis - the body is much more of a given. We may not like it; we may erect all sorts of defences against it, but we do know what the difference is between men and women and we know what it's about.

TRANSFERENCE AND COUNTER-TRANSFERENCE

R D Hinshelwood

I will simply try to convey the way that a contemporary psycho-analyst works. But first of all to make a distinction with the past, it is important to consider Freud's initial thought that the person of the analyst came to resemble, to the Unconscious of the patient, some actual figure in the patient's past - typically mother or father.

> What are transferences? They are new editions or facsimiles of the impulses and phantasies which are aroused and made conscious during the process of analysis; but they have this peculiarity, which is characteristic for their species, that they replace some earlier person by the person of the physician. (Freud 1905, p 116)

Dora

In the early days transference was simply the acting out of a drama with a figure from the past in the form of the analyst. When Dora was kissed without invitation by Herr K, the girl was affected by the pressure of his body on her, and aware of his erect member, as Freud coyly put it. She recoiled and left the holiday resort early. Freud realised that this negative reaction to Herr K was transferred to him, when Dora abruptly left her treatment. In turn Herr K rep-resented an earlier figure of her father. His patient's abrupt termi-nation of her treatment, you remember, had been quite a blow to Freud who had intended this analysis to be an exemplary analysis to supplement, as an illustration, his previous more generalised and theoretical accounts of hysteria. It took him four years eventually to publish this failed analysis.

The Total Situation

However, today, we do not think quite as Freud did then. The transference is not the recurrence of a drama in quite the sense that Freud originally meant it in the Dora case. The material the patient produces is regarded as provoked in the immediate present. Figures outside the analysis are regarded as a means of expressing what is *inside* the setting, but disowned and displaced there. What is in the analysis *and* in the extra-analytic situation are both regard-ed as transference phenomena.

... the transference situation permeates the whole actual life of the patient during the analysis. When the analytic situation has been established, the analyst takes the place of the original objects, and the patient, as we know, deals again with the feelings and conflicts which are being revived, with the very defences he used in the original situation. While repeating, therefore, in relation to the analyst some of his early feelings, phantasies, and sexual desires, he displaces others from the analyst to different people and situations. The result is that the transference phenomena are in part being diverted from the analysis. In other words, the patient is 'acting out' part of his transference feelings in a different setting outside the analysis.

These facts have an important bearing on technique. In my view, what the patient shows or expresses consciously about his relations with the analyst is only one small part of the feelings, thoughts and phantasies which he experiences towards him. These have, therefore, to be uncovered in the unconscious material of the patient by the analyst following up by means of interpretation the many ways of escape from the conflicts revived in the transference situation. (Klein 1943, 635-6)

Central therefore to this view of the transference is the way that the patient is struggling to cope with his own anxieties in his own way. What may be transferred from the past is just as much the kinds of defences he uses as the kind of objects he sees in front of him. '... it is essential to think in terms of *total situations* transferred from the past into the present, as well as of emotions, defences, and object-relations.' (Klein 1952, p. 55)

Thus, Klein drew a fuller attention to the nature of the transference. All the patient's associations fill in a picture or a part picture of what is being experienced by the patient with his *current* objects. And since, in the moment that the analyst encounters the patient the current object is the analyst, it is important to understand that the material concerns the analyst - however much it may seem distant from the here-and-now.

... the patient is bound to deal with conflicts and anxieties re-experienced towards the analyst by the same methods he used in the past. That is to say, he turns away from the analyst as he attempted to turn away from his primal objects; he tries to split the relations to him, keeping him either as a good or as a bad figure: he deflects some of the feelings and attitudes experienced towards the analyst on to other people in his current life, and this is part of 'acting out'. (Klein 1952, p. 55-56)

The patient also re-establishes characteristic ways of defending himself against anxiety.

Containing

Today, the transference is conceived in terms of *containment*, to use the term that has gained currency from the ideas of Bion and later Kleinians; or in terms of *holding*, to use Winnicott's idea. I shall take up the idea of 'containment'.

Non-Symbolic Contents

Psycho-analysts attempt to see the infant in the patient. This is not to ignore the adult. It is the adult in the patient that the analyst will address when he speaks. Instead he will proceed on the basis that there is something in the patient that for whatever reason, has remained as a child, that can at times take over the patient's experiencing - and indeed sometimes his functioning. The psycho-analyst looks out for those moments when it becomes apparent. But he does this in a particular way. The patient may indeed report childish feelings. But that is not such a problem, as we all have such things, and indeed enjoy them - Christmas time is a vivid example. What the analyst is interested in is what the patient does not know - does not consciously know. He is interested in a sudden moment when it is as if the patient relates to him as a child in distress. This moment can most easily be described by quoting from a recent account by a Kleinian of the transaction that goes on as it might between a *mother* and child:

> ...The infant's relation to his [mother] can be described as follows: When an infant has an intolerable anxiety, he deals with it by projecting it into the mother. The mother's response is to acknowledge the anxiety and do whatever is necessary to relieve the infant's distress. The infant's perception is that he has projected something intolerable into his

object, but the object was capable of containing it and dealing with it. He can then reintroject not only his original anxiety but an anxiety modified by having been contained. He also introjects an object capable of containing and dealing with anxiety... The mother may be unable to bear the infant's projected anxiety and he may introject an experience of even greater terror than the one he had projected. (Segal 1975, pp 134-5)

In this sketch the baby requires an anxiety to be modified. The baby believes it to be an intolerable anxiety. If the mother - or the analyst - can tolerate it then the baby has the opportunity for two things:

(i) firstly to experience a modified anxiety; and

(ii) secondly to learn from it to begin to develop its own modifying capacities.

These two outcomes may or may not fail - singly or together. In the analytic setting, the psycho-analyst addresses the distress that is being put across by the patient wherever that may be located by the patient. From the analyst's point of view the location is *inside* the patient.

It is important to understand that this process of pouring out something or other *into* the analyst is the key to the relationship. We can, then, describe this process as one of 'projection' - by the patient. Simultaneously a process of introjection by the analyst goes on.

Illustration

Patient A looked much younger than his 34 years.[1] He came for his jaded sense of purpose at work and in the first interview he found himself in tears - an occurrence, he told me afterwards, that had never happened before. It was occasioned by a link I made, a partial interpretation.

He explained about the death of his mother when he was around 8 years old and had been recently sent to a boarding school. The boarding school he described, vividly, as 'an English rose of a place'. This phrase had a condensed set of meanings, at the conscious level, almost a poetic condensation: it was a special place; it was set in beautiful English countryside; it was beautiful in surface appearance but with hidden thorns; it was an emblem of war (the Wars of the Roses); he remembered falling out of a tree in a part of the school estate known as the rose garden. I remarked that, the one connection that he did not make was that an English rose is a term often used about a beautiful young woman, and that perhaps unbeknown to him, he had been searching, all his time at school, for his beautiful young mother, and that besides his great respect for his school there was also a bitter hostility that he kept falling into despair about ever finding his mother again. I added that he might want to come to analysis for various reasons, one of which was a secret wish to find a mother here, and the other was that he might want to pour out some of the despair to me. He looked perplexed for a moment, and began to politely deny what I had said about despair - 'Despair? Curiously I never felt despair after she died. I was always a vigorous boy, a prankster. But then...' and he stopped in mid-sentence, as if suddenly taken by an urgent bowel motion forcing itself upon his attention; and suddenly his face puckered in the manner of a distraught boy, and a tight gulping sob came out of him. His eyes leaked tears for some minutes, though in a moment, through his tears, he was able to continue with a voice that remained measured and larded with aplomb. He complimented me on my astuteness at having divined something remarkably momentous.

The point of this incident is to show how a link made with words provided some context in which a powerful unfelt experience could achieve a conscious form - or rather it could begin to, since he clearly needed to make a fuller link between that emotional moment and his own use of appropriate words. But the relation between his feeling state, and my ability to form in words something about it, allowed it to have its form in him. This, I would call a moment of containment.

Counter-Transference - Using the Analyst's Mind

Today we are clear about two modes of impact on the analyst - one that is symbolic, with words. And one that is not symbolic and is loosely called 'acting-out' - though that has come to have unfortunate pejorative overtones.

Betty Joseph remarked on 'the way patients use us - analysts - to help them with anxiety' (Joseph 1978, p. 106). And this use may be of two kinds. Patients may seek to use the analyst's mind to help him evade his struggles - as well as enlighten his problems. The patient therefore sets about finding the appropriate ways to operate upon the analyst's mind - on his narcissism, on his despair, on his triumphant potency, and so on. Each psycho-analyst is different in his mind. And each patient has to explore the analyst he has in order to engage in ways that will effect a projection of his anxiety; and which will also involve the creation of a set of defences. In order for a patient to project his painful interest in knowing about himself, he has to have an analyst who does himself wish to know about the patient. Only then can the patient project into it. And only then could the patient, if he wanted to, split off that curiousity of his own and lodge it in his analyst.

Illustration

Patient A had worked on my mind, during the preceding moments before the emotional incident, in various ways, some of which I was sufficiently conscious of to allow me to make that link for him. I had been struck by his appearance of youthfulness and the seemingly ordered and almost poetic way in which he could describe the period around the death of his mother. The latter belied a turmoil of feelings which, it seemed to me at that moment, he must have had. I had more than a surmise that there must have been a wild turbulence in him, because I was myself experiencing a kind of agony about what it must have been like for an eight-year old boy to be sent away and then to receive news of his mother's death. I felt, I suppose a helpless bystander at someone else's tragedy - an experience that might almost make me want to fall out of a tree to put an end to it. And yet there was no visible tragedy in front of my eyes as I sat with him. I was addressing a situation in which my patient had been through profoundly disturbing events, and I was the one who was feeling disturbed. In this case, it was not difficult to put together my disturbance with his narrative. The link that I made was in the form of a note on the phrase 'English rose'; but it was, more profoundly, a link between my emotional disturbance and his story. What I achieved with my interpretative link was, to some degree, a re-entry of the disturbance back into Mr A. Although, to be sure, there was little link inside him at that point between his explosive tears and the verbal aplomb. Such a further link inside him had to be the work of on-going analysis, but at least we had taken the first step.

I add these details about the emotional incident with my patient, because they demonstrate the way my mind could be used to contain, momentarily, some experience that had proved intolerable for many years. The sense of containment comes through the engagement of two minds, a mating, as it were. Brenman Pick asserted how a state of mind seeks another state of mind like a mouth seeks a nipple. 'In part the patient seeks an enacting response, and in part, the analyst has an impulse to enact, and some of this will be expressed in the interpretation '(Brenman Pick, p 36). She remarks, about her own slipping into her motherly role:

> If we cannot take in and think about such a reac-
> tion in ourselves [i.e. the wish to mother], we either
> act out by indulging the patient with actual mother-
> ing (this may be done in verbal or other sympathet-
> ic gestures) or we may become so frightened of
> doing this, that we freeze and do not reach the
> patient's wish to be mothered'. (Brenman Pick, 1985,
> p 38)

This is a very important model for understanding the transfer-
ence/counter-transference interactions.

Now, we would see the occurrence in the Dora case as one in
which the patient projected a sexual guilt into the object. And that
what is repeated is the use of the object in that sense. Instead it can
be seen, in a number of ways, as an unconscious interpenetration of
two minds:

> as a communication out of desperation (of not
> understanding, exploiting)
> as an intention to hurt (revenge)
> as an erotic cruelty

How do we tell? The answer in the course of a current analysis
will turn partly on how the analyst feels when engaged with the
patient at that moment. In the case of Freud's encounter with Dora
we do not have proper corroborative evidence. However we can
mention one possibility. Freud's ambition was to make an exemplary success of this case. If this is so then the patient could have
been engaging with that intention in Freud and thwarting it in a
highly specific way. She could hurt him through his ambition. And
she could do so by cutting him off where it hurt most. This is an
engagement with her *current* object, not merely a repetition from the
past.

Conclusions

A contemporary view of transference and counter-transference
relies on the idea of containing (see Hinshelwood 1994). With a
brief clinical example I have illustrated how the mind of the analyst
attempts to take in the experiences of the patient, and then to give
them some form that can have a meaning that is usable for the
patient. I have indicated how, unconsciously, the patient *intends* to
make use of such an opportunity to put his experiences into a container. That kind of interaction is based on entirely familiar kinds

of processes that go on within human object-relations from birth onwards, although the technical aspects of raising it to a level of explicit, conscious reflection may be very sophisticated and outside the 'normal' range of human communication.

[1] This case material is so disguised as to render it merely illustrative rather than as being presented as supporting evidence.

ON COUNTER-TRANSFERENCE

Vicente Palomera

"Si peu que l'acte flanche, c'est l'analyste
qui devient le vrai psychanalysé"
Lacan. J., 'Raison d'un échec'.

Scilicet I

1. Introduction

Counter-transference is a psychoanalytic concept which made its full appearance in the fifties. It was no longer the analyst as a "blank screen" which was at stake, but an analyst who experiences feelings with regard to his patient. In the beginning it was thought that counter-transference was a personal disturbance to be analysed away in the analyst but in the fifties Paula Heimann, among others, also thought of it as having its causes and effects in the patient and, therefore as an indication of something to the analysed in him.

So far as I know, Freud scarcely ever spoke about counter-transference. I've just read the Correspondence between Freud and Binswanger, which has recently been issued in German (S Freud - L Binswanger Briefwechsel: 1908-1938, 1992), where I discovered what was Freud's position with regard to counter-transference. Freud explicitly states that the counter-transference is something to overcome. In a letter dated 20th February 1913, he writes that

Das Problem der Gegenübertragung, das Sie anrühren, gehört zu den technischen Schwierigkeiten der Psychoanalyse. Theoretisch halte ich es für leichter lösbar. Was man dem Patienten gibt, soll aber niemals unmittelbarer Affekt, sondern stets bewusst zugeteilter sein und dann je nach Notwendigkeit mehr oder weniger. Unter Umständen sehr viel, aber niemals aus dem eigenen Unbewussten. Dies hielte ich für die Formel. Man muss also sein Gegenübertragung jedesmal erkennen und überwinden, dann erst ist man selbst frei. Jemandem zu wenig zu geben, weil man zu sehr liebt, ist ein Unrecht an dem Kranken und ein technischer Fehler.

(Translation: 'The problem of counter-transference, which you touch on, is one of the technical difficulties of psychoanalysis. I think it is easier to solve theoretically. However, what one gives to the patient must never be a spontaneous affect but always a consciously communicated one, more or less according to need. In some circumstances a great deal, but never

out of one's own unconscious. That seems to me to be the rule. One must always recognize and overcome one's counter-transference; only then can one be free oneself. To give someone too little because one loves him too much is unfair to the patient and a technical error.)

As you see, Freud establishes no relation between the counter-transference and the psychoanalyst's unconscious. On the contrary, if he invites analysts to overcome their counter-transference, it is because he considers it a symptom with which it is not difficult to come to terms.

2. The laws of intersubjectivity

What do we mean by counter-transference?

First of all, the effect produced by the analyst on the patient. It is basically the consequence of a Freudian observation: the person of the analyst intervenes in the interpretation which justifies the argument that the analysis of the analyst must be carried out rather far.

Secondly, the counter-transference no longer refers to the feelings that the analyst inspires, but rather to those which he experiences.

Actually, if the analysand can be the cause of a desire in the analyst, if a passion is eventually stirred up, one might ask whether these feelings, when passed through an analysis, are equivalent or not to those which the analyst himself produced. If the response to this is affirmative, it is nothing but a case of transference. In this sense, the term counter-transference does not serve for anything except to identify the analyst with himself, and the main question here is: who is in analysis with whom?

This is the cul-de-sac that one reaches when the analytical cure is reduced to a dual relationship.

If one makes the categories of intersubjectivity (the laws of communication which rule inter-human exchange) intervene in the field of analysis, nothing escapes from reciprocity: just as there are two people, there are similarly two transferences, two resistances, two narcissisms and two unconsciouses.

The Kleinians who questioned the counter-transference found, in their way, a finer articulation than that which leads inevitably to the dual confrontation.

In his *Le Séminaire Livre VIII:Le Transfert*, Jacques Lacan devoted a full chapter to the subject of counter-transference. He took Money-Kyrle's article "Normal Counter-transference and some of its Deviations" as his text for criticism. I'm going to talk about it later on but I suggest you read it thoroughly because it shows that what is presented as "feeling" in the analyst does not belong to him, and is no more than an aspect of the patient's transference: it is no longer an obstacle put up against the transference of the analysand, but rather its manifestation in another place, and one could even say that it is continued in the analyst. The feelings or formulae which come to the mind of the analyst represent an anticipation of repressed elements in the analysand. One could speak in this way of a transference from the Unconscious of the analysand to the analyst rather than an interaction of two unconsciouses, which always evokes a mutual affective handling.

In 1954, Lacan located the transference as a phenomenon in which both the subject and the psychoanalyst are included(*The Seminar, Book II*). Experience shows that we are not dealing with anything more than a single subject, the subject of the Unconscious, in which there are two individuals. That's why, Lacan, like Freud, speaks very little about the counter-transference.

Lacan spoke of the counter-transference with regard to Freud in the case of Dora ('Intervention on the transference') and defined it as the sum of prejudices, and even errors; a lack of information, that is to say, the lack of certain signifiers coming from the analysand. It is the lack of the very signifier of the analyst which leads to counter-transference, which for Lacan is a deviation. The orientation that he gives in order to fill the absence of this signifier is summed up in his formula of the *subject who is supposed to know* , a formula which does not in fact designate anyone.

Lacan points out that in the end the only resistance which has to be taken into account is that of the analyst: the resistance of psychoanalysis is in the analyst himself and proceeds from his legitimate uneasiness with respect to the position of considering what the analyst wants to do with his patient, says Lacan in *Seminar XI;* but there is also the question of what the analyst wants his patient to do to him. All these formulae basically make the analyst's desire the axis of the cure: however, they frustrate any pretension to reciprocity and intersubjectivity with respect to the Unconscious. On the contrary, Lacan's position ends in a reabsorption of the category of counter-transference.

Finally, in the 1966 edition of *Ecrits,* a note corrects this obsolete terminology. According to Lacan, it should henceforth be said that the analyst's transference is, in fact, his resistance.

Lacan says that this does not prevent there being feelings. It is a fact that analysts not only have feelings with respect to their patients, and that they treat them with much circumspection and consideration; they also love them or hate them. Is there basically anything which prevents a patient from being the object *a* of his analyst? In fact the idea of getting the analyst to share feelings that he has not yet felt agrees entirely with the Lacanian thesis of communication of feelings. These are always reciprocal, and it's not that they are contagious or shared necessarily, but that they respond to the logic of imputation.

By definition, it is supposed that the Other always responds to the feeling that is directed toward him. As an individual I may well remain indifferent before the demand of love that is directed to me, but as an analyst, this is not the case. It is enough to place oneself in the locus of the Other in whom desire is supposed. It is enough to identify oneself with this place.

There are even symptoms which analysts borrow from their patients by means of 'imaginary identification'. Is this not an effect of the word rather than the consequence of a shared sympathy? This identification of the analyst with his patient may very well be the result of the law that says that one receives from the Other his own message in an inverted form.

Lacan affirms in *Seminar I* that feelings are always reciprocal. To say to a patient: 'you think that I am angry with you' or 'you believe you have seduced me' necessarily converts the analyst into a subject that desires, that is to say, identical to his enunciation. From which follows the well founded reply: 'You're the one who says it'. However, by trusting the feelings rather than the word that determines them, psychoanalysts came to trust their own feelings as the place of the manifestation of a truth repressed in the Other, as indisputable testimony of unconscious knowledge. The problem is, as we have just seen, that the reciprocal is equally true.

If the Unconscious is the discourse of the Other, why wouldn't the analyst have to be this Other, and why wouldn't he be considered as the transmitter of the message that is directed toward him?

He who listens, is heard to speak because it is the very locus of the Other whence he is addressed; even more reason perhaps, why he keeps his mouth shut. One could maintain that it is as an analysand that one listens to one's patient, then one is at the mercy of the listener when speaking ...

What Lacan called the crossing over of the plane of identifications at the end of analysis *(Seminar XI)* implies that he does not identify himself with the place where the message is addressed to him, that of the subject who is supposed to know, a function which is in fact entirely reversible.

3. Lacan and Money-Kyrle

In *Séminaire VIII: Le Transfert* Lacan points out the characteristic way in which the analysts of the Kleinian school perceived the 'impasses' caused by a practice of analysis supported by such a conception of symmetry. The question he puts is: how can one overcome the illusion of a dual relationship when the transference is handled starting from the fluctuation of introjection and projection? To illustrate this point Lacan takes an interesting clinical case presented by Roger Money-Kyrle.

In his article 'Normal counter-transference and some of its deviations' (1956) Money-Kyrle describes the process in the following terms: while the patient speaks, the analyst can identify by introjection with him, and having understood from the interior, he 'reprojects' it and interprets.

Lacan takes this illusion of identification very seriously. This illusion is of itself an effect of discourse that puts the analyst in a particular position with respect to the signifier of the analyst: he desires to understand, and to understand is to identify.

Money-Kyrle tells us about an episode of an analysis that at one moment ends in a difficulty for the analyst himself. He tells us that for a short while after he had finished his week's work, he was consciously preoccupied with an unsolved problem of his patient and that the period of conscious concern was followed by a period of listlessness in which he was deprived of the private interests which usually occupied his leisure. As a matter of fact, Money-Kyrle confesses that he experienced a sense of being robbed of his wits by the patient:

> A neurotic patient, in whom paranoid and schizoid mechanisms were prominent, arrived for a session in considerable anxiety because he had not been able to work in his office. He had also felt vague on the way as if he might get lost or run over; and he despised himself for being useless. Remembering a similar occasion, on which he had felt depersonalized over a weekend and dreamed that he had left his 'radar' set in a shop and would be unable to get it before Monday, I thought he had, in phantasy, left parts of his 'good self' in me. But I was not very sure of this, or of other interpretations I began to give. And he, for his part, soon began to reject them all with a mounting degree

of anger; and, at the same time he abused me for not helping. By the end of the session he was no longer depersonalized, but very angry and contemptuous instead. It was I who felt useless and bemused.

When I eventually recognized my state at the end as so similar to that he had described as his at the beginning, I could almost feel the relief of a re-projection. By then the session was over. But he was in the same mood at the beginning of the next one - still very angry and contemptuous. I then told him I thought he felt he had reduced me to the state of useless vagueness he himself had been in; and that he felt he had done this by having me "on the mat", asking questions and rejecting the answers, in the way his legal father did. His response was striking. For the first time in two days, he became quiet and thoughtful. He then said this explained why he had been so angry with me yesterday: he had felt that all my interpretations referred to my illness and not to his.

I suggest that, as in a slow motion picture, we can see here several distinct processes which, in an ideal or "normal" analytic period, should occur extremely quickly. I think I began, as it were, to take my patient in, to identify introjectively with him, as soon as he lay down and spoke about his very acute distress. But I could not at once recognize it as corresponding with anything already understood in myself: and, for this reason, I was slow to get it out of me in the process of explaining, and so relieving it in him. He, for his part, felt frustrated at not getting effective interpretations, and reacted by projecting his sense of mental impotence into me, at the same time behaving as if he had taken from me what he felt he had lost, his father's clear, but aggressive, intellect, with which he attacked his impotent self in me. By this time, of course, it was useless to try to pick up the thread where I had first dropped it. A new situation had arisen which had affected us both. And before my patient's part in bringing it about could be interpreted, I had to do a silent piece of self-analysis involving the discrimination of two things which can be felt as very similar: my own sense of incompetence at having lost the thread, and my patient's contempt for his impotent self, which he felt to be in me. Having made this interpretation to myself, I was eventually able to pass the second half of it on to my patient, and, by so doing, restored the normal analytic situation.

As you see, the analyst is in a situation of impasse; he is depressed because he doesn't understand. The depressive position in which he finds his patient in the beginning of the cure, and from which he wanted to extract him, is now his. What happens then is that the analyst loses track and can no longer pass on to the phase of 'reprojection': he can no longer provide effective interpretations.

During the weekend his patient had dreamed that he had forgotten his 'radar' in a shop and couldn't recover it until Monday. For Money-Kyrle this is what points him to the path of the interpretation of definite symptoms, and particularly of anxiety. 'I thought', says the analyst, 'that he had left parts of his "good self" in me'. The analysand doesn't like this intervention at all, he becomes disdainful and aggressive, but is no longer 'depersonalised'.

It is Money-Kyrle who takes over this place. His patient, he says, reduces him to a useless object, the same state in which the patient found himself before, and he adds that by this way of producing questions and at the same time rejecting the answers, he did the same thing as his father. Two days go by and the analysand then says that such interpretations don't concern him, and that on the contrary, it was the analyst who was ill.

Money-Kyrle thus tries to give an account of this irritating upset in the situation. He tries by means of introjection to identify with his patient at the moment when the latter has fallen to pieces, but then is incapable of recognising in this state anything that could correspond to that which he could have already understood in and of itself.

One can see how the situation makes a 180° turn. This patient is converted into the analyst's analyst. In fact this type of cure can deviate to the point of a hostile crystallisation.

If Lacan took this clinical example for a reason, it was to illustrate the effects on the feelings of the analyst of a demand that can run parallel with his own. If the demand of the subject represents the psychoanalyst's own demand in an inverted form, one comes up against the powerful effects of the severity of the superego, and this is what Money-Kyrle experienced. In his failed attempt at introjection, he found nothing more than his own superego. The identification with defeat in the failure of the parental drive is the depressive position of the psychoanalyst.

The depression of the psychoanalyst is presented then as an effect of shortsightedness with respect to the location that he occupies, and of his incomprehension of the patient's unconscious: it is the traumatism of misunderstanding.

Lacan drew consequences from this relation. There is a necessary link between not understanding, not being able to respond to the demand, on one hand, and the analyst's identification with ruin and defeat in the absence of the reparative patient, on the other. This is precisely the Lacanian definition of the analyst and the result of the annulment of his ego ('*moi* '): not looking for understanding implies that one abandons the locus of the Other of good faith. This is what Lacan actually says:

il ne s'agit (dans ce cas) que d'un effet irréductible de la situation de transfert, simplement ... c'est un effet légitime du transfert ... Il faut que l'analyste sache ... en particulier que le critère de sa position correcte n'est pas qu'il comprenne ou qu'il ne comprenne pas. Il n'est pas absolument essentiel qu'il comprenne. Je dirai même que jusqu'à un certain point, qu'il ne comprenne pas, peut-être préférable à une trop grande confiance dans sa compréhension. (Lacan 1991 p229).

(Translation: In this case it is only a question of an irreducible effect of the transference situation; simply ... it is a legitimate effect of the transference. In particular, the analyst has to know that the criterion for his correct positioning is not whether he does or does not understand. It is not absolutely essential that he understands: I would even say that up to a certain point, if he does not understand, this would be preferable to too great a confidence in his own understanding.)

---

[1]However little the action fails, it's the analyst who becomes the truly analysed.

THE UNCONSCIOUS: A KLEINIAN PERSPECTIVE

Robin Anderson

What is unconscious is the field of study for all psychoanalysts. All our work is about showing our patients how what they know of themselves is part of a larger pattern of which they are not aware. Freud described consciousness as being like the tip of an iceberg showing above the water: the larger part of the mind remains hidden. This larger part has a far greater influence on our lives than we ever realise, and all analytic work by all psychoanalysts is about helping patients to discover more about this, and in so doing help them to modify it. The differences between different analytic theories are, I think, more in the nature of what is unconscious, how it arises, and the way it relates to what is conscious.

I will try to say something about how Melanie Klein and those analysts using her theories have come to view the Unconscious and its relationship to consciousness, and something of how her ideas influence the way that we work.

In Freud's original topographical model he assigned a psychic space to what is dynamically unconscious. He put in this 'place' all that was unconscious, which he equated with the Id. The Ego was located in the systems preconscious and conscious. Later he began to realise that the boundary between conscious and unconscious was not the same as the boundary between the Ego and the Id: some of the Ego was unconscious and the same was true of the Superego, which his theory had now to accommodate. He therefore developed the Structural Model of Id, Ego and Superego, each of which might have components which were conscious and others which were unconscious (or preconscious). It was from this model of the mind that the Object relations view of the mind (including the Kleinian) developed. Melanie Klein came to view the mind as more of an internal world consisting of internal objects some of which are more or less stably clustered around the Self, and are identified with and related to who we think we are. Some of them are primitive and extreme, and these are unconscious. Some are more linked to figures of authority or fear by whom we are influenced, and which correspond to the Superego and sometimes can be described like that - not as a single introject, as Freud thought, but as a number of objects of varying degrees of resemblance to the actual parents in the past. Yet other objects are more primitive, more phantastic, more archaic, which might be compared more with the contents of the Id. We will be conscious of some parts of these objects, but mostly we are unaware of them. We know, for example, that we are influenced by our parents: we can think about how, and feel ourselves to be like them or influenced by them in certain ways. But most of what they mean to us is hidden. On the whole, the more archaic and primitive, the more knowledge of them would threaten our sense of who we are, the more likely we are to remain unconscious of them, and to repudiate, and repress such knowledge.

A patient, who had been brought up on a strict Truby King regime at the start of her analysis had dreamed that she was being chased by a man who was going to murder her, and she had stabbed him in self-defence. It was clear that allowing someone, that is her analyst, access to her mind was experienced unconsciously as a murderous attack on her which she had to defend herself against by all means at her disposal. She was horribly shocked, that she could harbour such ideas - such objects in her mind - indeed she remembered her father as a very caring man. But the shock of starting analysis had mobilised a quite different experience which felt quite unrelated to the memory of her benign father.

But how do we see the raw material of the Unconscious? Melanie Klein, like Freud, saw the basis of the mind as biological. Freud felt that the engine, so to speak, of the mind was instinct. Klein took this very seriously. She felt that the mind is active from birth, under the pressure of instinctual wishes - of hunger, of desire, of envy, the life and death instincts- all of which had to find mental expression. The manifestation of this was phantasy - phantasy is the mental representation of instinct. Freud had implied such ideas when he had written of hallucinatory wish-fulfilment: the baby is hungry and to relieve himself of this painful experience, hallucinates the means of relieving himself, the breast. Klein, however, took this much further, and felt that every drive, every impulse, gives rise to a phantasy that will satisfy it. A reasonably contented baby, who begins to experience hunger, will phantasise, like 'Freud's baby', a good and nurturing breast that is loved and which will satisfy him. If he is left, his experience of frustration and rage will be manifest as a phantasy which will become more disturbing, perhaps now an image of the breast as a mouth attacking him.

A patient who had been left for several hours in a pram outside between feeds, irrespective of her distress, dreamed, during an early weekend separation in her analysis, that she was witnessing a machine which was chopping up a breast: there was skin and tissue and chunks of breast all in a terrifying confusion. It was as though an archaic phantasy had been manifest in her dreams, probably a phantasy of biting up a breast which had perhaps been her experience, as she was left in a state of greater and greater distress, hunger and rage. The machine of the dream, I think, represented her way of trying to separate herself from this process and keep such a disturbing part of her inner world isolated as a piece of machinery. Her analysis had mobilised this archaic part of her unconscious, which had perhaps wanted to communicate itself (see below) to an understanding object, so that she felt both disturbed and relieved at this communication.

Of course, if we think of the mental life of unconscious phantasy as existing from birth, then there is the interesting question of what is the origin of such ideation. Klein herself never really went into this question, but some of those following her have. Freud had spoken of 'primal phantasy', particularly in relation to the primal scene, and had thought of it in a Lamarckian way as a kind of race memory which was inherited and was present as a given in the mind. Of course this raises all the objections of our present understanding of how characteristics are inherited. Money-Kyrle addressed this, and simply felt that certain aspects of mental life must have come about through the ordinarily accepted evolutionary means - by mutation and natural selection - to produce these mental images which attach themselves to the actual external objects when these are finally encountered. He gives examples from ethological studies - imprinting, etc; and we could now use the findings from infant psychology, for example, the rooting 'reflex', when the baby searches for the breast for the first time.

Money-Kyrle was also using the ideas of Wilfred Bion, who had addressed this issue in some detail. Bion described these unconscious phantasies about objects not yet experienced as preconceptions. When a preconception meets with the object that 'fits' it then the mental experience is called a realisation - a this-is-what-I have-been-waiting-for, I always-knew-it kind of feeling.

To come back to the issue of unconscious phantasy *per se*, clearly its raw materials - that is, the form of it - will draw on later experience to express whatever the phantasy might be. In analysis, we would see every utterance, every action, as having a possible link to an unconscious phantasy or to be a response to an unconscious phantasy. So that the analyst is trying to notice everything that the patient brings, irrespective of how relevant or irrelevant it may appear. A patient may be giving an account of something from the past, something that happened on the way to the session, a dream, a conscious fantasy - all these things will have some bearing on what is actually going on in the room at that moment.

I will come back to this question of how we relate to our patients' material, but before I do I would like to consider the way we deal with what is unconscious. Another way of considering this might be to ask the question: What do we mean by repression? Freud saw repression as being a force - originally the censor, later the superego - which held unacceptable unconscious ideas down and prevented them from becoming conscious. If we put this in object relations language we could say that an internal object which has power over the self, will by its power, its authority, forbid certain parts of the self or another object from certain activities, eg violence, sexual activity, etc. This kind of situation might be present in the mind which has reached the depressive position. We might add other details, but we would be seeing a mental organisation in which control is possible. But of course we also think of a more primitive state, in which the organisation is rather different, ie, the paranoid-schizoid position. Here we have a situation in which those unacceptable feelings and impulses which are too powerful, too dangerous to bear, are felt to be ejected from the self, split-off and projected. The experience of their location is therefore not felt to be in the self at all, but in the object. In early life there is a state in which anything that is unwanted is projected, leaving the baby's mind depleted but in fear of the return of which is felt to be located outside the self. Melanie Klein described how this situation developed into one of more consistent splitting between good and bad, the establishment of the paranoid-schizoid position, moving eventually towards the depressive position. Bion greatly enriched our understanding of this process because he showed what happens to this unbearable world - this unconscious which so threatens the self. He realised that we not only want to be rid of it - to hell with it - but we *also don't want to be rid of it;* and we even seek a special kind of object into which we can put our 'unconscious'. This object is of course the Mother, and the process is Bion's description of the container-contained. So, when the baby rids himself of his unbearable mental experiences - what Bion describes as ß elements - raw unbearable mental experiences these are felt to be in the mother who, if she can, if she is a 'good-enough' mother, accepts these projections - allows herself to be made uncomfortable. But then, instead of pushing them back at the baby, who will be fearing this, she will respond in a calmer, more benign way, so that what is taken back by the baby is not as bad as what was projected. The baby can re-accept back into himself, into his own unconscious as it were, a more benign version of what he projects (a process). This very special, and of course essential, type of object relationship is gradually internalised.

This relationship to a containing object is the environment in which development is taking place, and especially the negotiation of the paranoid-schizoid position. The necessity for this, I think, underlines the state of dependency on the object at this time. Bion felt the baby's hunger to have an object that could not only take what could not be borne but also an object that could make sense of it and give it back, was as important as feeding itself. He often speaks of it as being the mental equivalent of the breast - 'mental food'.

In an analysis, we see this process manifesting itself in the relationship between patient and analyst. So how do we see and think about the unconscious communications of the patient? When the patient is persistently in the paranoid-schizoid position then we know that we will be likely to be seeing a patient who feels less together.

There will be a sense of something missing in what the patient is telling us, because of course, from the patient's point of view there will be a sense that some pieces of experience have nothing to do with him -they will have been split-off and projected.

The patient brought up on the strict Truby King regime came to a Friday session after some hard work in the analysis, saying that she was feeling much better. She spoke of how, unusually, she had come by bus to the session, and how good that had felt, as she used to know this bus-route very well: the stops were familiar, and she felt as though she was coming home.

All this felt very benign, and linked very clearly for the patient with the recent analytic work which had resulted in her feeling much better in herself. She felt herself in a familiar place, and even though it was a weekend, such stops felt familiar and benign.

What had no connection for her with this good state of mind were some other things she had spoken of. She had made no direct link with why she did not have her car - her dog had a tumour and her husband was taking it to the vet. It was not clear whether the dog could be treated or would have to be put down. She had spoken too of saying goodbye to a friend who was depressed and whose life was full of losses.

When I raised these issues with her, in relation to her saying goodbye, at first she was reluctant to think about them. She said that the dog was more her husband's and son's than hers. I interpreted to her that she felt very pleased about her improvement, which she felt was very genuine, and hated the thought of it being undermined by losses which were associated with depression and death. She was able to think more about this, and realised that though she had protested that the dog was not really hers, she could relate to the loss and sympathise with the loss that her husband and son were facing.

I think the process of allowing a split to be linked together - the good feeling on the one hand, and the feelings of depression and death on the other - could happen partly because I had been able to recognise her anxiety about losing her better state of mind, to contain that anxiety and show her I understood that, and I think partly because of her own relationship to what she had split-off and projected. Although I would think of this material as evoking splitting and projection - and therefore in that respect the paranoid-schizoid position - the splitting was not too wide: she had not so hated her feelings of loss and fear of damage that she had wanted them as far away from herself as possible. Her sympathy with her husband and son showed that although she had split-off and projected the part of herself that felt anxiety about a damaged and dying object, she was still interested and indeed concerned about its welfare. The same was true of her friend. Although she was feeling more distant from her emotionally, she was very pleased to be looking after a piece of her furniture in her own house.

Moreover, she had used the session to tell me about these things. I had not found it too impossible either to think or to interpret to her. She had used me as a containing object with which she wanted to gather up these, for her, disparate, but also related, feelings which were important to her. There were symbolic links to what was split-off which both maintained her own connection with these parts of her and allowed me to help her to feel less split.

This issue of the degree of connectedness to what is unconscious is something that Kleinian analysts are very interested in. So it is not simply a question of whether something is conscious or unconscious, but how far away is what is unconscious, what symbolic relationship exists with what is unconscious.

Bion was very interested in the kind of link that the self made towards an object. He felt that not only was there a question of love or hate - was it a loved or a hated object? - but also, was it one that the self wanted to know about? - he called it the K link: +K for a wish to know and -K for a wish not to know.

A central question that Kleinian analysts think about in their patients' material is what is the degree of reluctance to know. Consciousness is really 'knowing about'. The question of whether what is not 'known about' is conscious or not, is an interesting one. In Freud's Preconscious, it was mainly a question of turning one's attention on a part of the preconscious, like shining a light and being able to see what is in its beam. But the question is then, what if there is a powerful wish not to look, not to know? This kind of unconsciousness is what Steiner refers to a 'turning a blind eye'. At the other extreme is the psychotic who has a hatred and fear of reality and also of the means of perceiving it, and resorts to extreme splitting and projection to be rid of it, which is so powerful, so omnipotent that what is not wanted is felt to have nothing to do with the self at all. Could we think of Freud's Censor as a variable filter which is controlled by a spectrum of emotion from a powerful hatred of knowledge or a piece of knowledge at one end, through reluctance, to a desire for self-knowledge despite the pain and distress this causes?

We think these attitudes towards wanting to know are found in the early relationship to a containing object where part of this unconscious which is projected is what the baby cannot bear to 'know'. If the mother can bear to know and receive these projections then the baby will have the opportunity to internalise an object which will support his or her wish to know about him- or herself. If, for some reason, the mother cannot, or will not, receive this projection, the baby, instead of internalising an object which will help him to know, will internalise an object that hates reality and is felt to take meaning away. In more perverse patients, this relation to the truth is more complex: there is an unconscious attempt to distort the truth as a means of defence.

From the point of view of the mother or the analyst, we are often at least partially conscious of what our patients want us to deal with. Occasionally one has the flash 'I can't bear this, if I start to face all this it will be overwhelming for me and the patient', and sometimes we do turn away. With patients who are fragmented, and hate and fear what is in their minds, we are indeed aware of the sense of how hard it is for us to bear to make connections or even to think. We do not feel our own symbolic functioning is mobilised by what we hear. With my example of the patient on the bus, I could feel my mind to be lively and functioning well. I had to deal with a certain anxiety about destroying her peace of mind. But this was not too difficult to stay with, to bear. We might think that this is about our own state of mind, about how well or badly we are functioning as analysts. But while our state of mind of course plays a large part, it is often when the patients' communications are richer, in the sense of 'full of symbolic meaning', that we can more easily explore the associative connections around what the patient brings. These are symbolic links, (which are the patients' relationship with what they have projected, with where the patients' unconscious is, one could say). Like the association to the piece of furniture, they are very much +K links.

On the other hand, with patients who are more fragmented, or more actively disintegrated, the analytic work is more like an ordeal in which we are told things which do not make sense. We make links in our mind, but then they do not seem to make any sense because the patient may themselves see the possible connections and steer us away from them, or say something to put us off the scent, or more violently to attack our perceptions, so that the dreaded knowledge/consciousness will not emerge. Because if the analyst begins to make sense of what is happening, the patient will feel this to be a great threat and has to destroy it as soon as the slightest hint of this is seen to be emerging, even in the mind of the analyst.

I will give a brief example of this kind of communication. Where is the Unconscious here? The task of tracing it was very difficult and disturbing.

The patient is an ll-year-old boy who is very ill, barely managing at school, and who probably has a severe borderline personality. His sexual identity is quite disturbed. He dresses up in his mother's clothes. I am supervising the psychotherapy, which is carried out by a junior colleague. For the previous week's supervision there had been a very demoralised therapist and possibly even more demoralised supervisor. I had been quite unable to understand the material, and felt myself to be quite useless. In this session the therapist noticed how drab his clothes were, which reminded her of how he had said they were 'nice and dull'. Eric began 'What we've been doing this week ... A black cat jumped up at the window-sill. It had a bird in its mouth. My mother and I chased it. We tried to get it to open its mouth. The bird flew off; then another cat caught it. It was not a dirty bird: it had a red beak and nice colours. My mother hit the cat, I did. Cats are wicked and unclean. The bible says cats are unclean.'.

He went off into a long obsessive account of which animals were unclean in the Bible. The therapist made some tentative comments about something very upsetting having happened. Which led Eric to speak of a funeral for the little bird, but very quickly this was taken over by a flood of associations about his grandmother's cremation and about his preoccupation with empty graves.

All this had the quality of a flood of anxieties that he could only rid himself of.

When the therapist interpreted how disturbed he was by these horrible thoughts in his mind he became calmer for a moment, and then managed to speak to the therapist about his terrors in a much more communicative way: his fear of Hell, his fear of Eternity, and how scared he was. But what we noticed was that when he had seemed to feel held by the therapist he immediately followed it by complaining about the rich people who sit at the front of churches and leave the poor at the back, and about the rich Pope and the clergy who should give to the poor.

After struggling to think about this type of communication in the supervision, I realised that the therapist was wearing a black dress and that might link with the black cat. She often wears black. There was also a contrast between the brightly-coloured bird with the red beak and the patient's 'dull' clothes. Gradually we began to wonder if the patient experienced the therapist as a highly destructive predator, black and deathly, who would pounce on him if he showed any signs of life, and probably also accuse him of stealing his mother's clothes and lipstick (the coloured bird with the red beak) and that to protect himself he has to live a colourless life, locked in his church, which offers him a kind of sanctuary, as long as he obeys its rules.

What I want to emphasise is the tremendous effort this work involves. Moreover, when he does feel less afraid of the therapist as the containing object he then cannot bear her richer mind (the rich clergy) and so even retreats from this. In other words, he has a terrible and unhappy relationship to the containing object and a dislike of his own mental experience - his unconscious phantasies - so that he projects them and does not make it easy for us to recover them. In the supervision we did begin to recover some capacity to make symbolic links; but in the session his therapist found it almost impossible to think.

I realise that there is much that I have not touched on in this talk, which may come up in the discussion. The role of the relationship between one object and another - the parental couple as a container, the role of the father, the baby who has to ward off the Unconscious of the mother.

As Freud's theory of the mind developed, his interest in the difference between what is conscious and what is unconscious became more complex. The different agencies each had their own relationship to consciousness and unconsciousness. With Klein's concept of the maturing mind as gradually becoming more integrated, the question of unconsciousness becomes a consideration of increasing symbolic connectedness, in which the 'unconscious' becomes less unknown and more accepted; though just as our hold on the depressive position fluctuates throughout the vicissitudes of life, so does our relationship to what is unconscious.

THE UNCONSCIOUS FROM A LACANIAN POINT OF VIEW

Filip Geerardyn

'In the dream, in parapraxis, in the flash of wit - what is it that strikes one first? It is the sense of impediment to be found in all of them. (...) Freud is attracted by these phenomena, and it is there that he seeks the Unconscious'.[1]

Introduction

To begin with, we might ask ourselves in what sense and to what degree the Lacanian unconscious differs from the Freudian unconscious. At first sight, this is a rather difficult question to answer. For, it is true that, for example, we in Flanders have come to read Freud through Lacan's so-called 'return to Freud'. This movement obviously did not consist in a mere repetition of the Freudian hypotheses but on the contrary, gave the opportunity for a further theoretical elaboration and foundation of psychoanalytical experience. So, would it follow that the Lacanian unconscious would not be the same as the Freudian?

This reminds me of a statement Lacan once made to an audience he addressed: 'You may well call yourselves Lacanian, I am Freudian!'. Indeed, the Lacanian elaboration of the Unconscious is not a kind of *deus ex machina* , but witnesses, time and again, a rigorous discipline in revisiting Freud's writings.

For one thing, this revisiting resulted in a re-opening of the Freudian unconscious. For Lacan heavily deplored the fact that the second and third generations of analysts had come to close their eyes to the very discovery - or should we say, the very invention? - of Freud, i.e. the Unconscious. As Lacan puts it in his seminar on the *Four Fundamental Concepts of Psychoanalysis,* analysts had come to behave like Orpheus, who lost his beloved Eurydice twice, due to his own impatience, disbelief and uncertainty. There we find 'the most potent image we can find of the relation between Orpheus the analyst and the Unconscious'[2].

I particularly love this quotation because it contains a reference to what might be the result of the closing of the Unconscious: the establishment of the psychoanalytical movement as a kind of Orphism or religious sect, whereas the linguistic structure of the Unconscious 'assures us that there is, beneath the term unconscious, something definable, accessible and objectifiable'[3], which can lead us to consider psychoanalysis as the 'science of language' as it is 'inhabited by the subject'. What I want to say is this: whenever a psychoanalytic institution displays the characteristics of a sect, be it a Lacanian or a Freudian sect, we should withdraw from it and content ourselves, in order to re-open the Unconscious, with a revisiting of the writings of Freud and Lacan in reference to our psychoanalytic experience and that of some other analysts.

The Unconscious Presupposes The Other

With the notion of the linguistic structure of the Unconscious, we already find ourselves in the midst of the Lacanian conceptualisation of the Unconscious and it is this qualification *'the unconscious is structured like a language'* [4] that I would like to explore here with you.

To put it in other words, one might say that *the unconscious presupposes the Other*, and this in a two-fold way.

Firstly, it is clear that the discovery of the Unconscious necessitated someone who was listening with the third ear. That someone indeed was Sigmund Freud who was the first to pay attention, in a very systematic way, to what might be regarded as trivial phenomena like dreams, parapraxes and jokes. It was in these formations that the Freudian unconscious had to be looked for and it was in analysing them that Freud found evidence for the same psychical mechanisms which he held responsible for the formation of neurotic symptoms. This resulted, for example, in his recognition of the overwhelming importance of sexuality and its repression, discoveries which were confirmed, time and again, by his own clinical experience and that of his close collaborators.

Very soon however, by the time of the Great War, psychoanalysis came to a standstill due to the fact that his views on the human psyche and its functioning all too readily found acceptance. That is to say that Freud's neurotics were no longer naive and came to his consulting room with their knowledge of sexual symbolism: had the Unconscious closed itself again?[5] They reacted in the same way as Smiley Blanton, the American psychiatrist who so urgently wanted to become an analyst. To this end he came over to Vienna and started his training analysis with Freud. The brave man kept a diary of his sessions and there we can find a beautiful example of the closing of the Unconscious and of the way in which Freud tried to re-open it.

At a given moment of the treatment Freud questions his patient on the fact that he never comes up with a dream - for after all, did he want to become an analyst? As a reaction to this intervention -

we perfectly might qualify it as a suggestion - Blanton started to produce such an amount of dreams that during the sessions no time
was left for analysing them. To this fact Freud responds with another question: 'Don't you think all that dreaming is pretty boring ?'[6].

What had happened ? In order to prick the prejudice of his
patient who wanted so urgently to become an analyst, Freud questions his motivation, or, to put it more properly, his desire, and
therefore refers him to his own dreams, to the 'other scene' (*die
andere Schauplatz*). His patient however obviously remains captured
in the dual and imaginary relationship between pupil and master, a
relationship which is reigned by the passion of *the not-wanting-to-
know*. To this dual relationship and the continuously 'empty speaking' of his patient, Freud has no choice but to try to reintroduce the
function of the third ear, of the *Other* through which the
Unconscious realises itself. By the words 'don't you think all that
dreaming is pretty boring?', he again questions the desire of his
patient and in so doing, provides the *gap* necessary for the appearance of the Unconscious.

This sequence can be represented on the so-called L-schema
which Lacan developed during the early fifties, at the time when he
was vigorously criticising the way in which the Freudian unconscious had been barred in ego-analysis.

'Why don't you come up with a dream?'
'Don't you think all that dreaming is
pretty boring'

S — — → (a')
Subject   Other
a ○ ←——— (A)

I want to become an analyst'   'the other scene'

What in this schema is labelled as the imaginary relationship
between *a* and *a'*, between two egos, between the ego of the patient
or subject on the one hand and the ego of the analyst on the other
hand, is what tends to be established in every intersubjective relationship - be it therapeutic or not. Lacan criticized not so much the
appearance of it in so-called ego-analysis but rather its promotion as

the instrument to reach the final goal of the treatment: in the end, and with help of the 'sane' part of his own ego - whatever that may be - the patient had to identify himself with the ego of his analyst. This *exploitation* of the mirror-relation between *a* and *a'*, that is to say of the axis of 'understanding' and resistance, runs contrary to Freud's project which consisted precisely in the *exploration of* the 'other scene'.

It may be clear from our example that the two interventions of Freud tried to shift the discourse of his patient towards the symbolic axis on which something of the subject of the Unconscious could be revealed from the place of the *Other* - e.g. something of the desire which motivated his judgement: 'I want to become an analyst'.

This appearing of the Unconscious can never be a matter of course, nor is it lasting. The contrary is true: the Unconscious takes us by surprise, just like the rabbit of the magician - however, it presupposes the *presence* of the magician who catches it by the ears. Or as Lacan puts it: *'who* is speaking depends on its reception'.[7] This means that the analyst is at least responsible for the direction of the discourse of his patient. On his reception of that discourse - as an alter-ego or from the place of the *Other* - depends whether it will be trapped in a dual and imaginary relationship full of love and hatred or whether from time to time something of the Unconscious will be realized through the *Other.*

This takes us to another sense of our statement: 'the Unconscious presupposes the *Other'.* I have chosen a second example from my own psychopathology of everyday life. A few weeks ago, I got quite upset by some things that are happening in our faculty, things that have to do with... let us call it a kind of 'conspiracy' against clinical psychology. A recent restructuring of the faculty has given birth - no doubt in the name of democracy - to some commissions in which a coalition has been established as a result of which the old battle between hardline experimental psychology and clinical psychology has been revived. Last Monday, however, as I was preparing my lecture for today, I had managed to ban my thoughts about that out of my mind, when around noon my Professor phoned, asking me to come over to him to discuss some things concerning that 'conspiracy'. I apologised for not being able to come at once 'because I was cooking', which is, as a matter of fact, something I never manage to do. As a friend who, for many years, has been acquainted with me but foremost as an analyst, he replied: 'so, you are cooking?'. At that very moment, firstly, I realised how full of anger I really was - 'to cook with anger' we say in Dutch - and secondly, I could understand why precisely during the last days I had started to prepare meals.

To put it in a more formal way, one could say that the signifier 'to cook' represents the subject for another signifier - 'with anger' - and that it is in the *gap* between those two signifiers that something of the repressed, of the Unconscious is revealed. But foremost, my recognition or acknowledgement of that piece of truth presupposed the presence of another person who was listening with that third ear, that is to say who did not focus on some kind of message or significance but on the signifiers which constitute the *Other*.

$$S^1 \text{ 'to cook'} \quad \longrightarrow \quad S^2 \text{ 'with anger'}$$
$$\$$$

The Freudian unconscious will be open as long as an analyst, in his referring to the *Other*, preserves the *gap* which according to Lacan is precisely the dimension which far too often had been forgotten by second and third generation analysts: '(...) the Freudian unconscious is situated at that point, where between cause and that which it affects, there is always something wrong (...) For what the Unconscious does is to show us the gap through which neurosis recreates a harmony with a real (...)'.[8]

For in the end, the Unconscious is not something positive. It can not be considered as a mere collection of repressed pathogenic memories the repression of which has to be undone by way of free association and interpretation. At its limit, the Unconscious always has to do with the 'nonrealised'[9], with the 'unborn'[10], with 'impediment, failure, split'[11] , and with surprise.

'Return to Freud'

Evidence for this thesis on the Unconscious can be found from the very beginning of psychoanalysis and throughout Freud's writings. The manifest dream-content, for example, is to be considered as a translation or as a result of secondary elaboration which is definitely not to be equated with the Unconscious itself. Even the free associations connected with elements of the manifest dream-content do not bring the Unconscious to light. Rather, the production of signifiers makes nothing but a contour around the 'navel of the dream', around that which continuously tends to be realised through the *Other*, although never succeeding in this. In other words: the Unconscious that confronted Freud refers us to the *not-yet-symbolised*.

Now, it may be clear that this insight has important implications for the sense or direction of analytical practice. In analysis we do not dig for 'nuggets' or specific ideational contents, but try to give opportunity for symbolisation, for *judgement*. In order to give evidence for this view I would like to comment on a longer passage from the *Studies on Hysteria* which contains, in my opinion, a magnificent description of the relation between the symbolic, the Unconscious, and the direction of the cure.

In his chapter on the psychotherapy of hysteria, Freud describes the progress which is to be made in the course of therapy in the following way:

'Things that belong to the external strata are recognised without difficulty; they had indeed always remained in the ego's possession, and the only novelty to the ego is their connection with the deeper strata of pathological material. Things that are brought to light from these deeper strata are also recognised and acknowledged, but often only after considerable hesitations and doubts.' [12]

Obviously Freud here differentiates between contents which belong to several strata of the psychical apparatus. In that sense we might suppose that the 'hard labour' - Freud's qualification - which has to be done in therapy consists in overcoming the resistance or in making abstraction of the other (*a'*) in order *to remember* things which belong to the deepest strata. And indeed, we must admit that this to some extent bears witness to clinical experience: transference supports reminiscence - through new love the past returns. Freud continues:

'Visual memory-images are of course more difficult to disavow than the memory-traces of mere trains of thought. Not at all infrequently the patient begins by saying: 'It's possible that I thought this, but I can't remember having done so.' And it is not until he has been familiar with the hypothesis for some time that he comes to recognise it as well; he remembers - and confirms the fact, too, by subsidiary links - that he really did once have the thought.' [13]

From this passage it becomes clear that Freud is describing two different things: the *actual producing* of trains of thought during free association on the one hand, and the *recognition or acknowledgment* of them as *ancient memories* on the other. As for example when a patient, firstly, tells us that as a young boy he considered his mother to be the most beautiful woman on earth and, secondly, describes the visual memory-image or scene in which his one-year old little brother is sitting on the kitchen-floor consuming his paint box. It might happen that our patient has no problem at all in recognising that his first train of thought, the one concerning his mother, really did exist at the time. As for his second train of thought, however, he might well recognise his letting his little brother consume his paint box as a manifestation of a death-wish, he might even admit that probably such a death-wish did exist at the time, but he just cannot acknowledge it as a memory:

'The ideas which are derived from the greatest depth and which form the nucleus of the pathogenic organisation are also those which are acknowledged as memories by the patient with greatest difficulty. Even when everything is finished and the patients have been overborne by the force of logic and have been convinced by the therapeutic effect accompanying the emergence of precisely these ideas - when, I say, the patients themselves accept the fact that they thought this or that, they often add: "But I can't *remember* having thought it.". It is easy to come to terms with them by telling them that the thoughts were *unconscious*. But how is this state of affairs to be fitted into our own psychological views? Are we to disregard this withholding of recognition on the part of patients, when, now that the work is finished, there is no longer any motive for their doing so? *Or are we to suppose that we are really dealing with thoughts which never came about, which merely had a possibility of existing, so that the treatment would lie in the accomplishment of a psychical act which did not take place at the time ? '* [14]

The psychical act Freud is talking about can be nothing but the *subjective judgement* throughout the *Other* by which the subject of the Unconscious is actually revealed or even established, by which the nonrealised is symbolised.

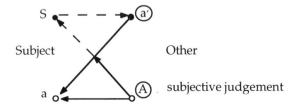

That is to say that what is presented as the discovery of the Unconscious, during the cure, is precisely what is produced in the *gap*. That is why Lacan states that the Unconscious is structured like a language or presupposes the *Other*. From this it can also be understood why Lacan urged analysts to study the linguistic field: 'In our time, in the historical period that has seen the foundation of a science that may be termed human, but which must be distinguished from any kind of psycho-sociology, namely, linguistics, whose model is the combinatory operation, functioning spontaneously, of itself, in a presubjective way - it is this linguistic structure that gives its status to the Unconscious.'[15].

However different the Unconscious might appear after the Lacanian elaboration with the help of modern linguistics, still it remains the case that throughout Freud's works, hints at the sense of that elaboration are manifold.

There is, first of all, Freud's study *On Aphasia* containing a theory of language which can be situated in the tradition of analytical philosophy, a theory of language which precisely was recognized by James Strachey as the logical complement to Freud's paper on the 'Unconscious'[16]. Secondly, there are the mechanisms of condensation and displacement which have been rightly identified as the linguistic categories of metaphor and metonymy. But perhaps most convincing is the figuring in Freud's work of the fundamental insight that there can be no *Other* of the *Other*, that is to say that there is no metalanguage which might reveal the truth of the *Other*, of the Unconscious.

There is no Other of the Other

That is the sense which must be attributed both to the passage quoted from Freud's *Studies on Hysteria* and to his paper on 'Negation', published thirty years later, a sense which was taken up again in 1937 in his paper on 'Constructions in Analysis'[17]. The revelation of the Unconscious can not be measured by the affirmation or disaffirmation by the subject, that is, as it were, by a 'judgement of the judgement'. Indeed, only the subsequent material appearing during free association can reveal the truth of what has been said before.

[1] J Lacan, *Four Fundamental Concepts of Psychoanalysis, Seminar XI*, (1964), p 25.

[2] *Ibid*, p 25.

[3] *Ibid*, p 21.

[4] *Ibid*, p 20.

[5] Cf. J Lacan, (1955), 'Variantes de la cure-type' , in: *Ecrits*, Paris, Seuil, 1966, pp 332-333.

[6] S Blanton, *Tagebuch meiner Analyse bei Sigmund Freud*, Frankfurt am Main, Ullstein, 1975, p 32

[7] 'Ainsi, non seulernent le sens de ce discours réside dans celui qui 1'écoute, mais c'est de son accueil que dépend *qui* le dit: c'est à savoir le sujet à qui il donne accord et foi, ou cet autre que son discours lui livre comme constitué.' J Lacan, (1955), 'Variantes de la cure-type', in *Ecrits*, Paris, Seuil, 1966, p 331.

[8] J Lacan, *Four Fundamental Concepts of Psychoanalysis*, op. cit. p 22.

[9] *Ibid*, p 22.

[10] *Ibid*, p 23.

[11] *Ibid*, p 25.

[12] J Breuer and S Freud, *Studies on Hysteria, S E* Vol II, p 299.

[13] *Ibid*, p 299.

[14] *Ibid*, p 300. (my italics)

[15] J Lacan, *Four Fundamental Concepts of Psychoanalysis*, op.cit., pp 20-2 1.

[16] S Freud, *On Aphasia, A Critical Study*, (1891), New York, International University Press, 1953; S Freud, the Unconscious, *(1915), S E* Vol. XIV, pp 159-215.

[17] S Freud, Negation, (1925), *S E* Vol XIX, pp 235-239; S. Freud, Constructions in Analysis, (1937), *S E* Vol. XXIII, pp 255-269.

DISCUSSION ON THE UNCONSCIOUS

Q: This is a question for Robin Anderson: conscious phantasy - are you using that as a synonym for 'the imagination'?

Anderson: Yes! In its broadest sense.

Q. Mary Sullivan: This may be a rather mischievous point... in the material from Eric there were two cats. Who, do you think, was the second cat?

Anderson: One might speculate it was the other parent. I could go off on that. I don't know. All I can say is I'm glad it's possible to think about what I've said. Perhaps it's the other parent. What I wanted to show was not in any way a full understanding or analysis of the material but to have a framework for thinking.

Sullivan: ... it's just interesting that you spoke about your difficulties with the supervision and I wonder whether you connected that to the idea of what that would mean to that boy.

Anderson: Oh I see what you mean! Yes. It may well have been that the boy had a sense of another object trying to cope with something, and that raises the notion of the couple in therapy.

Q: We have learned about the nature of the subjectivity of the analyst who has to understand the patient from their own experience and then give a subjective judgement, but from what you have said - and here of course comes the symbolism - the judgement required in therapy from the Lacanian point of view is from the side of the patient. When put that way the analyst is using understanding of what is happening in the patient and doesn't need to respond from the other side of the gap. There is no use of symbolism, no exchange of feelings, but of understanding alone. What do you think?

Geerardyn: If I understood your question, I used the notion of subjective judgement: just to put it firmly - subjective judgement is required in therapy on the side of the *patient!* From the Lacanian viewpoint this is not on the side of the analyst, who must not mingle his own history or even theory or subjectivity with the analysand - with the story of the analysand. The analyst has his own experience of therapy, and cannot mingle it. The analytical effects come from the speaking of the subject, which starts here in the register of the Symbolic. Mixing of one's own subjective judgement would maintain an imaginary discourse. The speaking of the analyst's subjective judgement gives a basis for discussion - a delusional dialogue - but this is not an analytic situation.

Sullivan: There is erosion from the other on the other side of the gap to understanding the patient without using subjectivity ...

Anderson: I'm interested in that whole notion. It had a lot of resonances for me. Your paper shows a picture of the Lacanian analyst being firm with themselves in relation to not mingling their subjectivity and being clear about that boundary. Of course *we* do all absolutely feel we have to lend our subjectivity to the patient. In a sense it's a risk - you can visit your own problems on the analysand in the session and the hope is you have been well enough analysed - there is a risk you can hand your own problems to the patient. What *we* would do - we need a firm analyst-object to help keep our mind on the task. I don't think from that example you would say Freud came to his understanding through his own humanity and unconscious but that he would be an Analyst with a big 'A' to enable him to respond to the patient in that way. We feel we have to be disciplined and have a strong analytic object derived from our own analysis alongside us to enable us to relate to our patients.

Geerardyn: In his 'Four Discourses' Lacan tried to formalise the position to be taken by the analyst. Just as you said, analysts from different kinds of backgrounds demand discipline with regard to one's own unconscious and preserving a distance from the story of your patient ...

Anderson: You need a structure to work with!

Geerardyn: Yes.

Sullivan: Where do you put the gap? In which place?

Geerardyn: Between two signifiers!

Sullivan: The patient and the analyst?

Geerardyn: Uhm... No! Between two signifiers *(laughter)*. What has not been said appears from the discourse of the patient constituted in signifiers - free association, if you want - of the patient. You want to say *this* but you say something else. In slips of the tongue something tends to be realised, symbolised. So when you make a mistake in symbolising what is trying to realise itself ...

Sullivan: In the gap the healing is taking place?

Geerardyn: The symbolic *needs* a gap to function! Lacan uses the metaphor of a little toy - all kinds of plastic parts you can move. In order to make sense of them, to move them, there must be one missing or you cannot move it. The gap is not overcome. The symbolic needs a gap, otherwise it cannot function.

Q. Joanna Swift: This is a question to Robin Anderson about a supervision I had, as I was curious to know how Kleinians would deal with this particular issue. At a given moment in a long piece of work the patient wants to take grapes from the front of my house... this is a patient who has a rather intense relationship with me. This is important to her symbolically - her actually doing it! She stole a bunch, tells me at the next session she put one in her mouth and tells me 'it was a sacrament'!

My interpretation was 'My body, my blood' - playing on the language of the communion service, playing on the signifier.

Now, what the Kleinian supervisor said was 'It's the nipple'!... It was translated into the language of primal phantasy. It ends up in the same place but what I had was a chain of associations with father's alcoholism, the past - which opened up a chain which was closed off by returning to the breast. Where is the place of language and chains of signifiers in relation to your notion of phantasy?

Anderson: I don't want to be an alternative supervisor, and I don't know enough about the details. If I make an interpretation which reduces the thing, giving meaning, then I'd question myself. It's a difficult one. I'd say we Kleinian analysts would be very sparing in interpretations like that now ... We'd have a prototype of where experience might begin. We'd have a starting point of the experience. You're saying it's a natural interpretation intended to open up thinking and awareness of experience ....

Swift: What I'm getting at is that I would question my ability to know where it's going, where it's leading. You Kleinians purport to *know* what precedes the material and I don't know where it's going and hope I can throw something in that might ....

Anderson: Sometimes one understands what the patient clearly doesn't. I might get a sense that they're caught up in something which I have a sense of, and that it might be important to give them something. I think to say 'that's the nipple' only has meaning if it's full of meaning for the patient. I vary; sometimes like Freud with Blanton I'm trying to open the gap - sometimes the gap is so closed there isn't a sense of you and them. One is trying to establish the possibility of dialogue and wouldn't be wanting to prematurely attempt to understand. A notion that influences many of us Kleinians is Keats's idea of negative capability - to tolerate an experience of not knowing. That's an essential prerequisite for any work - to tolerate not knowing. When one isn't aware of the gap, it's like with the patient who can't start analysis with Freud because he's too bound up with problems of relations with others. It's about establishing the conditions on which the analysis can start.

Q. David Mayers: I'm trying to think about the gap between signifiers in relation to Dr Anderson's black cats. There is a chain of associations when there are two. The point of view shifts. The cat with the bird in its mouth starts off clearly with oral sadism, teeth and claws, and then shifts to dirt and anal sadism. Perhaps the two cats are the boy's misconceived attempt to sort out these two points of view, the anal and oral, which have become confused. From the Kleinian/Bionic point of view we're interested not only in signifiers but in the patient's attitude to signifiers. For the Lacanians this might be rather a deluded attempt to bridge the gap between signifiers, and this could be one of the differences.

Geerardyn: In the passages to which I referred from Freud he refers to attitude: recognition and acknowledgemenet of judgement which is nothing else than what Lacan would say is the assumption of a desire. If we say the result of analysis presupposes the Other, then at the end of analysis the subject comes to a sense of acknowlegement of desire. What is this? This can only be acknowledged by signifying something - *by judgement!* For instance it is as the subject says at the end of the therapy: 'I have been this. It's finished. I am making a choice.' - or in an assumption of desire in another way: 'I will have become that.' And still this is through a judgement.

In the first example it's something you leave at your analyst's consulting room. It's finished! If you talk about attitude toward signifiers it is by speaking them out you symbolise them!

Anderson: I've got a problem. Before I could respond to you you would need to repeat to me what you mean by signifier. I think I still don't grasp that part? Is it a word?

Geerardyn: It's more than a word. A signifier can be lots of other things, for example a symptom is a signifier which has been partly articulated.

Anderson: So you'd be interested in how a signifier relates to something unconscious.

Geerardyn: Freud said the Unconscious is like an ever-expanding galaxy. So when I start my analysis I have no unconscious. As I proceed with my analysis my unconscious gets bigger. This is the relationship between the signifier and the Unconscious.

Anderson: You said the patient's associations are signifiers?

Geerardyn: Yes, and something will be symbolised which has never been symbolised before.

Anderson: (to Mayers) I can't do justice to your question about the black cats. I feel disorientated. I don't know how to make a bridge. The only thing that reverberates in my mind is how *we* would think of the unconscious world of the baby growing and developing and I suspect there would be a difference there. **(To Swift):** When you had your Kleinian supervision, I'm sure it was very good ....

Swift: It was Fantastic!

Anderson: Well, I've got far enough into the depressive position to be able to take that. I take your point about the connection between the grapes and the alcoholism of her father and that being more than the relationship between baby and mother, and if you interpret that it's an integrating experience for a patient. I suppose I would say symbolism doesn't start for us as language as it does for Lacanians, but from collecting these unbearable experiences which become bearable and linked with words as the baby gets meaning. The task of analysis is to create links and bridges between these areas.

I would be interested in *why* Blanton needed Freud in such a way, so clingy. Freud dealt with it by thinking the patient needed a bit of a push to create a gap where they could talk. We would think of it in terms of being afraid of being overwhelmed by something. We would be thinking 'why does the patient need to cling to Freud? What is he afraid of?'. We might feel that though he was a famous analyst he might have a mind that was afraid of being pushed away, of not being ready as an infant. We think of the infantile world starting off from a storm of primeval incoherent forces, with the baby pulled this way and that, and somehow that becomes meaningful and coherent, and sometimes one deals with that by restricting the area in analysis.

Q. Kirsty Hall: One problem is that Kleinian and Lacanian language is very different and there are hardly any equivalents. I was wondering if both speakers could relate this to the idea of the primal scene. There are differing Kleinian and Lacanian ideas of symbolism and its origins, and of the construction and functioning of the Unconscious. If you both spoke of the importance Freud put on the primal scene in The Wolf Man that might bring out some differences with respect to symbolism and the Unconscious.

Anderson: The idea of having a common piece of material and both looking at it is a good one, but it's a long time since I read The Wolf Man and I'd have to go back and read it again.

Geerardyn: There is a passage which reflects something of the discussion going on here relating to the function of the signifier. It's a passage commented on many times by Lacan, especially where he was developing the theory of foreclosure. He commented on this, on the rejection of the signifier when the Wolf Man was sitting in the garden, as a small boy, and saw one of his fingers hanging by a tiny piece of skin. It was an hallucination. That is reformulated when Lacan slowly spends the Third Seminar - a whole year - exploring what is the specific mechanism which establishes the structure of paranoia. He has some notions of how the mechanism should be named: rejection is the term he tries. What precisely has been *rejected?* During the whole academic year he tries to find the answer. The answer is - it is a *signifier* which has been rejected. But not just any signifier: within the Oedipus complex he locates the signifier of the Name-of-the-Father. In developing his reasoning he takes the case of the Wolf Man. In the hallucination he finds a similar thing, though the Wolf Man is definitely not a case of paranoia. The rejection of the signifier of sexual difference which has been rejected at that time by the Wolf Man *returns from the Real* in the form of visual or auditory hallucination. The relation between the signifier and the Wolf Man. Just a small example!

Q: Could the signifier be a psychic representative? In the Lacanian view the signifier has to be bound to something, it can't just be a feeling as with the Kleinian view where you can work with affect and see where that leads. Until a signifier arises from the Unconscious of the analysand the affect is looking for a signifier to bind it. It's not that Lacanians consider affect is unimportant. It's got to go into the chain of free associations before you can make any sense of it. Would that be right?

Geerardyn: As for the relationship between signifier and affect - affect is important! Whenever a patient comes and has a need for help all you can hear is free association, endless symbolisation and connection of signifiers - his 'story'. But there is always affect. See Lacan's Seminar on Anxiety - in the end there is only one affect: *anxiety!* All other kinds of emotions and affects are partial symbolisations of that one affect, anxiety. When I come to say I don't feel happy but discontent, this is manifestly not an anxiety attack, not physiological parameters, sweating, hyperventilation, palpitation. But I can't say *what I'm discontented about!* Still Lacan stresses the whole dictionary of emotions which we can borrow from psychologists. In every situation we are confronted by affect.

The other part of your question is the reference to Freud. If we look at Freud's first confrontation with neurosis this was the Clinic of the Real. Read his letters to Fliess, his *Studies on Hysteria.* In trying to deal with the problem of affect he generates a clinic of the excessively-intense representation or idea cathected with affect. What has not been symbolised is the Real - is the affect! We should give the patient the opportunity to symbolise. Between two signifiers there is always a chance that Real anxiety - for example the panic attack - can trigger the Real. In an anxiety attack someone just tries to master affect and put words on it. Then the affect is the establishment or rising up of certain meaning - as soon as I get the opportunity to add another signifier there is a shift in meaning. In clinical practice the anlysand says his story, repeats it, memories alter each time they are spoken. It is never the same story. There is not just one meaning. When you repeat the story it is never the same story. When a signifier is added, meaning shifts.

Robert M. Young: I have a contribution in the same spirit of running the risk of oversimplification. In Kleinian work if you have a series of words - feeling, experience, affect, utterance - there isn't a sense of hugh jumps as you go from one to another. You listen and interpret without any sense that language and signifier are in a special problematic intellectual space. If I'm good at my job I'm not saying there isn't a space for epistemology - but one doesn't feel fraught about these levels if the work is going well.

So much is made of this and I can't understand what all the fuss is about. Robin asks what is the signifier and everybody titters. I associate with him - part of me says 'I don't stumble over signifiers - I just try to do my job'. There is a huge difference of underlying assumptive words in the frameworks between these two positions. Would you like to respond.

Anderson: Yes! I can relate to that. I'm not quite at the stage of thinking what all the fuss is about but wondering what it is we feel our respective tasks are. It isn't that one idealises 'the moment of understanding'. The whole analytic process is what one is about. We often speak of moments of contact. It seemed to me that was important. I would say I think probably the moment Freud said 'your dreams are boring' is a moment of contact which breaks through, and one is after the conditions that make the contact that patients would have with themselves and the analyst more possible. One is trying to make interventions that will make the patient feel contained. That isn't just being 'loved'; that needn't be just love, but something that's brought them up short and might be quite difficult.

When I hear *you* (to Filip Geerardyn) I don't just hear a foreign language. What's difficult is I also hear something that feels familiar. We're ironing out these points about signifiers and differences. This is as far as I feel I can take it. I think something about the different positions we're coming from causes that difficulty ...

Geerardyn: It isn't that the only thing that matters from the Lacanian point of view is the signifier! But in the *clinical situation* all that *can* appear is signifiers! If you have two signifiers and the gap between them, what can appear between two signifiers is the Real: the affect, anxiety! But precisely that is the register of the Symbolic: there is not just the Real.

Lacan says the subject is so full of horror with the effects of the Real. There is something else - and it is the object - *objet a*. It is not good to introduce new theoretical concepts at the end. I want to make this shift - there is a link between the Other as object and the Other as Symbolic.

Things look different now because I am speaking in English. There is only one letter of difference between the Other and the M(Other) you (Robin Anderson) are talking about. In the very first attempt by Freud to make sense of the Unconscious he defined the mother, as Lacan so many years after defined the mother, as the first Other who from the point of her language and her own psyche interprets and gives significance to what the baby is doing. That's the importance of mother. A fresh little baby just born, crying and screaming: the mother thinks 'is it hungry, or is it wet, is it ill?' But she does this from *her own psyche:* Lacan says it is from her own desires that she symbolises something for that baby.

Anderson: That seems a very good point on which to end!

AN INTERVIEW WITH DONALD MELTZER[1]

Marc du Ry

M. du R. One characteristic of the British scene is that there are divergent ideas even within the British Psycho-Analytical Society itself. So what really distinguishes the Kleinian approach from other approaches with respect to training?

D.M. That depends on where you put it. The Kleinian approach has two centres really, I mean, the main centre, of course, is in the Institute of Psycho-Analysis and the other centre is in the Tavistock Clinic, especially the child aspect of Kleinian analysis. Now, to look at the Kleinian approach to training you would really have to consider what has happened since Mrs. Klein's death. Before Mrs. Klein's death there really was a gentleman's agreement, a Kleinian training in which people who were in Kleinian analysis and Kleinian supervision had a few seminars with the other two groups, but essentially their training programme was with Kleinian analysts. A few years after her death, the membership policies changed, the society changed in its population and its politics, the training was amalgamated and the Kleinian training was more or less swamped, in my opinion, by the general training.

Of course a person could still have a Kleinian analysis and Kleinian supervisors, but the didactic work was much more diffuse and the distinctness of the Kleinian approach was played down so that a sort of rapprochement with the Middle Group in particular was established, and people were encouraged to have at least one middle group supervisor and things of that sort. I think that in the British Society the distinctness of the Kleinian group has equally suffered because the assimilation of Bion's contribution has not really gone forward. It has been mainly at a lip service level and has not been assimilated into clinical practice, so that the Kleinian work at the British Society tends to be more or less at the level, in my opinion, that it was at in the middle or late sixties: moreover, with a certain push in a direction which I myself think is extremely unpleasant - rather combative, aggressive. It has earned the Kleinians a bad reputation really, people speak of the Kleinian gestapo and things of that sort, which is very unpleasant. But I think they have brought it on themselves by certain rather aggressive trends in technique.

M. du R. And in the Tavistock?

D.M. The work in the Tavistock is very different. It would much more conform to what I have said about the artistic and humane nature of psychoanalytic work, with much less emphasis on theory, and much more emphasis on observation. In fact the course is divided in two; we have a two year observation course and then two years of a course in clinical practice which makes it a very different kind of educational system. It also keeps the whole business of selection of candidates to a minimum. The whole atmosphere is one of work rather than of didactic units, and of course the motivation for people who want to work with children is often very different from the motivation of people who want to train as analysts of adult patients. The work has been largely under the influence of my wife and myself and people trained with and by us. It has remained so and has been very influenced by Bion's contributions. I think it has really developed very richly.

M. du R.   I'd like to contrast a little bit more organisations of the International Psycho-Analytical Association (IPA), and the Tavistock as far as training is concerned, because their relationship remains a puzzle for non-British readers. If we take supervision, there is a critique that the analyst rather than the analysis is taken as the object of supervision[2].

D.M.   Yes, that is probably true. And it probably is true that there is a widespread custom of the supervisor examining and discussing the counter-transference with the student analyst, and that is something that is never done at the Tavistock: that is left entirely to the person's personal analysis.

M. du R.   An important difference.

D.M.   I mean that would be viewed by us as such an intrusion on a person's privacy that it would simply not occur unless something flagrant in the nature of acting in the counter-transference was going on that had to be curbed. But that rarely occurs. Yes it certainly is true that in many institutes the supervision is primarily a teaching function, to train the student analyst in the techniques of psychoanalysis, and not a supervision of the therapy of the patient. In the Tavistock it has *always* been a supervision of the therapy of the patient. And the belief is that people learn to do psychoanalysis by treating patients and by having the experience. This is part, of course, of assimilating Bion's concept of learning from experience as opposed to learning 'about' things.

M. du R.   Now we have also seen with respect to the IPA, that the differences between the training analysis and the therapeutic or personal analysis are somewhat blurred: what is the policy at the Tavistock?

D.M.   Well, of course, the Tavistock's policy has always been to have virtually nothing to do with a person's training analysis; to set as few limits as possible on the person that can be chosen for the analysis; that if a person who applied for training is already in analysis, not to insist on their changing to somebody who is in some sense 'more respectable' and so on. Therefore people could have a Jungian analysis. They have sometimes been accepted with analysts who were not members of either the Jungian society or the British Society. Then eventually of course the Tavistock's own child analysts have become skilled and experienced adult analysts who have become acceptable as training analysts in their own right. It has become self-developing in that way. It also respects people who have had previous analyses and does not insist that they have to be in analysis during the duration of their training; that is, if they have had analyses that have been of adequate duration and in the patient's and analyst's opinion have been successful analyses therapeutically, the Tavistock accepts these as the training analysis. I think only the French have done anything like that.

M. du R. Well, to continue contrasting these two institutions, the question of knowledge and the transmission of knowledge arises. It has been said that an analysis each time calls into question a particular knowledge and its effects, and that each analysis is for that reason unique (whether therapeutic or didactic). How does this knowledge relate to the set body of knowledge which is taught or transmitted, in lectures for example?

D.M. The emphasis at the Tavistock has *always* been on clinical seminars and work on clinical material rather than any kind of theoretical lectures; the study of the literature has always been placed relatively late in the training so that people start work without a lot of theoretical ideas and preconceptions in their minds. It probably is true that people who have studied at the Tavistock are less enthusiastic and less widely read in cultural psychoanalytic literature, but they are much more widely read in cultural literature. And a good reason for that is quite simply that the people who work at the Tavistock are largely people who have been teachers, who've had history and literature degrees and who naturally in the course of their work use literary examples to clarify clinical problems and so on. And it naturally stirs students to read literature rather than psychoanalytic literature.

M. du R. You studied medicine in New York and psychiatry in St. Louis. But your final analytic training was here in Britain with Melanie Klein. Could you describe your own training a bit, what you remember as its truly formative effects?

D.M. Well ... for damn knows what reason I decided to be a psychoanalyst instead of an engineer when I was sixteen and first read some Freud. I had no idea what it was that moved me in that direction - some adolescent fantasy. As a medical student I worked with Loretta Bendor as an elective, and that decided me to be a child psychiatrist and child analyst. I went to St. Louis for my psychiatric training almost entirely for logistic reasons, because it was halfway between my family and my wife's family - not a good reason at all - and I trained there as a neuro-psychiatrist and a child psychiatrist. But my interest in Mrs. Klein started when I was helping out with schizophrenic and psychotic children on Loretta Bendor's ward at Bellevue. By that time I had read a fair amount of psychoanalytic literature and psychiatric literature as a medical student, and that absolutely clicked with me in the context of these psychotic children. It took me from then on, say, maybe from 1943 until 1954, to manage to arrange to come over here to do my psychoanalytic training and my formation as an analyst.

M. du R. What made the greatest impact on you at that time?

D.M. Although I had an analysis and quite a lot of psychoanalytic training during my years in St. Louis in a study group connected with the Chicago Institute, my formation really, as an analyst, is here doing cases under supervision, attending seminars, etc. and the main formation was undoubtedly through my analysis with Mrs. Klein. It was certainly the making of me, there's no question about it in my mind.

M. du R. The Tavistock seems to have played an important part in your career...

D.M. Oh yes, I started teaching at the Tavistock; I was associated with Esther Bick who stated the child training there; and, as I said, then I was married to Martha Harris and we worked together at the Tavistock, teaching. I'm sure we undoubtedly contributed to the structuring of that training.

M. du R. Now, at the moment, you don't seem to be working, correct me if I'm wrong, not for the British Society of course, but not for the Tavistock either. Do you prefer to work outside of these organisations?

D.M. Well, I don't lecture at the Institute. I probably wouldn't be accepted as a supervisor. Most of the people who come to me for supervision are qualified people. They are largely Kleinian analysts, Jungian analysts, also people who have trained at the British Association of Psychotherapists, and the London Centre for Psychotherapy, people of that sort. My work abroad is mostly with children and with people working with psychotic patients. I've been at universities, occasionally at institutes where I've been invited to talk, but I've actually no institutional, no formal institutional commitment.   Well, yes, I am a Visiting Professor at Milan University, but that is rather nominal.

M. du R.   How did it come about that the Tavistock became recognised as a 'specialist training' for child analysts?

D.M. Because child analysis died at the Institute. I mean, it was a pity. Winnicott, who was very keen on child analytic training, had a department of child analysis built with ten consulting rooms and they were never used. They finally became used by secretaries as the bureaucracy expanded. So child analysis just moved out to the Tavistock and Miss Freud's Hampstead Clinic.   There was an attempt to bring Miss Freud's clinic back into the Institute in a certain way later on, but it never really succeeded. One of the reasons was that it became fairly clear that people who trained initially as child therapists and then went on to do the adult training at the Institute disappeared from the children's field. They just disappeared. They might have retained membership in the Association of Child Psychotherapy, but they disappeared both as teachers and as therapists of children. The result was that people were no longer encouraged to do that, but were encouraged really - since people can work with children only for a certain number of years, by the time they get into their fifties they need to cut down on it - to do a sort of informal training in work with adult patients.   In the Tavistock this is just now being formalised as a training in adult analytic psychotherapy for experienced child psychotherapists.

M. du R.   So I hear, yes. To dwell on this question of specialisation a bit, I've asked you before about the qualities of child analysts, does this not pose a problem as to the identity or essence of an analyst? Can one separate a child analyst from an adult analyst?

D.M. No, absolutely not, but the thing is that people who have never worked with children do not see the child in the adult patient in the same way as people who have worked with children, and therefore their way of talking to them - of handling their patients, and their way of seeing the material - lacks this really infantile dimension. In so far as there is an infantile dimension, it tends to be terribly theoretical and not really based on an intimate knowledge of how children talk and think and play, and so on. And unfortunately people in raising their own children practically never devote the kind of systematic observation to a child that one gets in therapy. I mean one can raise half a dozen children and never know as much about how children think, feel and play and so on, as a child therapist does after a few years of work. So that makes a big difference in the quality of analytic work. Of course in the heyday of Mrs. Klein all the people in the Kleinian group trained as child and adolescent analysts as well. But that only meant a young child, a latency child, and an adolescent, and most people never saw children again; I mean, I was trained as a child psychiatrist so it was very easy and natural for me to go on working with children.

M. du R.   In your long experience in the field what qualities have you come to expect from psychoanalysts, indeed psychoanalytic psychotherapists, who work with psychotic and autistic children?

D.M.   Well, I suppose that my idea of the qualities that make for a good analyst have changed through the years. I used to think that it required a very high intelligence; I don't really think that anymore. I think any good intelligence is adequate because the kind of intelligence that is involved in psychoanalytic work really comes from the depths of the mind and not from the kind of levels that ordinarily manifest themselves in social and academic circles. The main thing that I look for when it comes to referring people and assessing which one of my students I feel free to refer patients to is kindness. This I learnt from Roger Money-Kyrle, and it seems to me to be the absolutely essential requirement for an analyst. Kindness means generosity, forbearance, a readiness for sacrifices, and a capacity for intense emotional interest in a person. It is a very complicated concept. I don't like people who are too steeped in theory, or too interested in theory, or who think that psychoanalytic theories are explanatory, and so on. My recommendations to anybody coming into this field would not be to study medicine but to study English literature or art history or things of that sort, the humanities, literature, but not philosophy...

M. du R.   Well, that can be defended...

D.M.   I really feel a philosophical training can be a great drawback, speaking from my experience with philosophers in this field.

M. du R.   To shift the point somewhat, you don't think that, at the training stage already, some form of theoretical creativity is a good thing?

D.M.   No, I think it's a great drawback; in so far as psychoanalysis is a science at all, it is a descriptive science; it is in no sense an explanatory science. The whole thrust of genuine advance in psychoanalysis was from accurate and sustained observation and accurate and honest description, and that is practically all that psychoanalytic research is, as far as I am concerned.

M. du R.   To move on from training let us look for a moment at the issue of institutions. How would you evaluate the psychoanalytic contribution to the work done in hospitals and the like, in comparison with other psychotherapeutic work?

D.M.   Well it is not my field. As far as I can see, the greatest value has come out of the development of ideas put forward by Bion in *Experiences in Groups* and developed through this conference up in the Midlands somewhere, an ongoing thing - I can't remember the name exactly - and people like Isabel Menzies Lyth and Elliott Jaques and so on. I haven't taken a great interest in that type of work because my interest in Bion's ideas about groups are mainly about how they can be applied in the analytic situation itself. I've never been a group therapist and I've never really participated in organisations politically any more than I've absolutely been forced to. It's just not my field.

M. du R.   But you've worked both in a clinic and in private practice, so...

D.M.   Well, I ran a clinic in the States: I ran a child psychiatry department. I ran the psychiatric services for the Air Force in the United Kingdom, for six years but under duress. I was never in organisational work, and I'm probably not good at it either.

M. du R.   Could we look at a larger context? What do you think are the most important characteristics or currents which distinguish the psychoanalytic milieu here in Britain from that in other countries, the US for instance?

D.M.   The US, of course, has followed a policy of very strong centralisation, controlling the institutes through the American IPA, whereas nothing of that sort has gone on in Great Britain; it has enabled American psychoanalysis to spread very widely, whereas the policy that has been followed in Britain has been one that has made it impossible for people outside London to train as psychoanalysts. Here the training takes so long that by the time people are trained, their families and lives and practices are established in London and they stay in London. Hence psychoanalysis has had a very unfortunate urban, mono-urban development in Britain, very different from Italy, very different from France, because the British Society has been unyielding in the question of allowing people to have analysis outside London, to name training analysts outside London, to have supervisons outside London. I remember even at a time when there were five of us in Oxford who were training analysts in the British Society, they insisted that our candidates must come to London for one of their two supervisions.

M. du R.   It sounds like a rather petty requirement, purely formal.

D.M.   They were convinced that we were going to form a breakaway society, whereas those of us who had come here had come to get away from the Society, and away from organisations of that sort, and nobody here would have dreamt of forming a psychoanalytical society, but they thought that if we had one more training analyst we'd have enough to start a blah, blah, blah.

M. du R. So what do you see as the most urgent problem facing psychoanalysis here?

D.M. Well the most urgent problem is the dissemination of psychoanalysis in this country. It won't happen. What will happen is that psychoanalysis will be disseminated through new training organisations of variable quality, run by people of varying qualifications who are trained psychotherapists. And that is what is happening already. There are training groups springing up in many centres in this country and of course what they do is to get people to come and lecture to them, and so on, and try to improve their quality.   I have seen some in the South West, Birmingham, Cambridge, places like that, which are developing and will develop further, and the whole mythology of the monopoly of psychoanalysis by the British Society will evaporate eventually, and they will price themselves out of the field.

M. du R. Now you said this development will be of variable quality. This doesn't mean you see the need for some more centralised authority, I presume.

D.M.   No, absolutely not. I'm in favour of people learning together and helping one another to develop. And they will develop. They'll read, they'll get people to come and lecture to them as they do, they'll set up study weekends and things of that sort and they will develop, because it is with their patients that they will develop. There's plenty of literature available to them, and plenty of people who are prepared to come and help them with lectures and seminars and so on, and the Psycho-Analytical Society will just be left behind as a little elitist organisation that eventually I'm afraid, will be rather despised by people.

M. du R. Do you see this as applying to the IPA worldwide?

D.M. Well, there are tendencies in other countries. In Denmark there is a simliar tendency, but not in Germany. I think Germany has developed remarkably, partly because it has at least two centres, and partly because it has been blessed with a very good president. But in the Low Countries, and in Scandinavia, these same sorts of restrictive measures have been followed, and the societies have remained small and controlled by old people, and haven't developed: psychotherapy is developing and psychoanalysis is developing but again it is outside these so-called official groups. I think Spain has had this problem to some extent; I know in Barcelona and in Madrid the societies have remained rather small and elitist and restrictive. And this is partly because of the influence coming from Britain, which is actually mainly a Kleinian influence.

M. du R.   As a last question, perhaps a difficult one, how would you evaluate your own influence, which has some weight, on developments in Britain?

D.M.   These are historical judgements. I think what I have contributed is a strong emphasis on clinical work, on clinical observation. I think I have helped people assimilate Bion's work, which is the next great step in psychoanalysis. I think there are some original bits and pieces in my work, in my thought, and so on, but I don't think that is how psychoanalysis develops. I think that is part of what used to be called the 'stepbook' theory of its development. I mean there have been very few people who have made extraordinary contributions, I would say maybe six or seven altogether, Freud, Abraham, Mrs. Klein, Bion - and I would include people like Paul Schilder and the early Wilhelm Reich. It is only a handful of people who've had original ideas. I'm not a person with original ideas.

M. du R.   Some people would contradict you on that.

D.M.   Well, that is because it's new to them. I say it in a different way, and they don't know where it comes from. That's not modesty, but that's my idea of how psychoanalysis grows. It grows in the consulting rooms, where gradually people become more experienced and able to talk to one another. So long as they stay close to the clinical material, they can talk to one another with more and more understanding. As soon as they start talking theories, pfftt, schools, conflict, politics and so on. I think my contribution has been one of attitude only.

M. du R.   Dr. Meltzer, thank you very much.

1. This article originally appeared in Italian, as *The Kleinian Inheritance of Donald Meltzer* published by La Bottega dell' Anima, and has been translated into English by Marc du Ry. It is reprinted with their permission.

2 D'un discours à l'autre, l'institution dite du contrôle', in *Scilicet* , 6/7, p213.

RETHINKING KLEINIAN INTERPRETATION: WHAT DIFFERENCE DOES IT MAKE?

Eric Laurent

Text commissioned and translated by Marc du Ry

The Use of Speech

In a beautiful paragraph of his *Seminar IV*, p 112, Lacan compares and contrasts Melanie Klein and Anna Freud. What he found lacking at that period, which was actually hyper-interpretative, was the taking into account of the function of speech. It is paradoxical since it was a time in which psychoanalysis produced the richest texts, richest in interpretations which translate: they have the form *"I say this and it is translated into that."* It was a time when analysis had no shame and no modesty. Everything that patients said was translated - a practice based on a naive conception of language which no longer carried the culture of Freud - yet was full of a positivistic conception of language making the Unconscious exist as reference, as the direct denotation of this interpretative flowering. Lacan situated the lack differently for Melanie Klein and Anna Freud.

Anna Freud thought that the child was entirely taken up in the actual moment - the parents are the real and actual parents - so that it is not possible to interpret, only to play. The analyst has to enter the game. Lacan says the following: *I would say that the engagement of the analyst in a relation other than that of speech, leaves the field of speech, if not developed, or even actually conceived, nevertheless indicated* - negatively in fact. By refusing speech Anna Freud demonstrates its scope. That is the credit he gives her. It is kind. By commenting on her work, Lacan learns from her.

Melanie Klein's idea is strictly opposed. Lacan: *Melanie Klein argues that nothing is more similar to an adult analysis than a child analysis, and that even at an extremely precocious age, what is at issue in the unconscious of a child already has nothing to do with the real parents, whatever Anna Freud says. Already between two and a half and three years, the situation is completely changed in relation to what one can see in the real relation.*

We have here an authorisation to interpret from the age of two and a half onwards. There is no doubt about this. But one had to notice it first of all. Now everybody is convinced that at two and a half, three years, one speaks to a child of parents who are already no longer the parents in reality. What has to be revealed in analysis is not an immediate relation, purely and simply, with the real, but one already inscribed in a symbolisation.

Lacan introduced this debate between the two women on the use of speech, within a pragmatic perspective linked to an analytic practice. The express references are on page 98 of *Seminar IV*. Lacan confides that he has reread all the literature of the Anglo-Saxon debate on the phallic stage in the child during the Christmas break. He says: *All the authors agree that in a turning point of her development, when the little girl enters the Oedipus, she begins to desire a child from the father as a substitute for the missing phallus, and that the disappointment of not receiving it plays an essential role in making her return from the paradoxical path with which she entered the Oedipus [...], back towards the feminine position. In order to show that the privation of the child desired from the father can enter into play with effects in the present [...] one author cites the example of a young girl who, since she was in analysis, could shed more light than others on what was happening in her unconscious. Following on from some piece of enlightenment she had been given, she got up every morning to ask if the father's little child had arrived yet, and whether it was going to happen today or tomorrow. And it was with anger and tears that she asked it each morning.*

Lacan speaks here of a *deviation from analytic practice.* One cannot consider this function of a knowledge transmitted as an interpretation. Far from having an interpretative effect, it only feeds the anxiety of the child, who demands the father's child instead of the phallus.

The Moment to Interpret

Lacan continues: *this makes it very clear that interpretation only comes into play after another stage in the evolution of the child.* He is addressing himself to people who have an unshakeable belief in stages, in changes of stage, etc. He explains to them that one can only interpret if, in one stage, one speaks of another. In other words, it needs a metalanguage and an object-language. It seems to me this was especially aimed at the pupils of Mme Dolto whose explicit doctrine was that one interprets the oral stage from the anal stage and the latter in terms of the phallic stage.

For example, a very devouring child, when touching modelling clay with her hand, smears it all over her. One does not say to her: *you are covering yourself in shit.* One says: *you are devouring the clay with your hand's mouth.* Why? Because she is actually in the anal stage. One cannot interpret to her that she is covering herself in shit because it is her object. One goes via the stage that she has got through, the oral stage. This is not stupid. It means at least considering that one has to know who one is speaking to. To speak in oral terms - the hand's mouth - to the child who is taken up in this position of being the object which falls or is retained, who is the anal object, to speak to her of her hand's mouth rather than her sphincter, is clever. It seems to me one has to take this into account, not in a mechanical way - isolating the current stage and always addressing the child in terms of the previous one - but to address oneself to a moment where the child has a chance to respond, to rise to the level of the response to the real in which the child finds itself.

That is why Lacan can say on page 99: *One can only put the phallus into play afterwards or even at a current moment, on condition that the child, insofar as the subject has to deal with him, enters into the game of a series of symbolic resonances concerning what the child has tried out [...].*

Action of the Symbolic

Lacan pays homage to Melanie Klein on p 112 and immediately takes his distance. *Should we agree,* he says, *with the affirmations of Mrs Klein? These statements rest on her experience, and this experience is communicated to us in observations which sometimes push things in a strange direction. Look at this witch's cauldron [..] at the bottom of which stir, in a global imaginary world [...], the container of the mother's body, all the primordial phantasies present from the beginning and tending to structure themselves in a drama which seems prefigured [...] We cannot not [...] ask ourselves what we are in front of here, and what it wants to say, this dramatic symbolisation which seems the more fulfilled the further one goes back. It is as if the closer we get to the origin, the more the Oedipus complex was already there, articulated and ready to spring into action. It seems worth at least a question. This question, if one asks it, springs up everywhere [...].*

Lacan puts a question to Melanie Klein: choosing between origin and structure, is it a question of origin, is it a question of structure?

The whole doctrine of *Seminar IV* is to offer a complete alternative to Klein's approach on a specific concept, that of the phallus, which is completely absent from her work. We shall see it is absent from both the cases of Dick and Richard, where, instead, there is present a metonymic penis which is rather cumbersome.

How does Melanie Klein place herself in relation to these pointers of Lacan, to speak only of what has been symbolised, of what has already happened, of what the subject is no longer? Or, in terms of what can one speak to him within the resonances of what he says?

Dick is a psychotic child. For Melanie Klein this is a schizophrenia. Lacan, commenting on the case in *Seminar I*, holds back on the diagnosis, but notes that this child is totally in reality - a term he uses at the time to cover the real too. Dick is in the real. In *Seminars I to IV*, reality and real are straddled, imbricated, distinguished at times, conflated at others. He will speak of Rosine Lefort's Wolf Child as a child who is in the real. This does not prevent the action of the symbolic since Robert is led to a baptism, to an action of the symbolic.

What is this action in the case of Dick? From the very first session, Melanie Klein names *daddy, mummy and copulation*, the primal scene in other words. Lacan says: this is amazing, she establishes the Oedipus. In what sense can he say that? There is no Oedipal dramatisation whatsoever. More precisely, what she has installed is the primal scene: daddy and mummy copulate.

Lacan points out that in the apparent installation of this description of the primal scene, four terms are in play: daddy, mummy, the phallus and the subject. There is a quaternary. So Oedipus is introduced in the sense of four terms, not that of an Oedipal drama.

The nomination of the primal scene is precisely what Lacan seeks to avoid when he says that Melanie Klein installs the Oedipus. He is aiming therewith to make us forget the necessity of naming the primal scene from the beginning and of confronting the psychotic child with an enjoyment which he has no means of symbolising, thus making him suffer all the more.

This raises the question: do we say in a psychotic child's first session, 'daddy and mummy copulate, are you aware of this?'? All psychotic children make something go into a hole - it is rare that there is a session where there is not some such action. Do you use that and say, 'there you are, that is what daddy does to mummy.'? How do we act in the case of a psychosis, when we think we are dealing with, to varying degrees, an F_0, a hole in phallic signification? Even if it is in varying degrees, we know that at the heart of psychosis there is an annulation - let us call it that rather than naming it foreclosure. F_0, this hole, produces traumatism[1] in the sense in which there really is a hole in the real, which for the child cannot be filled.

One hopes, it seems to me, to construct some metonymic chain which can lead the child to symbolise the enjoyment which invades him, in order to afterwards, why not, name things by their name and name sex.

So when we say that Melanie Klein establishes the Oedipus in the case of Dick, what has to be installed is a quaternary. It produces the effects of the constitution of a metonymic chain. As Lacan says, the child enlarges his world: there is a train, then two trains, trains which bump into each other, and door handles. There is a kind of metonymic chain which allows this child who is enclosed in his autistic fold to get out of it. Hats off, in any case, for the action produced. Likewise, in the case of Rosine Lefort, once there is this nomination, this baptism, there follow certain effects of constructing a metonymic chain of objects which will allow the child to get out of his anguished fascination with the hole in the toilet.

The Setting Up of an Interpretation

Let us see now how interpretation is put in place in the case of Richard. If we look at in detail we will see it is very close to the case of Dick.

Melanie Klein analysed this case in 1940. She kept it carefully, in good order, and it was almost ready for publication at the time of her death. It was published as a testament, as an example of what to do. Richard was a child of ten whom she saw for about four months, and who was going to be cured of a school phobia, of fears - of going into the street, of going to school, to the point of hating school. Straight away, in the first session, he speaks of school, of the boys in the street, of Hitler doing such bad things to the Poles and to the Austrians - Richard knew Melanie Klein was Austrian. A bomb fell not very far off, and scared the kitchen maid. He talks of Hitler again and then asks himself: *how does blood flow? And if one stands on one's head and all the blood goes there, would one not die?* Melanie Klein grasps his anxiety about death and says: *Do you worry about your mummy?* First step in the setting up: mummy. Little footnote: the mother had told her that the child was hyper-anxious about everything that could happen to her, he couldn't let go of her. Melanie Klein says: *One has to beware of the information given by parents. One should only use it in interpretation if it is very close to the material. I prefer, therefore, to use the material of the child, except that in this case I found the child exceptionally ready to speak of his worries.* She waits until he touches on a bodily preoccupation, until he invokes the fear of death, a bodily anxiety, in order for it to have meaning for him.

Richard tells her that *he is very afraid at night, that until four or five years ago he was absolutely terrified.* He thinks that until six he had lived in this nightmare. This kid has a history, it wasn't triggered yesterday. It is not the war which made him ill. He suffered from his earliest age. He uses a very beautiful expression. He says that *lately he has felt solidarity with the deserted. He was very worried about his mother's health. Sometimes she was not well. Once she was brought on a stretcher after an accident. She had been knocked down in the street. It was before he was born. He often thinks of it. At night, he thinks that a bad man, a type of tramp, wiould come and kidnap her. Then he would help her. He would pour hot water on the tramp -* you can see he has read the chivalrous romances of the Middle Ages. *He would make him uncon- scious. If he was killed, too bad: he would have saved his mother.*

Melanie Klein asks him - we haven't got to the first interpreta- tion yet - firstly: *Do you worry about your mother?;* secondly: *How would the tramp get into mummy's room? - He would break the window;* and the third intervention: *Would the tramp hurt mummy? - Yes.*

Then follows Melanie Klein's first interpretation, through a series of equivalences. Melanie Klein suggests that *the tramp hurt- ing mummy is very much like Hitler who scared the cook during the air- raid and treated the Austrians badly. At night* - this is the interpreta- tion - *he might have been scared -* there is a conditional and hence a modalisation - *of the fact that, when his parents go to bed together, some- thing could happen between them with their genitals which would hurt mummy.*

No Words With Which to Speak Sex

A small note of Melanie Klein's: *I had asked Richard's mother what term he used for his genital. She told me he used none.* A child of ten! *And he never referred to it. He seemed to have no name for urination and defe- cation either.* Melanie Klein adds: *when I introduced the word, 'big job' and 'little job' and later 'faeces', he understood them very quickly.* So she says: *in a case where repression, encouraged by the environment, has gone so far that no name for the genital or for bodily functions, exist, the ana- lyst has to introduce words for them. Doubtless the child knows he has a genital, as he knows that he produces urine and faeces and the words intro- duced will bring up the association with this knowledge, as was shown in this case. Similarly, the expression for sexual intercourse had to be intro- duced to begin with by describing what he actually unconsciously expect- ed his parents were doing at night. Gradually I used the expression* 'sex- ual relations' *and later also* 'sexual intercourse'.

What we have here is a particular use of speech. It starts from this: the child knows that he pisses and shits. If he does not use words for this, one has to give them to him. Look at the context: a ten year old child plunged into a world sick enough - there is no other word for it - a family where they don't know what to piss or to shit means, and in which there is no word for genitals. Melanie

Klein thinks it is a basic element and introduces it at once, in a manner which might seem a little arbitrary. In fact, *Richard seemed surprised and frightened. He did not seem to know what the word 'genital' means. Up to then he had understood.* She asks him: *Do you understand what I mean when I say 'genital'?.* He says: *No.* Then he says:*Yes, all right.* He thinks he knows *because mummy had said that babies grew inside her, that she had little eggs and that daddy supplied some kind of fluid which made them grow.* Melanie Klein says rightly: consciously Richard didn't seem to be aware of having a penis, but that he had a sexual theory. In an arbitrary manner, which is that of the signifier, she introduces words which will begin to signify.

This is not the daddy-train and the mummy-train, but it is similar. Right from the first session Melanie Klein very quickly introduces daddy, mummy and the primal scene. This she afterwards describes as a simple tool, the phallus. Of course she stops at the question: *sexual organs, do you understand what I am saying?.* So it is not only the primal scene but, here too, a quaternary articulation: daddy, mummy, the phallus and the subject, which is put in place from the start.

The Father, Bearer of the Phallus

On the other hand, Melanie Klein very quickly introduces the father as bearer of the phallus but not as the bearer of speech. He is immediately the father who harms.

Melanie Klein follows by interpreting that *he has contradictory ideas about his father. Whereas he knows that his father is a kind man, he might fear that at night daddy was doing some harm to mummy. When he thought of the tramp, he did not remember that daddy, who was in the bedroom with mummy, would protect her. He felt that it was daddy himself who might hurt mummy.* Here are two interpretations which Melanie Klein made. The first introduces daddy, mummy and sex; the second brings in the father as bearer of the phallus. That is moreover the function he will be assimilated to for most of the treatment. She adds that analysts diverge on the fact of giving transference interpretations from the first session onwards. Should she speak to him of her? Indeed, it is striking that in the first session she doesn't. She does not speak to him of the here and now. And she has to justify it: the patient may already be deeply engrossed in the relation with his father, mother and brother. The reference to the analyst has to come after. In the second session she will in effect speak of herself: she will make a further leap. She will only speak of herself after something else.

First the child speaks of the earth which will be bombed by the evil Hitler, the precious earth, and then of small countries: little Portugal, little Switzerland, etc. Melanie Klein translates to him at once, she interprets: *The earth is mummy, the people living on it, her children.* That is called interpreting, but it is really a translation. The Oedipus had been installed in the first session. In the second, one makes a mapping. Everything he says is transposed onto each of the terms - it is a systematic process followed up rigorously. Thus 'It is very far' means in fact that 'It is very close', in the parents' bedroom. When he speaks of the planets being pulverised, it is he himself; the small countries, they are him too. And finally, this catastrophe is exactly the way the parents can hurt each other when they encounter each other. Richard agrees but makes a correction - which is terrific. He says: *I agree, and I have heard of the expression, 'Mother Earth'.* He says: *This interpretation is right, it exists in language.* Wonderful! On the other hand he says that *he would like to correct something. Yesterday he told her he had seen his mummy on a stretcher before he was born, but he asked his mother and she said it happened when he was two.*

This child has a concern for exactitude and ciphering, for symbolic mapping, which contrasts with the imaginary handling of the Oedipal frame. The child already starts saying in the second session: *No, I was two when it happened.* He does things precisely, he relocates them in a symbolic framework.

The Part he Plays in it

After this Melanie Klein goes further. This child is telling her he has thought a lot about what she has said to him, and in particular about the interpretation that if he had made a mistake about his two years, it was probably out of guilt - and here she introduces the term *feeling of guilt*. The child is silent and says: *Yes, I think a lot about it.* He tells her he is irritated by the love his mother shows towards his older brother, who is a soldier, on the front; he is mad with rage when he returns on leave. He also tells her that he sometimes detests his brother. Melanie Klein interprets to him his jealousy in relation to what he has said about his mother's love for his brother, and tells him how it is he who is aggressive. She tells him - it is in the notes of the session : *In the second session I concentrated on the role his own aggression played in his anxieties. This suggests that my first aim in the analysis of children is to analyse the anxieties that are activated. But one has to be on one's guard. It is impossible to analyse anxieties without recognising the defences which operate against them...*

So, first defence - *You feel guilty,* which is a defence against his aggression. She recognises the guilt, and thereafter hands over to aggression the part that it plays.

In these two sessions we have not only a Melanie Klein who introduces this quaternary, included in an imaginary way, who names this quaternary, but also a Melanie Klein who asks him what role he plays in it. It is like the question Freud puts to Dora: *You tell me there is a great disorder in the world, but what is your part in it?* For Melanie Klein the part each child plays in analysis is what she calls analysing aggression, aiming at their anxieties and aggression. - *And you, what part do you play in this?* He speaks to her of the state of the world. She asks him what he does in it. She does not do this in the same way in the case of the autistic Dick as she does for Richard, who is not at all autistic.

Around an Umbrella: The Last Sessions

I will now take up two of the last three sessions. I will refer you, for the context, to the works I published in *Ornicar?,* 'What Melanie Klein knew' and 'The three guises of the object', where I comment on the unfolding of the treatment.

To introduce the last session, I must remind you what happened two days previously when everything turned around an umbrella. Umbrellas are very English. The child tells her about a scene with an umbrella. One day he is out walking with his mother and it is very windy. He opens the umbrella and it turns inside-out. She tells him off; it was the wrong moment to open it. He tells Klein this and then, in the last sessions, he plays with the umbrella. Melanie Klein tells him: *The umbrella is the good object, the stick is daddy's penis and the open umbrella is mummy's breast, the good breast.* The boy had said to her: *This is a good umbrella, it is made in England.* For Melanie Klein this shows that it is no longer one of these foreign countries which terrorised him, it is a good object. The child is telling her it is part of his world. He admits that he and the umbrella belong to the same world, they are in England. This is central. She is saying to him: Once, your mummy told you off about the umbrella, now you are showing it to me and that it is allowed to play with the umbrella.

In the last session the interpretation continues. He arrives and tells her that he has made friends with the bus conductress. This is a key personage. She tells him: - *He is trying to make friends wherever he could; in that way he would prevent being attacked by hostile people.* She takes up in the last session the terms from the beginning of the analysis. This child, who could not go out into the street, now

196   *The Klein - Lacan Dialogues*

smiles at everybody. She does not make a pastoral idyll out of it. She tells him: You smile so they won't attack you. This is very reasonable.

On the other hand, Richard is playing with flies, he puts them outside - he has killed many flies during the analysis and sometimes he has set them free. She interprets that to let these flies go towards the 'Bear's' garden, is to let them go - these flies which are like children - towards a fairly harmless daddy.

In You, The Penis of the Father

The child then goes into the kitchen to drink some water. She says that *since he could not have the good breast, he now wants to take the good penis of the father inside him.* Can you imagine saying that to a child of ten? It is the last session, he is cured, he is drinking water and you tell him: *you will take inside you the good penis of the father.*

One really has to count on forgetfulness, on the fact that the child does not understand what he is being told. If the child keeps this in memory without forgetting, when he is an adolescent he will have problems with sexual identity - Am I really a man? Do the girls want me? etc. - he will remember the last interpretation given to him, that he carries inside himself his father's penis. Luckily all this is easily forgotten. As with little Hans, once he is some way from it, for the child it has no more meaning. For the duration of the treatment he speaks the language of Melanie Klein; afterwards he takes his distance.

Then Richard plays with the clock, delves into the handbag of the analyst and says: *You don't mind do you?* - and takes her purse. He looks inside and asks *whether this is all she possessed or whether she had any more in the bank.* She interprets that before leaving *he wants to take as much milk and shit as he can. The fact that he had killed all the flies meant that he wanted to protect Melanie Klein or Mummy from all the bad babies which could put her in danger.* Richard also used every opportunity to touch Melanie Klein. Not only the umbrella now, but her. She interprets that *if he wants touch her it is not only in order to caress her but to take her into himself and keep her there.*

The notion of phallus which Lacan outlines in *Seminar IV*, with the help of Winnicott, is constructed against against this notion of phallic incorporation, of "keeping inside oneself".

The transitional object is the object created by Winnicott to put a spoke in the wheel of Melanie Klein's theory of the drive, which he considered inadequate. It is an object such that one doesn't know whether it is hallucinated, whether it comes from the child or from the outside. Lacan says: *this is what I would call imaginary*. The imaginary here is very particular: it is an imaginary like hallucination, it cannot be assigned a place, we cannot know whether it is real or symbolic. This object, which comes from the Other and yet, however, is not in the Other, is not the place of the symbolic. With this idea of saying "the phallus is this", one can deduce the doctrine that the phallus structures the position of the child but that the child cannot have it inside. This is the obstacle to interpretations in phallic terms on the lines of *you want the good phallus inside you*. It cannot be a relation of an inside, a relation of container-contained defined apart from a topology. Lacan will say of Winnicott's transitional object that it is one which defies interior and exterior, in the representation that he takes of a projective plane in terms of a Moebius strip stuck onto a disk. This is an object where one does not know whether one is inside or outside, on one side or another. This continues an elaboration of what Winnicott had put forward on this point.

The end of the analysis, with Melanie Klein, comes down to saying: *you take the phallus with you.*

An American psychotherapist, Milton Erickson, would end his treatments with: *My voice goes with you.* You will not leave empty handed, you will pocket my voice which will always calm you. Here we do not have the *voice* - in Melanie Klein's case, we have the phallus. *You are leaving, you cannot take the good breast with you, so you will take your father's penis. You drank it, it is inside you.* It is like a sacrament, a kind of baptism, a Eucharist. Yet Melanie Klein belongs to the Jewish tradition. So there is a special libation - *You ate it and you carry it away with you.*

Melanie Klein's perspective in fixing the child to his umbrella - *you are leaving with your umbrella* - is to fix him to a phallic object. He became a commercial traveller when he grew up, little Richard. We know this from Phyllis Grosskurth, who found him and interviewed him. He has a tramp side, he became himself a kind of very civilised tramp, going from town to town. This is an identification with the aggressor. And he has his umbrella.

This fixation to the fantasy derives from the same perspective that Lacan criticised in relation to Kris and the post-Freudians in general. The interpretation that the 'fresh brains' man carries away with him is a fixation to the fantasy of devoration. *If you are afraid of plagiarising, of stealing the ideas of others, it is because when you were young, you stole food, you ate the others. It is your urge to eat which makes you afraid of plagiarising and which gives you this defence. So you do not recognise what is yours.* This urge to eat, to which he responds by saying he is going to eat some brains, is of the order of a fixation, which allows an acting out as the only possible exit.

Lacan insisted on the endings to analysis, which have to termi-
nate - this is what he says at the time, he will reformulate it - on a
question. The certainty obtained is not one of fixation, a *You are this*.
It's the whole question of the dialogue which ends *The Function and
Field of Speech and Language in Psychoanalysis* - Prajapâti who
answers: *Da, da*. What does this mean? We don't know. Even the
Asuras surrounding Prajapâti do not understand clearly what he
says, but he leaves them with the significatory aspect of speech, on
a gigantic question mark, a signification to complete[2].

Crossing the fantasy is also to cross these significations, so that
they no longer fixate, so that one can refer them back to the enigma
of the primordial signifiers which remain perfectly enigmatic. Why
these in particular? Why is it like this in your life? Why do you find
yourself always with the same phenomenal signifying coincidences
which rule your life? That remains the great mystery to which you
are stuck. The crossing, the forcing of the fantasy, is to put this series
of signifiers in the fantasy into a chain, and to be ready to encounter
them, so that a new love can result rather than the old fantasy. Let
us say it is a first formulation of 'outside-sense'.

This enigma is not deduced from the handling of the transference proposed by Melanie Klein. The great contribution of
Winnicott has been to make the Kleinian world breathable. He was
an obstacle to it, but thanks to him, it has remained a strong current
in England. He introduced a great question mark. The transitional
object is the enigmatic object: one cannot disgorge it. One cannot
make it admit whether it belongs to the Other or to the real. Each
analysis that it directs, therefore, stumbles on enigmas and questions.

Compare, for example, the end of analysis with Richard and the
end of the analysis of the little Piggle, or even other cases, bizarre,
atypical, of analyses conducted in a hospital, in a little corner with
a patient always falling asleep. Winnicott has described a host of
unlikely cases. He who had conducted many standard cases, published none of them. He insisted on publishing only cases which are
non-standard. All are centred on enigmas, on incomplete endings,
and are deliberately conceived that way.

Let us see what happens to the continuation of Kleinianism
when the Winnicottian question mark is not integrated.

A Contemporary Kleinian

I should like to examine with care an ambitious and programmatic text written in 1990 by the president of the IPA Horatio Etchegoyen. 'Psychoanalysis During the Last Decade: Clinical and Theoretical Aspects' is an ambitious text because it is both a practical and an epistemological answer to the question of what it is to interpret, while on the other hand, it presents a direction which goes against the American way. It is a programmatic text insofar as it is part of a presidential program: at the time Etchegoyen was about to become President Elect of the IPA.

Looking at ten years of psychoanalysis, Etchegoyen intervenes with this text in a debate which started within the IPA in 1987 at the Montreal Congress, and was continued in Rome, where Robert Wallerstein responded to Heinz Kohut, specifically to Chapter VI of his book *How does Psychoanalysis Cure?* .

In the sixth chapter Kohut opposed the Kleinian conception of psychoanalysis, especially its Argentinian variant, to the theory of *self* (particularly his own), wanting to show that there are two ways of formulating an interpretation: either in Kleinian (or neo-Kleinian) language, or in the language of self-psychology. To this fact that different languages of interpretation existed in the IPA, Wallerstein responded both theoretically and epistemologically by saying that one should not consider these different languages in terms of exactitude or inexactitude (a torment introduced by Glover in 1930), or in terms of depth or surface, but that they should be apprehended in terms of *metaphor.*

This idea of metaphor came in the main from a debate which took place in the 1960s in epistemology, indeed in psychoanalysis, on the basis of readings of Lacan by the intellectual circles of the East Coast of the United States. This was specially felt in psychoanalysis in the magazine *Psychoanalytic Quarterly*, whereas in philosophy, it joined up with epistemological issues as discussed by Richard Rorty, for example.

Wallerstein's position was that languages of interpretation which appeal to theories of a high level of abstraction (those which concern subject, object and aim, etc.) are metaphors. The common grounding, the reference, is clinical theory, minimal, of a low level of abstraction. So there is a clinic, and and one interprets clinical facts in different languages all of which are metaphors. That is how Wallerstein gets out of it, with this fairly simplistic epistemological model which gives him a point of reference. Metaphor here means that there is a signifier, which is perhaps better signified in the *common ground* which is clinical theory. This is precisely what Etchegoyen will respond to, because he considers it a dangerous position.

Etchegoyen proposes the necessity of maintaining the idea that a real interpretation is not a metaphor referring back to a clinical theory, even one of a low level of abstraction. A true interpretation refers back truly to something real. In his words: 'it must account for the psychic reality which exists at that moment in the Unconscious of the patient'.

This is to maintain a theory of truth such that, according to the Polish logician Tarski, '"Snow is white" is true if and only if snow is white'. It is a statement of the type: 'The sentence "P" is true if and only if P'.

Adapted to Etchegoyen's perspective things take a more 'realist' turn, since he considers that an interpretation is true if and only if it describes exactly what the subject has in mind at the moment it is made.

We will see where this leads him. It is in fact what Lacan marked off as the danger of a theory of truth which is a theory of correspondence between ego and reality. It is to construct the ego as the place of what really happens. There would be a place where someone has something in his head. That is already quite a lot, for saying that the drive is acephalic means that one does not know what there is in its head, nor even if it has a head at all. It is very difficult to think a psychic reality in terms of there being a place where one could know what was in it. It is a topology of inside/outside with a strict boundary, and a place such that one knows what is in it. These are the things Lacan excluded from the theory he wanted to transmit.

It is therefore rather interesting to see how the years of the 1950s and 60s find an epistemological enrichment in the 1990s. Etchegoyen is a cultivated man, very open to Lacanian currents, and who knows the present state of theory. This makes his choice of maintaining the necessity of a correspondence all the more interesting.

He enters the debate with an article in three parts. In the first part he recalls the past debate and its issues; in the second, he marks his differences with Wallerstein, reformulates the problem, explains what he would have done, and this in a very reasonable way; in the third, he presents a clinical vignette taken from his own practice, and gives the interpretation that he made, from the end of an analysis. That is where things no longer seem reasonable to me, and I would like to show, courteously and reasonably, a point of disagreement about what is really in question, and about the consequences of such a view of the end of analysis.

'You Are Deeply Troubled ...'

The very reasonable part is the following. In chapter VI of his book, Kohut spoke of the following session, which he had supervised, and which was conducted by an analyst presented as belonging to a South American Kleinian orientation. 'At the end of a session, this analyst informed her patient that she would have to cancel an appointment in the near future. When the patient came to the next session, she was silent and withdrawn and did not repond to the analyst's promptings to tell her what she was experiencing. The analyst finally said to the patient, obviously in a warmly understanding tone of voice, that she felt her announcement about being away had decisively shifted the patient's perception of her. Formerly the analyst said, she had been the good, warm, feeding breast, but now she had become the bad, cold, non-feeding one. She added that the patient had come to feel intense sadistic rage against her, qua bad breast; that the patient wanted to tear the analyst apart and, furthermore, that she defended herself against these impulses to bite and tear by inhibiting her activity, in general, and by her oral activity (i.e. talking via 'biting' words) in particular.'.

We therefore have here: oral drive, inhibition. One refinds here the same principle of interpretation (presented as a South American Kleinian one) that had guided Melitta Schmideberg in the case of the 'fresh brains' man - he had a drive to eat; in his childhood he stole food from the fridge; this was followed by inhibition, since transformed into intellectual inhibition.

Kohut, on the contrary, thinks that it would have been better to formulate things in terms either of self-psychology or of ego-psychology. In ego-psychology one does not go immediately to the object without passing through the Oedipal conflict. One says to the patient: 'You felt the same way about my announcement yesterday as you did when your mother shut the bedroom door in order to sleep with your father.' There is the Oedipal conflict: the patient is mad with rage to see that her mother is interested in something other than her.

Or, in the words that self-psychology employs with narcissistic patients, one should have reformulated things in terms of an interpretation centred on the self, saying for example: 'Your self esteem...'. (Self esteem is the closest equivalent in English to the '*amour-propre*' of the French moralists. As for narcissistic patients, they are the ones who do not tolerate conflict: they have not elaborated the Oedipal conflict properly, and, walled in by narcissism, they wander alone in the world, complaining at not being valued properly - hence with a slightly megalomaniac quality. Here is the category of narcissistic patient, always so difficult to handle ...). One should therefore formulate 'Your self esteem has been dented by what I told you yesterday, in the same way as on the day in which your cold and distant mother dismissed the cook who was so warm, and who allowed you to help her, and who sang your praises.'

The analyst, reporting what followed, notes that after the interpretation the patient was more relaxed: she spoke more freely. But Kohut gives the following comment: whatever the positive effect of the interpretation, the point is that although the message was right, the theory was deficient.

What was the central message? It was 'You are profoundly troubled by the fact that one of your sessions has been cancelled'; I register it. That is what should have been said.

Kohut's idea is that one should have said to her: 'All right, it is allowed, you had every right: there was reason to.'. The great theory of Kohut - his basic message - is the empathy that is to be transmitted to the other. *How does psychoanalysis cure?* With the smile of the mother. To be cold, distant, chasing the other away, saying it isn't good, or that it is bad, to tell somebody off, rapping on the knuckles, etc. : all that is no good. One has to be welcoming to the other, and it is not by rebuking the neurotic that one gets anywhere. This is not false, of course, and it allows some things to be understood. The idea therefore is to say 'OK': it is this fundamental yes which Kohut considers as the essential psychoanalytic operation.

Etchegoyen on the other hand, thinks it is the opposite: the theory was right (that of the good and bad breast) - he carries the Kleinian torch - but the formulation wasn't correct. He then presents what should have been done.

First point, not to say 'it is legitimate' (the cancelled session had not been evoked by the patient), but simply to say (putting words to silence): 'something troubles you and you are incapable of expressing it'. And there, 'if she had said that she was silent because since the previous session her jaws had contracted, and if she had added some biting words addressed to the analyst, then there would have been verification' - when the jaws are in question it is certain that the oral object is present in the mind: the proof is that they decontract. Only then could one have said: 'You have felt yesterday's announcement as if the breast had been withdrawn from you, and you reacted with fear and the wish to bite, by clenching your teeth and saying things which could bite too.'

He continues:

'If the patient had said that while silent she was thinking of some disagreeable incident which had occurred the evening before, with her 5 year old daughter who had wanted to remain in her parents' bedroom rather than sleeping in her room; that the patient had ended up getting angry, and taken her daughter to her own bed by force; and if she had added that she was already irritated because in leaving the session she had had an argument with a taxi driver who had refused to give her change; then I would not have hesitated in telling her this anger she spoke of in relation to her daughter was her way of informing me of her reaction to the news I had given her (...); that she had had an argument with the taxi driver because he had not wanted to give her something; and that, in speaking of her daughter, she was expressing her own infantile reaction: she felt I was the mother chasing her from the room in order to sleep with the father.'.

Lastly: If the patient had brought me a dream, reproducing the traumatic infantile situation in which the mother had dismissed the nice cook, (I would have said) 'indeed, it was like your mother...'.

But Etchegoyen adds: 'I would never have had the audacity to say "your cold and distant mother", because an interpretation must always bear on the subject, never on the people in the environment. There, my disagreement is definite'. That is very nice, but, all the same, some parents are monsters! And in spite of everything, one has to say so. When the talk is on the theme of: 'Is it I who really...? I wonder if my mother...', one must be able sometimes to guide the subject on that. It must come from the patient, but one has to take a position at times. That is a big difference with Kohut. Etchegoyen considers that one must absolutely respect that: not a word. One can see that on this point he cuts out several orientations within the languages of interpretation, and their consequences.

So he notes 'the three hypothetical interpretations contain fragments of theory of a high level of abstraction, but they are not metaphors insofar as they strictly correspond to the material of the supposed session.'. Thus, according to him, the problem is not to discuss either the profundity, or the efficacy of these interpretations, but to know - once they have been uttered, or their different versions expounded - whether one thinks or not that they really refer to something, a state of mind, formulated in the psychic reality of the patient. Etchegoyen considers that that is what one has to uphold, and he's going to give an example of it: not the scholastic case which he takes up - a scholastic example because it is Kohut taking up the interpretation of another analyst, then taken up by Wallerstein in a conference, then himself. There is dovetailing here:

Etchegoyen is going to give an example from his own practice, and he does so in the third part of the article.

'And We Continue...'

It concerns a patient who, he says, is at the end of an analysis and this is of interest to us. It is not a training analysis, but a patient on the point of ending. The patient dreams that he is in a prison cell with a curving wall.

The context is as follows. The patient is in business. The idea of a prison is linked to the fact that, even though the transaction he has to conclude is perfectly legal, he could be punished for it. Actually, if he succeeds, he will become much richer, and earn much more than his analyst; that makes him guilty. So he has some idea about why he has this dream. But at the same time he is surprised because he considers that one of the signs that his analysis is ending is that he has managed to handle this financial speculation in a much more relaxed state than usual: it has not put him in a state and he has not taken himself for the master of the universe either. Etchegoyen says: 'He had an inner peace which reminded him of Kipling's poem *If.*'.

Soon after there emerges an important anxiety, centred on the idea of ending analysis. 'He was afraid of deceiving himself and me, thought that I wanted to get rid of him as soon as possible, and in this anxiety he dreamt of *someone giving birth*': without any detail, anonymously.

'I interpreted to him that the end of his analysis was to him as if I gave birth to him, and he accepted this interpretation as a metaphor of the end, which is in effect what I had wanted to say in offering it to him'.

This first interpretation is thus a metaphorical one in the author's sense: the idea of birth is replaced by 'it is the end of the analysis'.

'After that session, he again felt acute anxiety, complained of thoracic oppressions and of having difficulty breathing'. Thoracic oppression and suffocation: 'He associated this too with the idea of ending analysis'. And here comes the profound interpretation: 'I told him that, *confronted with the fear of ending analysis, he had to get back inside me* to annul the feared birth; but in doing so, he became a prisoner, and could hardly breathe'.

How authentic! The phrase used is 'he had to get inside me'. Etchegoyen continues 'this interpretation was obviously not proffered as metaphor, but as an explanation of what really happened at that point'. Here we have *explanation* and no longer *interpretation*.

The term is used in its strong epistemological sense: as in the natural sciences. 'I explained to him what was really happening: at the theoretical level this rested (...) on the theory of projective identification (Melanie Klein 1946). Having said that, I would not dispute an explanation made in relation to another framework (return to the womb, birth trauma, stage of individuation - separation, etc.). All these theories succeed in explaining the material, and one would need more clinical material to verify which one would have been most adequate in this case. After my interpretation the *patient laughed*, then charily asked me if I was referring to his dream from the week before where he was a prisoner. I did not answer directly, for (...) it was a purely rhetorical question. Yet it is worth mentioning here that when I had made this interpretation, I did not remember this dream, or, if you will, I had repressed it. I simply answered that his association with the dream was very appropriate, because it gave a convincing explanation of his fear of remaining imprisoned inside me (claustrophobia).

- But this dream had nothing to do with your body, said the analysand, it was a room, a dungeon, and I remember that it was a very special cell, with a curved wall, as in a watch tower.

- Yes, like this turret. And I pointed to the wall facing the couch in front of which he had lain during his twelve years of analysis.

The analysand was very surprised. He said he never thought of it, and confirmed that the wall in his dream was exactly like that of my consulting room. Soon after, he remarked calmly that the oppression (...) had lifted.

Examples like this, frequent in the practice of any analyst (this is an analyst's modesty), are interesting because they show how our technique can reach deep unconscious levels, which are illustrated by our highly abstract theories, when these emerge spontaneously and unexpectedly in the material. *What is most important to demonstrate is that my interpretation here has to be heard as more than a metaphor,* which is justified by the associations of the analysand. So our work as analysts does not simply consist in offering heuristic models so that the patient can resolve his problems, or in applying our favourite metaphors to the material. There is more: our work consists in helping the analysand to overcome his resistances, *so he can get to what he really thinks.'*.

This is how the operation of correspondence is done: one formulates what the analysand really thinks, and that is why it works. As Etchegoyen says: at that precise moment, 'analytic work' establishes truth conditions in psychic reality'. It is very subtle: if one has a psychic reality, one still has to furnish it with a truth table. The analytic work must effect - magically? - the creation of a truth table. 'At that moment, the interpretation ceases to be a figure of speech, and takes on a very precise signification, isomorphic with what (really) happens in the mind of he who receives it'.

Everything is given in this sentence. Firstly, 'truth tables introduce themselves into a reality'. How does one do that, introduce truth tables into a reality? It seems a bit hard. Secondly, 'an isomorphic signification'. Perfect. What is the morphology of the phenomenon? How does one arrive at transforming an isomorphic phenomenon into truth tables, which presupposes a language? By using the terms *isomorphic* and *truth conditions*, Etchegoyen is holding onto a denotative theory of truth.

His article continues in the following way: 'The thesis here finds a convincing confirmation because the analysand had dreamt that he was in a cell with a curved wall, like that of the turret in my room. When I interpreted that he wanted to get back inside my stomach to annul the end of analysis lived as a birth, I did not remember his dream. It was he who invoked it, paradoxically in order to deny my interpretation. No, he had said, it has nothing to do with your body: it was a cell with a curved wall.'.

Thus the patient is convinced that the interpretation in terms of the body of the analyst, extended to the consulting room, was the right one.

I also will now play the game of putting on Dupin's green spectacles and ask: what doesn't work here?

First of all, I have to say that I do not think at all that the analysis of this person is at its end, even if it is not a training analysis. I will apply the method that Dr Lacan used in the Seminar on *Transference*, that is: one has to know from where somebody is laughing. It was Kojève's method. When Lacan wanted him to speak on Plato's *Symposium*, Kojève only said: 'the key of the text is in the laugh of Aristophanes, transformed into hiccup'. Well, the patient laughed. One can see that laughing has an effect of liberation from oppression. In good Freudian theory, there is in laughter a liberation from the chains of signification, which frees the patient from what enclosed him.

But I do not have the same idea as the author about what he was enclosed in. To say it at once, my idea is that probably the central conflict of this patient is with his father.

Indeed, the patient for his part speaks above all of the Kipling poem *If*, which, in Anglo-Saxon spheres, is the prototype of a father-son relation. The poem ends with: 'If you can do a whole string of totally unlikely things, *then you will be a man my son*'. It is a list which is partly contradictory and inconsistent. Imagine having that on one's shoulders! Specifically, on the list, it says one has to be able to win and lose. It could be the credo of the business man: 'if you can win and lose with the same indifference...' This is valid for the casino: there are also people who try to rediscover a link with their father by proving to themselves that the condition *if and only if* is realised when they lose everything. The correct usage here is clearly: one can win *or* lose.

In a demonstrable way (which I think plays a part in the choice of this case) there is in this story an element of *if ... then:* in the very construction of the patient there is an *if ... then*, a deduction. And if the analyst has the feeling of approaching a conclusion, the end of the analysis, it is because he has formulated the conditions of this *if ... then:* the patient wants to be a son, and he tries to sketch out his own particular conditions, the *if and only if* which might lead him to deduce that *then* he is a son. In this perspective, it seems to me that the object - not only the oral object (fundamental in Kleinian theory) but the anal object - is in play. There is in this circuit of the drives, in this prison, in fact, a note of anal retention, of something cornered. This, it seems to me, is to answer also to the oral character, maternal breast etc., to which the explanation of *'he wanted to get inside me'* refers.

It seems to me then, that this patient has to deal with a ferocious Other, from whom he expects the *if ... then*, the *if* taking the form of this list of prohibitions, prescriptions and recommendations of Kipling. He awaits the oracle: 'Then I'll be'.

The problem is, and it must be a torment, that he feels he spends his time deceiving this Other. That is why he is guilty. It is not only because he will earn more than his analyst. There is in effect this anal note: the little extra profit. It is enough for the analyst not to feel impressed, not to care whether his patients are richer than him, for this feeling to find its place. Of course, that has nothing to do with it. The analyst does not seem to be preoccupied with it. He notes that subjective guilt stems from there.

To answer this with *'he wanted to get inside me'*, is, all the same, there is no other word for it, to penetrate him anally. That is the fantasy which is authenticated. Indeed, I agree with the analyst here, that this is in question, but not in order to be inside his body and imprisoned. He is anxious because he is busy conning him. His relation to the Other is to deceive him, and he is doing so here. His torment is that once again, his relation to the Other is going to end in such a way that he cannot conclude *if ... then*. In essence, his conclusion is: 'If I do that I will have deceived you once more. I got out of it. I got more than you and I can leave in peace: you did not see anything'. That is why he laughed when the analyst, very precisely, told him what he was doing and when the pressure on the chest was eased. Because he saw that the other saw nothing.

It is very different, at such a moment, to increase the cost of sessions on exit and to tell him: 'and we continue', from opining 'of course, you need to feel at home here because you do not want to leave'. It is very different.

My disagreement concerns the fact that with a theory according to which there is a correspondence between interpretation and what 'really' happens in the mind, when one is aiming at the drive, one cannot fail to refind the same aporias which Lacan pointed to in his commentary on Kris's case. One finds again 'what one should have got the analysand to understand'. To take up what Lacan said ('one should have made him understand that he was stealing nothing'), one should, in this case, have got him to see that everything he thought he had more of than his father, and his having deceived him, well, in relation to that Other that he is concerned with, that is nothing at all. And as it is nothing, one has to pay dearly for it. So he would have paid for it a bit more dearly, the nothing he was busy stealing from the analysis.

Obviously, I am being clever here, because I am coming from behind, as well - if I may say so. As Lacan said, there is always someone who can pluck a feather from one's behind while one is looking at the ground. I do not know the ins and outs of this analysis. So I give this commentary in the same scholastic spirit with which the case of Kohut and the remarks of Wallerstein were made. It seems to me that the logic of the case, as I see it, would have benefited from being put in this perspective.

The epistemological interest of the case, over and above this revival, this additional stake that I bring to the debate, is the issue of knowing what it means to say 'what happens in psychic reality'. What does one call psychic reality? Why does the phrase 'he wanted to get inside me' describe a psychic reality for this analyst, according to the theory of projective identification?

What is 'Really' in the Mind?

The question of knowing what has to be considered as real and in what way a theory can be adequate to the real world is not new. I read about this in Alexander Koyré's writing on the question of the void and infinite space in the XIVth century.

In this article of 1949, anterior to *From the Closed World to the*

Infinite Universe, a fundamental work which explains the Galilean break, Koyré, - who was, like Kojève, a master of Lacan's - confronts an adversary, Pierre Duhem, another French university epistemologist and author of a large and very serious work on the birth of science . He was a noble and respected adversary for Koyré, as also Etchegoyen is a a respectable man and a respected president.

Duhem said the following: 'If we had to give a precise date to the birth of science we would doubtless choose 1277, when the Archbishop of Paris solemnly declared that there could exist several different worlds, and that the set of celestial circles could, without contradiction, be animated by a rectilinear movement.'

'A curious assertion', Koyré wrote, 'which places at the origin of science, the proclamation by the Archbishop of Paris of two absurdities'. You can see the tone: to Duhem, the most serious of epistemologists, Koyré said: a curious assertion, because they are two absurdities. Hence Mr Gilson (Etienne Gilson, the great philosopher of the Middle Ages and of the sciences) had good reason to clarify matters and to remind us that 'the Archbishop of Paris did not care about the sciences: he only declared that one could not prevent God, in the name of the necessities of the Greek world then held as real, from creating one or more worlds with a different structure, and he said so in the name of divine omnipotence, as theologian.'.

The thesis was as follows: during the Middle Ages, everybody had the idea that Ptolemy's astronomy perfectly described the movement of the stars, according to very complex spherical models established by the great Greek science of around the third century in Alexandria. While on the one hand there were these perfect and complex spheres, regulating the stars (the sphere above us, the stars, the fixed ones), there was, on the other hand, a great theological debate which one can formulate as follows: 'Can God move the world? Could he shift it?'.

We no longer grasp the issue of this debate very well because at present the notion of space is for us coexistence with the universe. But the question asked was 'can one move the world?'. For Aristotle, there was no place, no point outside the universe. But for there to be movement there has to be a point outside the universe, a place of departure and a place of arrival. Therefore, in order to move the universe, there would have to be a place outside the universe. As this place does not exist, it was necessary to prove that God could not move the universe. This Christian theologians opposed by saying that God could do as He pleased. He can absolutely unsettle the order of the world if He feels like it. So there is no reason for God not to create other worlds than this Greek one held as real.

What did the Archbishop of Paris say in this debate? He said: God can create several languages of interpretation, if I may say so. He can create several possible worlds: a world in which we speak self-psychology, a world in which we speak Lacanian, etc. He can create possible worlds, and he can even operate movements on a reference point, on what is held to be real. And it is possible to verify a correspondence. There are possible languages and there is a correspondence: everything depends on what is taken as real. Archbishop Tempier's declaration is crucial because it shows that what one called real was a theory: the Greek theory, Ptolemy's theory. That shattered the conception of the real.

Gilson, who was a Christian, tried to say: nevertheless 'if modern science was not born in 1277, it was the date when the birth of modern cosmologies became possible in the Christian world'; it is the opening of all those possibilities. Koyré demolished this whole construction by showing that it was all in vain, that no-one had invented anything at all, and that one had to wait two centuries before one could think a little more on the question. Koyré thus put forward an opposition to the theory of a liberating Christianity presented by Gilson. I refer you to his objections, which are very funny; it is an amusing and well founded intellectual debate. But the important point is really what is considered as real.

This idea of correspondence with psychic reality is what Lacan has freed us from with a fundamental notion, which is that, at the horizon of psychic reality, we do not have a structure of correspondence.

We have the idea that there is a signifier which is missing and that the real at issue is what this missing signifier comes to inscribe: that there is no sexual rapport. Certainly, we say that there are metaphors, but these metaphors refer in the last instance, either to a symbolic place (this is what Lacan upheld first: the Name-of-the-Father as a principle guaranteeing the separations, the possible metaphors), or, more profoundly (his second theory) to an inconsistent Other, because supported by a point which can never be inscribed: sexual non-rapport. There is no possibility of referring to a denotation there: it is not inscribed. You have no way of using it in that way, of checking to see whether it is yes or no. A modality has to appear, which is that of the impossible, and which answers to this inexistence, to this 'there is not'. What there is 'really' in the mind is 'nothing', the logical consistency of the object *a*, 'isomorphic' to the drive .

Winding Up the Clock

There is moreover a remarkable book which addresses the question of 'what there is' or 'what there is not' in the minds of men. It is The *Life and Opinions of Tristram Shandy* by Thomas Sterne. I have found this book enchanting. It is hilarious and the most beautiful book, together with *Jacques le Fataliste*, which the 18th century has produced. It is too funny for words.

To give you a taste I shall read the first page of the book which precisely concerns the question of what one has really in one's mind:

'I wish either my father or my mother, or indeed both of them, as they were in duty both equally bound to it, *(you see already the logical turn of mind of this boy)* had minded what they were about when they begot me; had they duly considered how much depended upon what they were then doing; - that not only the production of a rational Being was concerned in it, but that possibly the happy formation and temperature of his body, perhaps his genius and the very cast of his mind *(you see how all this relates to the analytical commentary)*; - and, for aught they knew to the contrary, even the fortunes of his whole house might take their turn from the humours and dispositions which were then uppermost: - Had they duly weighed and considered all this, and proceeded accordingly, - I am verily persuaded I should have made a quite different figure in the world, from that, in which the reader is likely to see me. - Believe me, good folks, this is not so inconsiderable a thing as many of you may think it; - you have all, I dare say, heard of the animal spirits, as how they are transfused from father to son &c. &c. - and a great deal to that purpose (*Vital [animal] spirits transmitted from father to son, that was the dominant theory of transmission in the XVIII Century. Nowadays, we adopt a new theory - you've possibly heard talk of the Oedipus complex*): - Well, you may take my word, that nine parts in ten of a man's sense or his nonsense, his successes and miscarriages in this world depend upon their motions and activity, and the different tracts and trains you put them into, so that when they are once set a-going, whether right or wrong, 'tis not a halfpenny matter, - away they go cluttering like hey-go mad; and by treading the same steps over and over again, they presently make a road of it, as plain and as smooth as a garden-walk, which, when they are once used to, the Devil himself sometimes shall not be able to drive them off it. *Pray, my dear*, quoth my mother, *have you not forgot to wind up the clock?* - *Good G* -! cried my father, making an exclamation, but taking care to moderate his voice at the same time, - *Did ever woman, since the creation of the world, interrupt a man with such a silly question? Pray, what was your father saying? - Nothing.'*.

End of chapter! And it continues like that for 580 pages.. I will leave you to discover the plan of the fortifications of Namur by Uncle Toby...

This first chapter exactly describes the sexual relations between the parents, and the mother who says to the father, at the crucial moment in which Tristram Shandy is engendered, 'did you wind up the clock?' It is amazing, this function of putting everything back under the sign of exactitude, including the exactitude of the hour of generation (exactitude is indeed the perspective of the XVIIIth century), and this comical piece of letting man-machine bear the vital spirits which transmit themselves, etc. this determination weighing on him, is frightening.

The horror of the XVIIIth century was to see oneself as a great machine entirely determined. How to get out of that? That is what haunted Diderot, and it haunted the novel of the XVIIIth century, through all these references which try to get out of these determinations, and at the same time to invent a new world, with that naturalism which was to provoke a fundamental moral crisis.

What is admirable is that Sterne refers this naturalism, this determinism to the mother. It is the mother who interrupts the father and who unsettles the order of the world. She disturbs the father in his phallic enjoyment, and she does this in the name of the order of the world. It is very funny to see women in this role of winding up the clocks. Not to do it, but to say to the man 'did you do it?' And the man finds himself with an imperative on his shoulders at the very moment, if I may say so, when he is thinking of something else. She calmly puts an imperative on his shoulders, with her *'did you wind up the clocks?'*

Well, perhaps it is always useful to keep in mind that each time one poses to oneself the question of what there really is in the mind, one always finds this: an imperative which entails that, in the moment of sexual rapport, it is women who really have in mind winding up the clocks.

[1] *trou* makes *troumatisme:* pun in the original (translator).

[2] See the commentary on the end of this text in the Seminar of Jacques-Alain Miller of 1995-96, *La Fuite du Sens*, especially the sessions of June 1996.

LIST OF CONTRIBUTORS

Robin Anderson is a Child and Adult Analyst and a Training Analyst at the Institute of Psycho-Analysis, London. He is also Chair of the Adolescent Department at the Tavistock Clinic.

Catalina Bronstein is a full member of the British Psycho-Analytical Society and a member of the Association of Child Psychotherapists. Over the last ten years she has been working with adolescents at the Brent Adolescent Centre, is Hon. Senior Lecturer in psychoanalytic theory at University College London and lectures at the Tavistock Clinic, in other psychotherapeutic organizations and abroad.

Bice Benvenuto is a psychoanalyst, a founder member of the Centre for Freudian Analysis and Research and a member of the European School of Psychoanalysis.

Bernard Burgoyne is Reader in Psychoanalysis and Head of the Centre for Psychoanalysis at Middlesex University. He is a founder member of the Centre for Freudian Analysis and Research and a member of European School of Psychoanalysis.

Marc Du Ry is a practising psychoanalyst in London, a member of the European School of Psychoanalysis and of the Centre for Freudian Analysis and Research.

Filip Geerardyn is a doctoral assistant at the Department of Psychoanalysis and Clinical Consultation at the University of Ghent, Belgium. He is a member of the European School for Psychoanalysis, the International Association for the History of Psychoanalysis and vice-director of the Gezelschap voor Psychoanalyse en Psychotherapie.

Guy Hall is an analytical psychotherapist in private practice. He is a rabbi. He is a member of the Forum for Independent Psychotherapists.

Robert Hinshelwood is a member of the Institute of Psycho-analysis. He founded the British Journal of Psychotherapy. He is the Clinical Director of the Cassel Hospital. He is taking up a post as Professor in the Centre of Psychoanalytic Studies at the University of Essex.

Eric Laurent is a psychoanalyst and a psychologist at the Sainte-Anne

Hospital in Paris. He is the current President of the European School of Psychoanalysis and a Member of the World Psychoanalytic Association.

Darian Leader is a psychoanalyst practising in London and Leeds and is a founder member of the Centre for Freudian Analysis and Research.

Donald Meltzer trained in medicine and child psychiatry in the United States but came to London in 1954 specifically to train in psychoanalysis with Melanie Klein. He remained in analysis with her until her death in 1960.

Dany Nobus is a lecturer in Psychology and Psychoanalytic Studies at Brunel University. He is a member of the Universities Association for Psychoanalytic Studies and the European Association for the History of Psychiatry.

Vicente Palomera is a psychoanalyst and psychologist. He is a member of the European School of Psychoanalysis and the World Psychoanalytic Association.

Liz Reid is Chair of THERIP, a member for the Centre for Freudian Analysis and Research and a Lacanian analyst in private practice in London.

Margaret Rustin is Consultant Child Psychotherapist at the Tavistock Clinic, London. She is the Organising Tutor of the Tavistock Child Psychotherapy training.

E. Mary Sullivan is a lecturer at the School of Psychotherapy & Counselling, Regent's College; she is Secretary of the European Society for Communicative Psychotherapy and has a private practice specialising in communicative psychotherapy with patients diagnosed as psychotic.

Jane Temperley is a member of the British Psycho-Analytical Society. She is a Kleinian psycho-analyst in private practice.

Robert M. Young is Professor of Psychotherapy and Psychoanalytic Studies at the University of Sheffield. He is a member of the Lincoln Centre and Institute of Psychotherapy and the Institute for Psychotherapy and Social Studies.

BIBLIOGRAPHY

Adams, P. (1992), 'Waiving the Phallus', Differences: *A Journal of Feminist Cultural Studies*, IV, no 1, pp 76-83.

Ariès, P. (1979), *Centuries of Childhood*, London: Penguin.

Armstrong-Perlman, E. (1987), 'The Child's Psyche and the Nature of its Experience', *British Journal of Psychotherapy*, Vol 4, No. 2.

Assoun, P-L. (1995), *Freud, la philosophie, et les philosophes*, Paris: Presses Universitaires de France.

Benvenuto, B. (1985), 'Oedipus, a myth in development: the case of Little Hans'. *Syngraphia* no 1: London.

Benvenuto, B. (1994), *Concerning the Rites of Psychoanalysis or the Villa of the Mysteries*, Cambridge: Polity.

Benvenuto, B. and Kennedy, R. (1986), *The Works of Jacques Lacan: An Introduction*, London: Free Association Books.

Bion, W. (1955)[1977], 'Group Dynamics - a Re-view' in (Eds.) Klein et al. *New Directions in Psycho-Analysis*, London: Karnac.

Bion, W. (1961), *Experiences in Groups and Other Papers*, London: Tavistock.

Bion, W. (1967) [1984], *Second Thoughts: Selected Papers on Psycho-Analysis*, London: Heinemann.

Bion, W. (1980), *Bion in New York and Sao Paulo*, Perthshire: Clunie Press.

Blanton, S. (1975), *Tagebuch meiner Analyse bei Sigmund Freud*, Frankfurt am Main: Ulstein.

Bott Spillius, E. (1988), *Melanie Klein Today*, 2 Vols., London: Routledge.

Bott Spillius, E. (1994), 'Developments in Kleinian Thought: Overview and Personal View', *Psychoanalytic Inquiry*, Vol 14, Number 3.

Brenkman, J. (1993), *Straight Male, Modern: A Cultural Critique of Psychoanalysis*, New York-London: Routledge.

Brenman Pick, I. (1985), 'Working through in the counter-transference'. *Int .J . Psycho-Analysis* , Vol. 66: pp 157-66.

Breuer, J. and Freud,S. (1895), *Studies on Hysteria*, S.E . II, London:Hogarth.

Britton, R. (1989), 'The Missing Link: parental sexuality in the Oedipus Complex' - in *The Oedipus Complex Today*, London: Karnac Books.

Chasseguet-Smirgel, J. (1976),'Freud and Female Sexuality: Blind Spots in the Dark Continent', *Int. J. Psycho-Analysis*, Vol. 57, pp. 275-286.

Cooper, D. (1972), *The Death of the Family*. London: Penguin.

Copjec, J. (1994), 'Sex and the Euthanasia of Reason' in *Read my Desire: Lacan against the Historicists*. Cambridge Mass. -London, MIT .

Diderot, D. (1796) *Jacques le Fataliste et sa Maître*, Paris: Flammarion.

Duhem, P. (1913-59) *Le Système du Monde*, 10 Vols., Paris: Hermann.

Etchegoyen, H. (1991), 'Psychoanalysis During the Last Decade: Clinical and Theoretical Aspects', Psychoanalytic Enquiry, Vol.11, No.1, pp 88-106.

Etchegoyen, H. (1991), *The Fundamentals of Psycho-Analytic Technique*, London: Karnac.

Fairbairn, W. (1952), *Psychoanalytic Studies of the Personality*, London: Tavistock.

Foucault, M. (1967), *Madness and Civilisation: A History of Insanity in the Age of Reason*, London: Tavistock.

Freud, S. (1891) [1953], *On Aphasia, A Critical Study*, New York: International University Press.

Freud, S. (1905), 'Fragment of an Analysis of a Case of Hysteria', S.E. VII, London: Hogarth.

Freud, S. (1909), 'Analysis of a Phobia in a Five-year-old Boy', S.E. IX, London: Hogarth.

Freud, S. (1914), 'On Narcissism: an Introduction', S.E. XIV, London: Hogarth.

Freud, S. (1915), 'The Unconscious', S.E. XIV, London: Hogarth.

Freud, S. (1915), 'Instincts and their Viscissitudes', S.E. XIV, London: Hogarth.

Freud, S. (1916-1917), Lecture 21, 'The Development of the Libido', in *Introductory Lectures on Psychoanalysis*, S.E. XV and XVI, London: Hogarth.

Freud, S. (1917), 'A Difficulty in the Path of Psychoanalysis' S.E. XVII London: Hogarth.

Freud, S. (1918), 'From the History of an Infantile Neurosis', S.E. XVII, London: Hogarth.

Freud, S. (1919), 'A Child is Being Beaten', S.E. XVII, London: Hogarth.

Freud, S. (1920), 'Beyond the Pleasure Principle', S.E. XVIII, London: Hogarth.

Freud S. (1920), 'Three Essays on the Theory of Sexuality', (4th Edition) S.E. VII, London: Hogarth.

Freud, S. (1923), 'The Infantile Genital Organisation: an Interpolation into the Theory of Sexuality', S.E. XXI, London: Hogarth.

Freud, S. (1925), 'Negation', S.E. XIX, London: Hogarth.

Freud, S. (1926/27), 'The Question of Lay Analysis', S.E. XX, London: Hogarth.

Freud, S. (1930), 'Civilisation and Its Discontents', S.E. XXI, London: Hogarth.

Freud, S. (1931), 'Female Sexuality', S.E. Vol. XXI, London: Hogarth.

Freud, S. (1932), 'The Acquisition and Control of Fire', S.E. XXII, London: Hogarth.

Freud, S. (1933), 'New Introductory Lectures on Psychoanalysis', S.E. XXII, London: Hogarth.

Freud, S. (1937), 'Constructions in Analysis', S.E. XXIII, London: Hogarth.

Freud, S. (1953-73), *The Standard Edition of the Complete Psychological Works of Sigmund Freud*, 24 Vols., London: Hogarth.

Freud, S. & Binswanger, L. (1992), *Briefwechsel 1908-1938,* Berlin: Fischer.

Gedo, J. (1986), *Conceptual Issues in Psychoanalysis: Essays in History and Method,* New York: Analytic Press.

Glover, E. (1931), 'The Therapeutic Effect of Inexact Interpretation: A Contribution to the Theory of Suggestion', *Int. J. Psycho-Analysis,* Vol. 12, pp 397-411.

Gordon, C. (1990), 'Histoire de la Folie: An Unknown Book by Michel Foucault', *History of the Human Sciences,* 3, pp 3-26 (with several responses, pp 27-67).

Gorgias, [1995] 'Encomium of Helen', in (Eds.) Gagarin and Woodruff *Early Greek Political Thought from Homer to the Sophists,* Cambridge: Cambridge University Press.

Hartmann, H. (1939), *Ego Psychology and the Problem of Adaptation,* New York: International University Press.

Heimann P. (1950), 'On Counter-transference', *Int. J. Psycho-Analysis,* Vol. 31.

Hinshelwood, R. (1987), *What Happens in Groups: Psychoanalysis, the Individual and the Community,* London: Free Association Books.

Hinshelwood, R. (1991), *A Dictionary of Kleinian Thought,* London: Free Association Books.

Hinshelwood, R. (1994), *Clinical Klein,* London: Free Association Books.

Hoffmann, C. (1991), 'Mystérion, les deux jouissances', *Apertura,* V, pp 33-36.

Isaacs, S. (1943) [1991], Discussion of "The Nature and Function of Phantasy", read at a Scientific Meeting of the British Psycho-Analytic Society, January 27th 1943, in (Eds.) King, P. and Steiner, R.,*The Freud-Klein Controversies 1941-45,* London: Tavistock/Routledge.

Isaacs, S. (1948), 'The Nature and Function of Phantasy', *Int. J. Psycho-Analysis* 29: pp 73-97.

Isaacs, S. (1952)[1989], 'The Nature and Function of Phantasy', in *Developments in Psycho-Analysis,*   Klein M., Heimann P., Isaacs S. and Riviere J., London: Hogarth.

Jaques, E. (1955)[1977], 'Social Systems as Defence against Persecutory and Depressive Anxiety', in Eds. Klein et al *New Directions in Psycho-Analysis* pp 478-98.

Joseph, B. (1978)[1989], 'Different Types of Anxiety and their Handling in the Analytic Situation', in Joseph *Psychic Equilibrium and Psychic Change,* London: Routledge.

Joseph, B. (1985) [1989], 'Transference: The Total Situation', in Joseph *Psychic Equilibrum and Psychic Change,* London: Routledge.

King, P. and Steiner, R. (1991) (Eds.), *The Freud-Klein Controversies 1941-45.* London: Tavistock/Routledge.

Klein, M. (1927) [1975], 'The Importance of Words in Early Analysis', in *Envy and Gratitude and other works 1946 - 1963,* London: Hogarth.

Klein, M. (1928) [1975], 'Early Stages of the Oedipus Complex', in *Love, Guilt and Reparation and other works 1921-1945,*   London: Hogarth.

Klein, M. (1930) [1975], 'The Importance of Symbol-Formation in the Development of the Ego' in *Love, Guilt and Reparation and other works 1921-1945,* London: Hogarth.

Klein, M. (1932/1932) [1975], *Die Psychoanalyse des Kindes,* Vienna/*The Psycho-Analysis of Children*, London: Hogarth.

Klein, M. (1943) [1991], 'Memorandum on Technique', in (Eds.), King, P. and Steiner, R. *The Freud-Klein Controversies 1941-45,* pp 635-638. London: Tavistock/Routledge.

Klein, M. (1945) [1975], 'The Oedipus Complex in the Light of Early Activities' in *Love, Guilt and Reparation and other works 1921-1945* , London: Hogarth

Klein, M. (1946) [1975], 'Notes on Some Schizoid Mechanisms' in *Envy and Gratitude and other works 1921-1945,* London: Hogarth.

Klein, M. (1952) [1975], 'The Origins of Transference', in *Envy and Gratitude and other works 1921-1945,* London: Hogarth.

Klein, M. (1955) [1975],'On Identification', in *Envy and Gratitude and other works 1921-1945,* London: Hogarth.

Klein, M. et al. (1952) [1989], *Developments in Psycho-Analysis,* London: Hogarth.

Klein, M. et al. (Eds.) (1955) [1977] , *New Directions in Psycho-Analysis,* London: Tavistock.

Klein, M. (1961)[1975], *Narrative of a Child Analysis,* London: Hogarth.

Klein, M. (1975), *The Writings of Melanie Klein,* 4 vols., London: Hogarth.

Klein, S. (1980), 'Autistic Phenomena in Neurotic Patients', *Int. J. Psycho-Analysis*, vol.61, pp 395-402.

Kohut, H. (1984), *How Does Psychoanalysis Cure?*, Chicago: Chicago University Press.

Koyré, A. (1971) 'Le Vide et l'Espace Infini au XIVe Siècle', in *Etudes d'Histoire de la Pensée Philosophique*, Paris: Gallimard.

Kris , E. and Loewenstein, R. (1946), 'Comments on the Formation of Psychic Structure', *The Psychoanalytic Study of the Child*, 2, pp 11-38.

Kris, E. (1951), 'Ego Psychology and Interpretation in Psychoanalytic Therapy', in *The Psychoanalytic Quarterly*, Vol. XX.

Lacan, J. (1948)[1977], 'Aggressivity in Psychoanalysis', in *Ecrits: A Selection*, (trans. Sheridan A.), London: Routledge.

Lacan, J. (1949) [1994], 'The Mirror-phase as Formative of the Function of the I', translated by Roussel, J. in (Ed.) Zizek, S. *Mapping Ideology*, London: Verso.

Lacan, J. (1949) [1977], 'The Mirror Stage as Formative of the Function of the 'I' as revealed in Psychoanalytic Experience' in *Ecrits: A Selection,* (trans. Sheridan, A.), London: Routledge.

Lacan, J. (1951) [1982], 'Intervention on the Transference', in (Eds.) Mitchell J. & Rose J., *Feminine Sexuality: Jacques Lacan and the Ecole Freudienne*, London: McMillan.

Lacan, J. (1953)[1977], 'Function and Field of Speech and Language in Psychoanalysis' in *Ecrits: A Selection*, London: Routledge.

Lacan, J. (1955) [1966], 'Variantes de la cure-type' in *Ecrits*, Paris: Seuil.

Lacan, J. (1956-57) [1957], 'La relation d'objet'. Report by J.B. Pontalis in the *Bulletin de Psychologie.*, Vol X, No 7 (April 1957), pp 426-30; Vol X, No.10 (April 1957), pp 602-5; Vol X, No. 12 (May 1957) pp 742-43; Vol X, No 14 (June 1957) pp 851-54; Vol XI, No 1 (Sept. 1957) pp 31-4.

Lacan, J. (1957-1958) [1977], 'On a Question Preliminary to any Possible Treatment of Psychosis' in *Ecrits: A Selection*, London: Routledge.

Lacan, J. (1958) [1977], 'The Direction of the Treatment and the Principles of its Power', in *Ecrits: A Selection*, London: Routledge .

Lacan, J. (1958)[1982] 'The Meaning of the Phallus' in (Eds.) Mitchell J. & Rose J., *Feminine Sexuality: Jacques Lacan and the Ecole Freudienne*, London: McMillan.

Lacan, J. (1960)[1977], 'Subversion of the Subject and Dialectic of Desire', in *Ecrits: A Selection*, (trans. Sheridan, A.), London-New York: Routledge.

Lacan, J. (1964)[1995], 'Position of the Unconscious', (trans. Fink, B. in (Eds.) Feldstein, R., Fink, B. & Jaanus M.), *Reading Seminar XI: Lacan's Four Fundamental Concepts of Psychoanalysis*, New York: State University of New York Press.

Lacan, J. (1966), *Ecrits*, Paris: Seuil.

Lacan, J. (1966-67), *Le Séminaire, Livre XIV: La Logique du Fantasme*, (Unpublished).

Lacan, J. (1968), 'De Rome '53 à Rome '67: La Psychanalyse - Raison d'un Echec' in *Scilicet*, 1, Paris: Seuil.

Lacan, J. (1973), 'L'Etourdit' in *Scilicet*, 4, Paris: Seuil.

Lacan, J. (1973) [1979], *The Seminar, Book XI: The Four Fundamental Concepts of Psychoanalysis*, (Ed.) Miller, J.-A., trans. Sheridan, A., London: Penguin.

Lacan, J. (1974) [1990], *Television, A Challenge to the Psychoanalytic Establishment* (Ed.) Copjec, J., (trans. Hollier, D., Krauss R. and Michelson A.), New York-London: Norton.

Lacan, J. (1975) *Le Séminaire, Livre XX: Encore 1972-73*, Paris: Seuil.

Lacan, J. (1977), *Ecrits: A Selection* , (trans. Sheridan, A.), London: Tavistock/Routledge.

Lacan, J. (1979), 'The Neurotic's Individual Myth' (trans. Evans, M.), in *The Psychoanalytic Quarterly*, vol. XLVIII, no 3, pp 405-425.

Lacan, J. (1988), *The Seminar of Jacques Lacan, Book I: Freud's Papers on Technique 1953-1954*. Cambridge: Cambridge University Press.

Lacan, J. (1988), *The Seminar of Jacques Lacan, Book II: The Ego in Freud's Theory and in the Technique of Psychoanalysis, 1954 - 55*, Cambridge: Cambridge University Press.

Lacan, J. (1991), *Le Séminaire, Livre VIII: Le Transfert, 1960-61*, Paris: Seuil.

Lacan, J. (1991), *Le Séminaire, Livre XVII: L'Envers de la Psychanalyse, 1969-70*, Paris: Seuil.

Lacan, J. (1993), *The Psychoses: The Seminar of Jacques Lacan, Book III, 1955-1956*, (Ed.) Miller, J.-A., trans. with notes by Grigg, R., New York-London: Norton.

Lacan, J. (1994), *Le Séminaire, Livre IV: La Relation d'Objet, 1956-57*, Paris: Seuil.   Laing, R. (1970), *The Divided Self*, London: Penguin.

Laplanche, J. And Pontalis, J.-B., (1973), *The Language of Psychoanalysis*, London: Hogarth.

Laurent, E. (1978), 'Le Comité Castration', *Ornicar?*, No 16, pp 38-46, Paris.

Laurent, E. (1981), 'Lire Gabrielle et Richard à partir du Petit Hans', *Quarto* no 1., pp 3-23, Brussels.

Laurent, E. (1981), 'Ce que savait Mélanie', *Ornicar?*, No 24, pp 143-150, Paris.

Laurent, E. (1983), 'Trois Guises de l'Object', *Ornicar?*, No 26/27, pp 78-87, Paris.

Laurent, E. (1993-94), *Les Paradoxes de l'Identification,* seminars presented to the Clinical Section of the Department of Psychoanalysis at the University of Paris VIII.

Laurent, E. (1995), 'Phantasy in Klein and Lacan' in (Ed. E. M. Sullivan) *Psychoanalytic Seminars 1991-1994,* London: THERIP.

Lefort, R. (1980), *Naissance de l'Autre.* Paris: Seuil.

Lefort, R. (1988), *Les Structures de la Psychose*, Paris: Seuil.

Lemoine, G. (1987), *The Dividing of Women or Women's Lot*, London: Free Association Books.

Meltzer, D. et al (1975), *Explorations in Autism: A Psycho-Analytic Study*, Strath Tay: Clunie.

Meltzer, D. (1978), *The Kleinian Development. Parts 1-3,* Strath Tay: Clunie.

Meltzer, D. (1988), 'The Relation of Anal Masturbation to Projective Identification', in (Ed.) Bott Spillius, E., *Melanie Klein Today,* Vol 1, pp 102-16, London: Routledge.

Meltzer, D. (1991), Lecture on Projective Identification and the Claustrum (tape).

Meltzer, D. (1992), *The Claustrum*, Strath Tay: Clunie.

Menzies Lyth, I. (1951)[1988], 'The Functioning of Social Systems as a Defence against Anxiety' in *Containing Anxiety in Institutions: Selected Essays*, Vol 1., London: Free Association Books.

Miller, E. (1990), 'Experiential Learning Groups 1: The Development of the Leicester Model', in (Eds.) Trist E. and Murray H., *The Social Engagement of Social Science: A Tavistock Anthology. Vol 1: The Socio-Psychological Perspective*, London: Free Association Books.

Miller, J.-A. (1984), 'D'un autre Lacan', *Ornicar?*, no 28, pp 49-57, Paris.

Miller, J.-A. (1994-5), *Silet,* from the Seminar Series of Jacques-Alain Miller, (Unpublished).

Miller, J.-A. (1995-6), *La Fuite du Sens*, from the Seminar Series of Jacques-Alain Miller, (Unpublished).

Miller, J.-A. (1996), 'L'Interprétation à l'Envers', *La Cause Freudienne*, No. 32, pp 9-13, Paris,

Money-Kyrle, R. (1956) 'Normal Counter-Transference and some of its Deviations', *Int. J. Psycho-Analysis*, Vol. 37.

Morel, G. (1993), 'Conditions Féminines de Jouissance', *La Cause Freudienne, Revue de psychanalyse*, no 24, pp 96-106, Paris.

Nobus, D. (1993), 'El pudor - Un afecto feminino?', *Uno por Uno, Revista Mundial de Psicoanálisis*, No 37, pp 5-10, Barcelona.

Pfeiffer, E. [Ed.] (1966)[1972],   *Sigmund Freud and Lou Andreas-Salome: Letters,* (trans. Robson-Scott, W. and E.), London: Hogarth and Institute of Psycho-Analysis.

Plutarch [1941], *Life of Alcibiades,* Oxford: Loeb Classical Library.

Ragland, E. (1995), *Essays on the Pleasures of Death. From Freud to Lacan,* New York - London: Routledge.

Rapaport, D. (1960), *The Structure of Psychoanalytic theory: A Systematizing Attempt,* Psychological Issues 2/2, Monograph 6. New York: International University Press.

Riviere, J. (1952), 'General Introduction' in (Eds.) M. Klein et al, *Developments in Psycho-Analysis,* pp 1-36, London: Hogarth.

Riviere, J. (1952), 'On the Genesis of Psychical Conflict in Earliest Infancy', in M. Klein et al, *Developments in Psycho-Analysis,* pp 37-66, London: Hogarth.

Rousseau, J-J. (1762) *Emile ou de L'Education,* Paris: Flammarion

Schmideberg, M. (1934) [1993], 'Intellectual Inhibition and Eating Disorders' in Rose, J., *Why War?,* London: Blackwell

Schmideberg , M. (1938) 'Intellectual Inhibition and Disturbances in Eating', *Int. J. Psycho-Analysis,* Vol. 19.

Schneiderman, S. (1993), *How Lacan's Ideas are Used in Clinical Practice,* New York: Aronson.

Schnurmann, A. (1949), 'Observation of a Phobia', *The Psychoanalytic Study of the Child,* Vol 5 pp 3-4.

Scilicet/Anon (1976), 'D'un discours à l'autre, l'institution dite du contrôle ', in *Scilicet,* 6/7, Paris: Seuil.

Schopenhauer A. (1819) [1995], *Die Welt als Wille und Vorstellung* trans. as *The World as Will and Representation,* New York:Dover.

Segal, H. (1973), *Introduction to the Work of Melanie Klein,* London: Hogarth.

Segal, H. (1975), 'A Psycho-Analytic Approach to the Treatment of Schizophrenia', in (Ed.) Lader, M., *Studies of Schizophrenia,* pp 94-7, Ashford: Headley Bros.

Silverman, K. (1992), 'The Lacanian Phallus', Differences: *A Journal of Feminist Cultural Studies,* IV, no. 1, pp 84-115.

Soler, C. (1994), 'Qu'est-ce que l'inconscient sait des femmes?', *Psychoanalytische Perspektieven,* no 23, pp 25 - 35.

Spitz, R. (1957), *No and Yes, On the Genesis of Human Communication,* New York: International Universities Press.

Sterne, L., (1759-67)[1983], *The Life and Times of Tristram Shandy, Gentleman,* Oxford: Oxford University Press

Strachey, J. (1958), 'Introduction' in Freud S., *Papers on Technique (1911-1915),* S.E. Vol XII, London: Hogarth.

Turquet, P. (1975), 'Threats to Identity in the Large Group', in (Ed.) Kreeger, L., *The Large Group: Dynamics and Therapy*, London: Constable.

Tustin, F. (1986), *Autistic Barriers in Neurotic Patients*, London: Karnac.

Wallerstein, R., (1988),   'One Psychoanalysis or Many?' *Int. J. Psycho-Analysis*, vol. 69, pp 5-21.

Wallerstein, R., (1986),   *Forty-Two Lives in Treatment: A Study of Psychoanalysis and Psychotherapy*, London-New York: Guilford.

Winnicott, D. (1971), 'Mirror Role of Mother and Family in Child Development'. *Playing and Reality*, London: Tavistock.

Wittgenstein, L. (1953),   *Philosophical Investigations*, Oxford: Blackwell.

Xenophon, [1990], *Memoirs of Socrates*, (trans. by H. Tredennick & R. Waterfield), in *Conversations of Socrates*, London: Penguin Classics.

Young, R. (1994), *Mental Space*, London: Process Press.

INDEX